MW01253045

Ethics in the Field

Studies of the Biosocial Society

General Editor: **Catherine Panter-Brick**, Professor of Anthropology, Yale University

The Biosocial Society is an international academic society engaged in fostering understanding of human biological and social diversity. It draws its membership from a wide range of academic disciplines, particularly those engaged in 'boundary disciplines' at the intersection between the natural and social sciences, such as biocultural anthropology, medical sociology, demography, social medicine, the history of science and bioethics. The aim of this series is to promote interdisciplinary research on how biology and society interact to shape human experience and to serve as advanced texts for undergraduate and postgraduate students.

Volume 1
Race, Ethnicity, and Nation: Perspectives from Kinship and Genetics
Edited by Peter Wade

Volume 2
Health, Risk, and Adversity
Edited by Catherine Panter-Brick and Agustín Fuentes

Volume 3
Substitute Parents: Biological and Social Perspectives on Alloparenting in Human Societies
Edited by Gillian Bentley and Ruth Mace

Volume 4
Centralizing Fieldwork: Critical Perspectives from Primatology, Biological and Social Anthropology
Edited by Jeremy MacClancy and Agustín Fuentes

Volume 5
Human Diet and Nutrition in Biocultural Perspective: Past Meets Present
Edited by Tina Moffat and Tracy Prowse

Volume 6
Identity Politics and the New Genetics: Re/Creating Categories of Difference and Belonging
Edited by Katharina Schramm, David Skinner and Richard Rottenburg

Volume 7
Ethics in the Field: Contemporary Challenges
Edited by Jeremy MacClancy and Agustín Fuentes

Ethics in the Field

Contemporary Challenges

Edited by
Jeremy MacClancy and Agustín Fuentes

berghahn
NEW YORK · OXFORD
www.berghahnbooks.com

First published in 2013 by
Berghahn Books
www.berghahnbooks.com

Library of Congress Cataloging-in-Publication Data

Ethics in the field: contemporary challenges / edited by Jeremy MacClancy and
Agustín Fuentes.
  p. cm. -- (Studies of the biosocial society; v. 7)
  ISBN 978-0-85745-962-6 (hardback) -- ISBN 978-0-85745-963-3
(institutional ebook)
  1. Anthropology--Moral and ethical aspects. I. MacClancy, Jeremy. II. Fuentes,
Agustin.
  BJ52.E725 2013
  174'.9301--dc23

                                                                2012037775

British Library Cataloguing in Publication Data

A catalogue record for this book is available from the British Library
Printed in the United States on acid-free paper.

ISBN 978-0-85745-962-6 (hardback)
ISBN 978-0-85745-963-3 (institutional ebook)

JAPANFOUNDATION

We are grateful to the Japan Foundation for providing funds to the
Biosocial Society, and for helping to meet the costs of producing this book.

Contents

List of Figures and Tables

Acknowledgements

This book is the product of a conference held by the Anthropology Centre for Conservation, the Environment and Development (ACCEND) at Oxford Brookes University, April 2009. This was the second in a planned series of interdisciplinary, international gatherings, organized by ACCEND, in its efforts to further the project of a transdisciplinary anthropology. Results of the first conference were published as *Centralizing Fieldwork: Critical Perspectives from Primatology, Biological and Social Anthropology*, co-edited by ourselves (Studies of the Biosocial Society, vol.4). Further volumes are in the process of publication.

The conference went well, and was praised by all. We are profoundly grateful to our generous supporters: the School of Social Sciences, Oxford Brookes University; the Japan Foundation; the Biosocial Society; the Royal Anthropological Institute; University of Notre Dame Institute for Scholarship in the Liberal Arts. We also thank our team at Berghahn Publishers, especially our editor Megan Palmer. Louis O'Carroll compiled the index.

Jeremy MacClancy
Agustín Fuentes

1

The Ethical Fieldworker, and Other Problems

Jeremy MacClancy and Agustín Fuentes

We are, by definition, moral beings. There are no human groups without morals, however vaguely formulated, however unsystematic these morals might be. There are no non-human groups with them: apes, great or small, might display creativity and fellow concern, and many other primates and social mammals may engage in diverse forms of social reciprocity, but they do not have culturally prescribed standards of ethical conduct. Morality, in this sense, is a distinctive, essential, integral aspect of humanity. Without it, we are regarded as not just inhumane, but as inhuman.

It is surprising, then, that a social anthropology of morality has only begun to emerge as a modern field of endeavour within the last few years (e.g. Howell 1996; Lambek 2010; Zigon 2010; Faubion 2011). It is as though anthropologists did not realize that morality could be studied productively, cross-culturally until very recent times, and had quietly forgotten that Westermarck had inaugurated the very project over a hundred years ago (Westermarck 1906–1908). In a similar manner the interest of most social anthropologists, in the UK and the US at least, in the ethical dimensions of their fieldwork practice has been patchy at best, rising and falling over the decades since the 1940s (Rynkiewich and Spradley 1976; Fluehr-Lobban 1991; Koepping 1994; Caplan 2003). The latest surge of interest appears to be the result of a professional reaction to recent cases of ethical misconduct in the discipline (e.g. Borofsky 2005), the rise in debates about the apparently competing claims of culture and rights (Cowan, Dembour and Wilson 2001), and the implementation of ethical regulation, via Institutional Review Boards (IRBs) in the US and University Research Ethics Committees (URECs) in the UK. Primatologists only seem to have taken ethical concerns on board even more recently. The exception appears to be biological anthropology where, perhaps because of its occasional association with clinical research, practitioners have for some time been aware of the need for rigorous ethical procedures when fieldworking.

However, what has not yet been attempted is the transdisciplinary comparison within anthropology, broadly conceived, of ethics in the field. In other words, until now there has been no consideration of what is common to the moral challenges faced by fieldworkers in social anthropology, biological anthropology, and primatology. Nor have practitioners questioned what might be distinctive to the moral field practice of each discipline, or pair of disciplines. They have similarly neglected to ask what are the significant commonalities, and the telling differences. The comparative investigation of these queries is the primary aim of this book.

A secondary aim is to contribute further towards the modern development of a transdisciplinary anthropology, one pitched, above all, at the level of methods. In this sense, this book is a further effort by the Anthropological Centre for Conservation, Development and the Environment (ACCEND), based at Oxford Brookes University, to give substance to a reinvigorated, broadly based anthropology. This book is a complementary successor to our *Centralizing Fieldwork* (MacClancy and Fuentes 2011), whose focus was on the nature, contexts, and process of fieldwork itself. To repeat a caveat stated there: our concern at revitalizing this cross-disciplinary exercise is not to reduce all forms of anthropology into a singular, dominant, scientific paradigm. We have no truck with any reductionist programme, however veiled. Rather, we seek to stimulate a lively and open dialogue across arenas of anthropological inquiry. Instead of trying to squeeze the variety of anthropologies into a single paradigm, we are more concerned with facilitating mutual interaction across sub-disciplinary and theoretical boundaries. We wish, in sum, to exploit, not to confine, the transdisciplinary potential of our subject.

The range covered by the chapters demonstrates this desire. Melissa Parker, a biological anthropologist, compares the challenges she encountered in two major fieldwork projects, one in a British teaching hospital on AIDS and sexual networks in the UK, the other in East Africa on neglected tropical diseases. Though the two projects were very different from each other, both highlighted the impossibility of predicting many of the ethical issues which may arise in the course of fieldwork, including the need to make decisions which could have life or death consequences for her informants. She argues that the solution is not to impose ever tighter controls on what can and cannot be researched. The following chapter by Matt McLennan, primatologist, and Catherine Hill, biological anthropologist, develops Parker's main finding in a different dimension. McLennan, supervised by Hill, conducted fieldwork in an East African territory. The government had not classified the area as protected, and the endangered resident chimpanzees often came into conflict with local farmers. What McLennan observed, to his alarm, was the effect his presence had on local social and political dynamics. Hill and he conclude that a clear ethical framework is needed for conducting primatology in landscapes which are increasingly dominated by humans.

Primatological concerns continue in the next four chapters. Karen Strier reviews the evolving ethical terrain of her long-term fieldsite. Both the research questions and the animals' demography have changed over time. However, what most concerns her is whether the continued presence of human observers over such an extended period of time means we can truly regard long-term observational studies of primates as being as non-invasive as they are touted to be. Her fear is that these studies become invasive, as they affect the spaces and ecologies around social landscapes in and around the fieldsites. She thus queries the ethical terrain at the core of primatology: the long-term study. Nobuyuki Kutsukake, in Chapter Five, broadens the debate. He considers just how many sets of ethics primatologists have to contend with: the researcher's personal morality, that of the community with whom he or she is residing, and that of their profession. These different codes may at times run in harmony; often they are at odds with each other. Kutsukake suggests that mutual communication, understanding and negotiation might well solve some of the ethical conundrums which arise during fieldwork, in an almost inevitable fashion. In their chapter, Katherine MacKinnon and Erin Riley review critically the outcomes of several recent symposia and publications dealing with broad questions about ethics in primatological fieldwork. For them, the key concerns are the need to incorporate more ethics-oriented considerations in research projects, and particularly in the teaching and professional training of primatology students. They challenge fellow primatologists to consider more seriously ethics as central to their enterprise. To that end, they propose the development of a formalized code of ethics to guide future primatological field research. Anna Nekaris and Vincent Nijman take a very different tack. Using statistical analysis of Great Ape field sites, they contend that the researchers there have concentrated their work on chimpanzees, gorillas or orang-utans and paid much less attention to primate conservation and other endangered primates inhabiting these sites. Nekaris and Nijman thus breach the usually unspoken wall and ask if it is indeed unethical to favour one species of primate over another at a given fieldsite. Because most primate species are today threatened with extinction, they argue that, to reduce the possibility of humans transmitting disease to primates, it is morally imperative that the use of established research sites be optimized.

We do not wish the reader to take our opening paragraph to mean that we are not aware of the rich emerging literature on non-human primate social complexity, recognition of inequity, and the possibilities of altruistic action, even justice, in multiple species (eg. Brosnan 2012; Pierce and Bekoff 2012; Sussman and Cloninger 2011). Such recent work demonstrates that other some primates (and species of social mammals) react, with some consistency, to experimentally produced inequities. They also seek out one another for a range of reciprocal support and create long-lasting robust social relationships that are behaviourally negotiated across time. Primates engage in apparently altruistic acts and rely extensively on social networks and relational partners throughout their life histories. So one can indeed argue that there are predictable patterns of social exchange and systems of expected, and negotiated, behaviour in the primates. However, these are not the same as the kinds of ethical challenges and contexts that emerge from our anthropological study of them or of each other. Our stance, and the point of this book, is to look more specifically at the ethical contexts that are produced by human anthropologists engaging in research on primates and other humans. It is in this sense that we see morality as a distinctive, essential, integral aspect of humanity that results in complex webs of ethical scenarios and conduct.

It is crucial that readers understand our focus. We are not saying that the ethical concerns of primatologists and social anthropologists are identical or interchangeable. We are saying that there is a great degree of overlap between the two, that they share many ethical quandaries, and that this commonality has been insufficiently recognized. At first glance, these research priorities might appear fundamentally different: primatologists by definition are primarily interested in non-human primates, whereas social and biological anthropologists work with humans. But no primatologist can study a group of primates without also taking into account local residents, whether they be hunters, foragers, farmers, villagers, forest wardens, official gatekeepers, regional administrators: whomever. And dealing with fellow humans means ethics is constitutive of any encounter between primatologist and local. Moreover, there are the broader ethical consequences of any anthropological study, again whether that be of one of the more hairy primates or naked apes.

The remaining chapters are by social scientists. Susie Kilshaw, a social anthropologist, considers the ethical dilemmas and issues she faced throughout her research into Gulf War Syndrome. She deals in particular on three challenges she had to contend with: how to present oneself to those whom we fieldwork; how to manage one's ongoing relationships with them; and how to balance both of those considerations with one's relationship with the funders of the research project. Tina Miller, a fieldworking sociologist, looks in particular at issues of access and consent, data collection, and that often neglected topic, leaving the field. What she finds is a misfit between complex social and cultural worlds. This leads her to propound that researchers are more in need of ethical support than regulation. Em Rundall, whose work was jointly supervised by a sociologist and an anthropologist, investigates the ethical dimensions of a new and rapidly expanding arena of study: the internet. In the course of an anonymous, asynchronous websurvey she carried out, she isolated five fundamental ethical principles which had to be confronted: the inequalities of internet accessibility; informed participation and consent; anonymity and confidentiality; the safety of participants and researchers; and security of data. Her chapter provides extremely useful guidelines for academics wishing to research in this field.

MacClancy closes the book with an ethnographic investigation into one of the greatest areas of contention within our broad theme: the process of ethical regulation by URECs in the UK. Given the agitated debate these committees have caused, it is surprising, perhaps sad, that this is the first ethnographic research on URECs. What MacClancy uncovers makes him argue that these committees should stop regulating social scientific research, and restrict themselves to the ethical training of fledgling fieldworkers.

We have chosen the various themes summarized above because they illuminate a host of trans-anthropological ethical concerns, common to primatology as well as to biological and social anthropologies: the centrality of ethics to the research methods of all three; the integral importance of ethical training to neophyte fieldworkers; persistent questions over the benefits and obstructive downsides of a prescribed code of ethics; the simultaneous presence of multiple moral codes and the quandaries their encounter cause; the dearth of easy, quick answers; the sustained need to constantly negotiate moral complexities, which may well prove irresolvable in a conclusive manner; the enduring ethical consequences of long-term fieldwork, and of their persistence, even after the academic has left the fieldsite. To summarize: as moral beings in morally complex settings, we have to learn to live with ambiguity.

While we wish to underline trans-anthropological commonalities, at the same time we do not expect a perfect dovetailing between the three areas of endeavour. Each has, after all, its own distinctive aims and specific institutional history. Primates do not object to what is written about them, although the repercussions can carry ethical weight for the author. However, the myriad of local humans that primatologists have to work with may well take exception to what is printed. Social anthropologists do not usually fear that studying one group long-term may affect neighbouring peoples, though it is marginally possible to imagine. Biological anthropologists tend to fit somewhere between practitioners of the two other pursuits, as they may study humans or the interactions between humans and primates. Given the medical funding of so much of their research, the majority of biological anthropologists these days tend to do problem-oriented work among those classed as 'vulnerable' groups; this has long made them particularly sensitive to ethical considerations. We are not trying to straitjacket these three modes of enquiry into one fitting. Rather, we recognize that each is distinct in some ways, but wish above all to explore the common challenges their practitioners are all forced to ponder today.

We also chose the above themes because they concern contemporary procedures, and illuminate the troublesome reality of present practice. Some contributors address questions about the increasing prevalence of formalized codes of ethics and the power of those who regulate their compliance (MacClancy, MacKinnon and Riley). Others investigate the ethical queries raised by the ever-more pervasive use of new technologies (Miller, Rundall). Yet others consider the consequences of having a private body fund one's research: an increasingly common and concerning phenomenon in these neo-liberal times (Parker, Kilshaw). To our knowledge, McLennan and Hill's contribution is among the first to consider how primatological fieldwork may inadvertently threaten the future survival of the very animals whose conservation they came to assist.

We have covered patches of, and interconnections across a broad ground. But we have not tried to broach all current ethical issues. Our aim was not to produce an encyclopaedia, but a provocative guidebook to today's problems for anthropologists of whatever ilk planning to go into the field.

Fielding ethical questions

It was perhaps the Nuremberg Trials of Nazi clinicians which most prompted debate about the ethics of research. Lawyers needed an explicit code of what was medically permissible and what not in order to be able to prosecute those who had committed evil acts under the guise of science. At much the same time medical research in the USA began to expand at a tremendous rate, and continued to do so for several decades. Some of this research was conducted unethically. The most notorious example was the Tuskegee Syphilis Study, where the effects of the disease on hundreds of African-Americans, over four decades, was observed by clinicians, even though penicillin had become available in the interim and could have been used. The example of the study, coupled with the revelation of the abuses committed by cavalier medical researchers, led first to legislation and then to the widespread establishment of Institutional Review Boards (IRBs) throughout American universities. Given the moral concerns about clinical experiments which underlay their creation, it is not surprising that the research model for IRBs was biomedical, and their monitoring procedures demonstrated this bias. Over time the remit of IRBs extended to include the social sciences as well. This extension has generated outrage among many social scientists, who see a biomedical model for research as grossly inappropriate when applied to the work of their disciplines. A parallel process of extension occurred in the UK at the turn of the millennium and has led to a similar degree of anger. But what, precisely, is going wrong here?

The key initial point is that the overwhelming majority of social anthropologists, as well as a significant number of biological anthropologists and primatologists, do not work in laboratories, in the traditional sense. Laboratories are highly controlled, artificial environments, and those scientists who choose to work in these settings do so in order to control variable factors as much as possible. Their aim is to enable minutely monitored, reproducible experiments whose results can be interpreted and repeated. Fieldworkers operate in radically different environments. They might wish to restrict the number and kind of people that they are researching but they are totally incapable at any time of controlling the movement of individuals, whether in the study group or not, in and out of the field site. Indeed, interaction with locals may well make an anthropologist researcher change her notion of the very boundaries of her designated site. Interaction may also make a fieldworker radically rethink the questions she wishes to pose, and even the very nature of her project. Further, a serendipitous event or comment may illuminate something she had hitherto not foreseen, and so force her to reconfigure her research agenda yet more. The dimensions of the unpredictable multiply. No wonder, then, that so many anthropologists see fieldwork as an essentially exploratory approach, especially in the dynamic contexts which characterize contemporary society, or that a fieldworker is expected to be resourceful, adaptable, ready to follow the data wherever they take her.

The only social anthropologists who do work in laboratories are there to study the culture of science. They are part of an increasing number of practitioners whose approach is more conceptual than physical. They may be working on biopolitics, technoscience, banking practices, public policy, among other topics. To Aihwa Ong and Stephen Collier, these contemporary anthropologists are investigating 'global assemblages': particular technologies, ethical regimes and administrative systems which articulate transformations in the world today (Collier and Ong 2005). To a significant extent, the concerns of these innovative ethnographers overlap with those of Miller and Rundall in this volume, for both of them had to face new sets of problems created by the ever-expanding use of online communication. If fieldwork is seen as an exploratory process whose endpoint may be hard to perceive, online anthropology is doubly exploratory as both the ethnographers and the studied are learning how to realize the potential of these technologies, increasingly well-established but constantly developing, at an accelerating rate (see, e.g. Boellstorff 2008).

One immediate question which follows is, what is the value, or function, of a code of ethics in research contexts which can evolve in surprising, unanticipated ways, whenever, wherever? Strong defenders of ethical codes argue that their aim is to protect the researched from potential abuse. For the sake of human dignity and physical integrity, the researched need to be safeguarded as carefully as possible. Thus what the researchers plan to do, when, why, how, to what end, needs to be specified beforehand in an extremely detailed manner. Furthermore the researched, as much as possible, must be informed of what is to be done to them. Otherwise, they are ignorant of what they are consenting to.

Fieldworking social scientists counter-argue that these safeguards may well be necessary and justified in the case of medical research but are unsuitable for the kind of investigations they carry out. They readily admit that it is possible that injecting a purple substance directly into a subject's veins could lead to physiological damage. Thus, experiments like this have to be planned with precision and equally carefully monitored. This is not questioned. What is disputed is whether such regulatory measures need to be imitated in the social sciences, whose practitioners do not usually put potentially nasty items physically inside human beings. It is true that exceptions have to be made for those classed as vulnerable, e.g. children, prisoners; statements about maintaining data confidentiality have to be upheld. But these can be seen as qualifying clauses which do not undercut the aims and values of most qualitative field research. Moreover, critics of ethical overregulation underline the incompatibility of forecasting precisely the trajectory of a research project, and fieldwork. In other words, because fieldworkers follow rather than confine others, they cannot predict with any exactitude what they will be doing when during the course of their research. So how can they fill in the forms?

Consent forms raise a further series of issues. The basic idea sounds at first plausible, indeed laudable: informing an interviewee of what is about to occur, why, and of their freedom to end the encounter, at any point, without giving a justification. Problems arise when people may not understand what they are consenting to, especially if they are from cultures or groups where forms are unknown. To many, both interviewers and interviewees, reading and signing preliminary forms is an intrusive formality, an unwanted opener to what they hope will be a relaxed discussion. Moreover, many peoples, particularly those from subaltern strata, are sceptical or wary of all forms. All too often, signing papers is seen as an extraneous bureaucratic exercise which further entangles the signatory in the meshes of the state. On top of that, the form itself implies mistrust, by the producers of the form, who refuse to rely on the professionalism of the interviewer, and by the interviewee, who feels the ethnographer sitting opposite him cannot take his trust as read. Oral consent, captured and preserved on a digital recorder, can suffer the same problems.

In other words, no matter how consent is formally given, the anthropologist ends up caught in the middle, in a situation not of her own choosing.

Of Vampires, Vultures and Other Fieldworking Blood-Suckers

In 1936 the anthropologist Geoffrey Gorer represented fieldwork in starkly superior tones: 'Anthropologists resemble society hostesses in many ways – an anthropologist talking to a "savage" is quite like a lady putting a "not quite quite" at her ease' (Gorer 1936: 27). His condescending attitude may be as out of date as his antique snobbery, but certain fundamental inequities within common fieldwork styles remain hard to shift.

When MacClancy first began fieldwork in Spain, in 1984, he was immediately informed how much indigenous colleagues disliked 'paracaidistas' (parachutists), i.e. foreigners who drop into an area, get the information they need, and then get out, usually never to be seen again. Spanish anthropologists felt their compatriots were being taken advantage of, and given little in return. When Fuentes began fieldwork in the Mentawai Islands, Indonesia, in 1989, he was immediately questioned by indigenous officials and locals whether or not he, like earlier researchers, would simply stay for a short while, gather information and then depart, or if he would be making some sort of tangible contributions to villagers' lives. Anthropologists in general are well aware of the potentially exploitative dimension of their work practice: gaining something in exchange for virtually nothing.

The Malinowskian model of fieldwork is all too open to this charge. The idea is that an ignorant outsider goes to live with a group, tries to make friends with them, participates in their daily activities, continually watches everything, and endlessly questions. The traditional justification for this practice was the archival value of the resulting ethnography, and the potential of ethnographically-grounded cross-cultural comparison to generate generalizations about the nature and variety of humanity. For an increasing number of anthropologists, that justification is no longer enough.

Critics of this style of fieldwork, for many decades almost dominant in anthropology, argue that it is unethical because fundamentally deceptive. A dutiful fieldworker strives to make friends, or something close to that; she and the subject of her fieldwork cannot keep up a formal academic relationship throughout the extended period of her stay. Both will relax and talk as though among friends. However, the key difference between the two parties with respect to those conversations is that at least one of them has an ulterior motive. To put this another way, many fieldworkers are uneasy that they are consciously entering into social relationships in bad faith. They might appear to be extending the hand of friendship, but in reality that is the sentimental cover for their hard-nosed end: to exploit this bond for their own instrumental desires. Defenders of this method might counter-argue that they are open in their aims from the very moment of their arrival; they are hiding nothing. The response is to query how many locals understand academic endeavour, whether they realize fieldworkers are never off-duty, and whether they comprehend that their fieldworker has no control whatsoever over what others may do with the information she publishes. In the 1960s the Anglo-Cypriot anthropologist Peter Loizos carried out doctoral fieldwork in a Cypriot village. When one of his key pundits read the resulting thesis, he said he was surprised at the detail, then added, 'I think you sociologists do exactly what you like'. Loizos took that to mean, 'You are powerful, and you follow your own interests without regard for others' (Loizos 1994: 45).

The exploitative possibilities go further than this. A fledgling fieldworker who does her job well and produces well-regarded publications gets a job and some prestige. The locals get nothing, usually. Worse, they may be left feeling betrayed. For in a face-to-face community where people know one another from birth until death, the idea of making friends with an outsider may well be very unusual, and the locals might not take on board the fact that their relationship with the incomer has, from the beginning, a time expiry date. So when the fieldworker does depart, they may be left feeling surprised, and hurt (MacClancy 2011). In addition, the presence of the fieldworker can easily raise locals' expectations about the benefits of her stay, over which she has little control. Her failure to meet those expectations may become another source of disappointment and pained feelings. In the 1950s several anthropologists in Papua New Guinea encountered locals clearing a landing strip, for the goods-laden plane the fieldworker had commanded (e.g. Lawrence 1964). More recently Catherine Panter-Brick, engaged in a study of Afghan schoolchildren, discovered that so many were turning up for interview because they thought they were being selected for a scholarship to the United States (Eggerman and Panter-Brick 2011).

The potential pitfalls for biological anthropologists can be even worse. Some self-critical social anthropologists, seeking a striking metaphor, call themselves 'vampires', as though going for the jugular of the studied, or 'vultures', because they treat others like corpses to be picked at (Loizos 1994; Koepping 1994: 105). But the term of abuse for biological anthropologists may be much more cutting, because it is far less metaphorical: blood-suckers, collecting sanguinary samples in the name of science. Unlike clinical researchers, biological anthropologists do not put anything into people's bodies. Instead they may take things out: blood, saliva, and other effluvia. The possible interpretations of this practice are manifold, with indigenous groups vigorously campaigning, on various grounds, for the return of any body part removed from a living person and still stored after their death. The biological anthropologist Alain Froment characterizes his colleagues caught in these disputes as trying to achieve a provisional balance between individual and community rights, and the rights of humankind (Froment 2011: 194–95). His colleague, Jonathan Marks, stakes a more resolute position:

> It could be argued that the major biomedical advance of the twentieth century was neither antibiotics or genomics, but rather the recognition that progress in science is great, but when it comes into conflict with human rights, human rights wins, hands down. The nature of those rights and

what constitutes a violation of them are necessarily evolving subjects, but if science is to flourish, it must do so in the context of public ideas about what is fair, decent and appropriate. (Marks 2010: 4)

For primatologists, the context of their impact is double: humans and non-humans. Most primatologists are faced with a number of ethical obligations: to source country collaborators, local communities in which they work, the actual primates that are the focus of the research, and the local ecologies where they ply their trade. In these ways primatologists are enmeshed in both a local human and a local primate community, and often also in a larger conservation community. Many of the contexts noted above for social anthropologists extend also to primatologists. Furthermore, as noted at the beginning, a primatologist must also consider the impact her presence has on the lives and ecologies of the local primates, who are themselves often threatened and/or endangered. All too frequently, the interests of local humans and of local non-human primates are opposed to one another, thus generating conflict over space, food and the use of local ecologies. This is especially true in the contexts of human hunting practices and the exploitation of tropical forests (Fuentes 2002, McLennan and Hill this volume).

Many anthropologists try to mitigate the imbalance commonly experienced in fieldwork by seeking a means to reciprocate. When MacClancy lived in a village on Tanna, Vanuatu, he offered to set up a small chicken-rearing business for his hosts in acknowledgement for his keep. He later overheard villagers explaining his presence to visitors by saying they were helping him in his studies, and he was assisting them with an economic project. The visitors replied, 'It is straight'. When Fuentes worked at the monkey forest site in the villages of Padangtegal and Ubud, in Bali, Indonesia, he helped them to develop resource management and educational programmes in addition to coordinating and providing scientific and veterinary advisory support. The limits of reciprocity, however, may be soon reached. Loizos recounts that one of his study group turned up in London with a sick child, and asked the anthropologist to fiddle his UK status so that his boy would be treated for free. To the man's anger, Loizos refused (Loizos 1994: 47). One partial means to redress the inherent imbalance in the Malinowskian fieldwork style is to take one's manuscript back to the group studied, describe or read out what is in it, and then take account of the comments made by locals. The underlying hope is that the final publication does not misrepresent the population studied and is a somewhat more equitable product of the encounter between fieldworker and the fieldworked. Of course, the final content of the resulting book is still decided by the author; only her name goes on its front; she alone bears the legal responsibility for its words. When MacClancy adopted this strategy with his book on Carlism, it seemed to work suspiciously well (MacClancy 2000). The villagers described made a few comments but accepted the vast majority of what was written. The supposed result was that the locals did not feel excluded from the production of information about them, and the ethnographer gained a more fine-grained account. The lingering suspicion MacClancy was left with was that the villagers had proved as exemplarily polite as ever: they had corrected a few points but were maybe reluctant to make more incisive comments for fear of, what exactly? MacClancy remains unsure.

The controversy in the early 2000s over the conduct, while among the Amazonian Yanomami, of the biological anthropologist James Neel and the social anthropologists Napoleon Chagnon and Jacques Lizot did much to develop anthropological debate about fieldwork ethics. Robert Borofsky, in his analysis of the issues raised, has argued that the old anthropological dictum 'Do no harm' is no longer sufficient. It is too passive, implying that anthropologists only need to avoid causing problems. Instead, he contends, anthropologists should be more actively engaged, by seeking to practice just compensation. As he admits, this approach is both 'far more involved and expensive'. It indicates that fieldworkers need to help improve the lives of those they live among, just as they, by giving information, help anthropologists build professional careers (Borofsky 2005: 87–89). How many contemporary practitioners are prepared to practise this is another question – a fact which raises its own question about the present constitution of social anthropology.

Some biological anthropologists seek to redress the imbalance of fieldwork by providing a degree of medical care to the population studied. This otherwise laudable aim has raised much controversy. Some argue that fieldworkers should aim to provide services which are adequate by local standards. Others contend that medically-oriented researchers are obliged to offer the best globally available treatment (Aagard-Hansen and Johansen 2008: 18). Anything less is not just patronizing, it is profoundly unethical.

In recent years, some anthropologists have attempted a seemingly more radical mode of redress: collaborative ethnography. The idea here is that a fieldworker does not go to a fieldsite with her research agenda already more or less clear, and with some ideas about how to reciprocate her hosts' assistance. Instead, she visits a group, states what she would like to do, and consults the locals about what research they would like carried out, what benefits the project could bring to the locals. They then enter a negotiation where a mutually agreed programme of research is formulated. The parties also establish an agreement that the field notes and material will not be used for any other purpose without the prior consent of the studied. The biological anthropologist, Lawrence Schell, who has practised this style of fieldwork with the Mohawk Nation of Akwesasane, upstate New York, states that the consequent research process was noticeably slower but the results richer, and executed in the knowledge that it was as ethically equitable as can at present be conceived. At the same time, and of equal importance, this style of ethnography may, or at least should, improve the lives of the people studied in some way, particularly the economic (Schell et al. 2005, 2007, personal communication, 2 May 2011). In social anthropology Serge Elie, among others, has argued for a comparable approach grounded on a 'reciprocity principle' which underpins his ethnographic practice in order to ensure that the final product has a practical effect on the social conditions of those studied. His wish is that his research product will 'serve as "resources of hope" for the improvement of my research subjects' lives (devoid of any condescending missionary intent), and not merely to fulfil the exigencies of making a living in an academic institution' (Elie 2006: 68). Some anthropologists have gone further. For instance, the Maori anthropologist Linda Tuhiwai Smith has argued that one effective way to 'decolonize' research methods and so help to redress the present ethical imbalance in anthropology is to enable more indigenous peoples to fieldwork their own communities, setting their own research priorities (Smith 1999). In reaction, several commentators on her highly successful *Decolonizing Methodologies* have worried what role her proposed strategy would leave for non-indigenous researchers (Staehelin 2000; Wilson 2001).

Perhaps this discussion is wrong-footed from the start, where what appears to be the anthropologists' general lack of commitment to the locals is in fact an Anglocentricity, a consequence of the anti-applied approach of Evans-Pritchard, the UK professoriate of his postwar time, and some of their transatlantic colleagues. In fact anthropologists in some other countries practise very different modes of fieldwork. In Brazil, Ramos emphasizes that she and the majority of her colleagues are expected to campaign on behalf of those they study (Ramos 1990). Many Argentinian social anthropologists regard their role as a political agent battling against the State and the powers that be (Guber 2008). In Israel, Emmanuel Marx stressed the commitment of fieldworkers to the fieldworked, the former acting as intermediaries between indigenes and the Government when the bureaucrats wanted to institute major change.[1] In South Africa, anthropologists are obliged to state in their research applications how the proposed fieldwork will benefit local populations (Ainslie, personal communication) In this case, it is the national government which enforces the committed style: it only funds fieldwork which is relevant to policy.

Fieldworkers like Schell and Elie have made an ethical point of collaboration. It can of course be argued that a collaborative approach has long grounded fieldwork. It has just not been placed at centre stage nor lauded as a central research method, until recently. Further, and to our collective shame, it is very likely that some anthropologists were formerly unwilling to acknowledge the extent to which locals themselves set the research agenda or themselves fulfilled the fieldworker's brief. While some late anthropologists are now infamous for hiding their debt to their key assistants, e.g. Melville Herskovits (Price and Price 2003), some others were ready to admit it. The best example here is Franz Boas, whose concern to acknowledge his local collaborator led him to name the latter as a co-author of some of his ethnographic works (e.g. Boas and Hunt 1905, 1906).

Concern that fieldwork be as ethically equitable as possible should not, of course, blind us to the long-known fact that some locals are working hard to take advantage of their fieldworker as much, or more, than she is exploiting them. Kummels and Schäfer recount how, although they went to work with all the inhabitants of one Amazonian village, they unknowingly fell in with one of its factions, whose members were only too willing to use the interlopers to strengthen their already powerful position (Kummels and Schäfer 1994). Such tales are common. MacClancy's original aim in Vanuatu was to do fieldwork among the Big Nambas of Malakula Island. Since they regard cultural information as property to be traded, he was immediately instructed that they consider anthropologists to be thieves; most doors were shut to him. When one independent chief did decide to take him into his village, he very quickly learnt that his task was to list the 'trouble-makers' there so the colonial officers could identify and remove them. MacClancy left within a week. The work of Fuentes and subsequent students in the Mentawai Islands resulted in significant financial support for one village, and one extended family in particular. This exacerbated a split among a prominent clan and villages, a split which preceded Fuentes' arrival at the site. This fact was only discovered a few years after the original project.

Some anthropologists argue that collaborative approaches do not go far enough, that it is to be expected, perhaps even encouraged, that locals should make the most of fieldworkers. They contend that anthropologists should be prepared to commit themselves to assisting those whom they fieldwork in their political struggles, indeed in whatever campaigns they may be engaged in. In 1990 Philippe Bourgois accused his mainstream colleagues of not merely dismissing researchers' responsibilities to uphold human rights, but of condemning these issues as ethically problematic. In pointed contrast to the then current postmodernist stand-offishness, he called for anthropologists to assume their 'historical responsibility' to address large moral issues because their traditional object of study – exotic peoples – were being violently, traumatically incorporated into the global capitalist economy (Bourgois 1990). Since then, an increasing number of anthropologists have advocated an activist approach (e.g. Hale 2007; Armbruster and Laerke 2008). But taking sides, however praiseworthy, has its own problematic. It is, for example, all too easy for a fieldworker to learn that the side she decided to work with is not as simple or simply identifiable as initially thought. Perhaps she has to choose between competing factions or viewpoints. She may have to ask the question, to whom is her primary allegiance due? Perhaps fieldworkers, especially those in conflictive zones, should be prepared to take a political stand, even if that means taking a choice between 'competing complicities' (Pettigrew, Shneiderman, and Harper 2004: 25). Shannon Speed, who conducted fieldwork in Chiapas, Mexico, tackles a related issue when she argues that 'one virtue of activist research is that it makes the interaction open to definition and the effects open to scrutiny by both the researcher and the community' (Speed 2006: 72). When the community she studied was divided on certain issues, she had to make a personal ethical decision about where her alliance lay. The difference, she contends, is that such decisions are more explicit and transparent. The result is not just an engaged activist anthropology, but a critical version as well.

A somewhat different issue emerges when 'studying up'. If a fieldworker sees her primary responsibility as lying with the vulnerable, the unvoiced, and the oppressed, then any study of an elite must, by definition, be critical. Moreover, it is unlikely that an elite is monolithic in operation and thought, but will be divided by debate and different interests. In these contexts, it is improbable that all members of the elite will approve the resulting ethnography (Stirrat 2005; Schwegler and Powell 2008: 6–7). Thus, we should not expect them to. When the British anthropologist David Mosse tried to get his analysis of a long-term aid project funded by the Department for International Development published, employees who had been criticized in the analysis tried, unsuccessfully, to halt its release. In his defence, Mosse argued that the publication of studies such as his is a precondition for the understanding that will assist international development to develop (Mosse 2005, 2006). Perhaps, as Tara Schwegler and Michael Powell suggest (Schwegler and Powell 2008: 7), we should rethink the nature of relationships between an anthropologist and those she studies, in ways which facilitate dialogue.

The upshot of all this is that not only is traditional distancing of anthropological fieldwork practice problematic, several of the proposed solutions are equally so. Some fieldworkers have become moral vigilantes to the point of no longer 'observing' the people they live among. Others have formed their own NGOs in order to take a more direct approach to advocacy. In the process the very nature of what it might mean to be an anthropologist is laid open to repeated question. The following is one example, among many: the Oxford-trained anthropologist John Palmer did his doctoral fieldwork with the Wichí of the north Argentinian Chaco. Post-doctoral, he returned in 1991 to 'accompany' them, as he puts it, in their sustained struggle through the hierarchy of courts to retain control over any of their resources which regional capitalists wished to exploit for their own ends: land, timber, oil, etc. His work is externally supported by Chacolinks, a small, international charitable organization. While he continues to write on anthropology, as well as dealing with his burdensome and diverse legal caseload, his publishing priority is to produce work of legal benefit to the Wichí. He remains an anthropologist, although one who is self-subordinated to the Wichí cause.[2]

The Malinowskian ideal was that one should participate as much as possible. But his professional charter was in fact always subject to limiting riders. Certain assumptions were not stated because it was understood by the gentlefolk majority who first filled the ranks of British anthropology that they did not need to be voiced. Perhaps the most notorious limitation was the taboo on sex with the locals: in the 1930s the only person prepared to openly dispute this, at Malinowski's seminar, was the self-promoting iconoclast Tom Harrisson, co-founder of Mass Observation (MacClancy 1995). It is true that a few anthropologists have entered into enduring relations with locals (e.g. Good 1991; Kulick and Wilson 1995; Guha 1999), but most have kept away from, or kept quiet about, such relations because they know they are generally viewed as exploitative. In contrast, in primatology there are at least a few well-known examples where the researcher has allied herself with prominent indigenous peoples via marriage, in order to subvert the hold of external, national authorities over local forests and primates. On top of that, there have always been some societies in which it has been difficult for fieldworking anthropologists to avoid matrimony or sexual relations with the locals. Among the nomadic Tuareg of sub-Saharan Africa, for instance, both marriage and divorce are easily entered into and all tents are owned by women. Thus a male anthropologist doing fieldwork with them has had to choose whether not to marry and so be regarded as a boy, or to enter a tent as its owner's husband. Moreover, there are today an increasing number of groups whose sexuality is central to their identity (e.g. Kirtsoglou 2004). For many of these peoples, a fieldworker who does not participate intimately is seen as stand-offish and guilty of an Olympian disregard for local mores. They are not wanted.

Anthropologies: Military, Commercial, Commissioned

July 1940: Evans-Pritchard, then an officer in the Sudan Defence Force, writes to his friend Meyer Fortes:

> Neither of us are under any illusions about the place which anthropology occupies in the minds of Government officials, but I was a little surprised they did not easily admit that such activities as intelligence and sabotage are those for which an anthropologist's training benefits him. (Quoted in Goody 1995: 65)

If there is one style of fieldwork which has raised controversy in recent years, it is the re-emergence of social scientists collaborating hand in glove with the military. To find anthropologists working for the army of their nation is nothing new. In 1919 Franz Boas publicly denounced the activity of a group of his American colleagues, who went unnamed, because they had used their field research as a cover for spying on behalf of the national government. During the Second World War many US-based anthropologists, openly and without apparent qualms, participated in the war effort. They thought the nature of the conflict justified the exploitation of their skills (Price 2008). In the postwar period many anthropologists continued to receive funding from US military organizations, though not quite so openly (Price 2004). During the Vietnam War anthropologists who did fieldwork among rural Vietnamese advised generals and Department of Defense officials on ways on achieving US objectives in the country. At much the same time, some anthropologists participated in Project Camelot, a research-grounded counterinsurgency project, which was much criticized by those who thought that it subverted the ideals of social science. The strength and number of these criticisms led to the cancellation of the project. It is not yet known how many British anthropologists have acted similarly. Evans-Pritchard, though frustrated in 1940, did eventually get his way, exploiting his anthropological skills for military ends, in the Middle East and North African campaigns.

These applied forms of anthropology have become, yet again, so polemical because in the mid-2000s, the US Army established a Human Terrain System. Its aim was to establish small Human Terrain Teams, mixed groups of military and social scientist personnel working in areas where US troops were deployed. Their task was to gain understanding of local socio-cultural conditions. Commanders would employ the information gained to achieve objectives pacifically, without the use of military force. Their level of success has been varied and questionable. Their defenders have argued that their use is ethical when their military superiors are engaged in a 'just war', that the Teams 'save lives', and that the application of 'socio-cultural knowledge reduces violence, creates stability, promotes better governance and improves military decision making' (McFate 2007; Lucas 2009). In response to the ensuing debate within academia, the American Anthropological Association established in 2006 a Commission on the Engagement of Anthropology with the US Security and Intelligence Communities to gather data on and assess the nature of the System and its Teams. In its Final Report, released in December 2010, the Commission highlighted 'the lack of a well-defined ethical framework of conduct for the program'.[3] As several had already pointed out, and the Commission iterated, given 'the inability of HTT researchers to maintain reliable control over data once collected, the program places researchers and their counterparts in the field in harm's way' (Gonzalez 2009; Network of Concerned Anthropologists 2009).[4] In other words, anthropologists who are embedded in the military cannot predict how the information they garner may be used and so potentially endanger themselves, their fieldworking colleagues, and the reputation of the discipline.

A key point generated by this debate about the Teams is that anthropologists in general have all too often been nonchalant about the possible uses of the information they publish. Too many have not thought through the consequences of including sensitive data in their papers and ethnographies (see Price 2004: 350). A central difficulty here is just how far into the future anthropologists need to think. Recent work has demonstrated the ways in which even ethnographic data published decades ago is today being exploited by locals in unexpected fashion. For instance, in Vanuatu, John Layard's *Stone Men of Malekula* (Layard 1942) is today being used by some Malakulans to strengthen their land claims, so deepening the rift between rival claimants (Geismar 2009). This might appear an extreme example (Layard did his fieldwork in 1914), but the point is still worryingly clear: we cannot accurately foresee how our words will be utilized, by whom, when, for what end, with what result.

These caveats apply not just to academic and military anthropology, but to all externally commissioned fieldwork. If the research of an anthropologist is funded not by an academically-oriented charitable foundation but by an external organization, the resulting data do not usually belong to their generators, but to the funders. Thus Judith Okely, whose fieldwork on gypsies in the UK was financed by the Department for the Environment, learnt to her surprise and shock on completion of her research that all her fieldnotes were the property of the British Government (Okely 1987). Working for a government department gave her access to otherwise confidential documents, but that generated yet more problems. When she learnt that a County Council was considering the creation of an inter-agency body of highly dubious legality, she felt too intimidated at the time to blow the whistle and only revealed the content of the relevant document decades later in a relatively unknown Scandinavian academic journal (Okely 1999). The ethics of anthropologists who work as consultants for business organizations can be just as complex (see examples in Cefkin 2009; Jordan 2010). The chapters by Parker and Kilshaw exemplify these moral quandaries in illuminating detail. The consequences of highlighting institutional incompetence may be all too clear. There is evidence that anthropologists employed as consultants on international aid projects can fail to win further contracts if they make their criticisms too loudly. One adaptive response to this negative outcome is for the suddenly underemployed anthropologist to re-present herself under the guise of a new consultancy group.

It is a general problem that many of the organizations for whom anthropologists act as consultants include gagging clauses in their contracts, which prohibit the publication of unwanted research conclusions. In addition, research funded by charitable bodies, who have their own funders to answer to, may be subject to ethical regulation by IRBs in which special interests are deeply problematic. The consequence is reactionary: here, institutional protection may be not just inhibiting academically, but in effect act as a gatekeeping procedure which ends up, over time, structuring bodies of knowledge. In other words, the desire of those who run institutions to keep the funders happy and the grant money rolling in frames and directs what kind of research activity are advanced. To put that another way, public-private neo-liberal tendencies shape the allowable. A systematic investigation of this skewing has yet to be carried out, although its significance is patent. One immediate question: who would fund this project?

The Virtuous Anthropologist, Robust Defender of the Moral Low Ground

Fieldworkers have to negotiate their research path simultaneously through at least three sets of ethics – their own personal one, that of their discipline, that of the locals – and maybe more, e.g. those of gatekeeper organizations who oversee access to the population studied, whether national, regional, provincial, ethnic, religious, professional, institutional, commercial, and so on. None of this negotiation is easy. In the same way that fieldworkers have to be prepared to question radically their research goals, methods and most cherished concepts, they must also be ready to revise their ethical parameters and be disposed to rethink their passage as they tiptoe across a complex moral terrain. To put this another way, if fieldwork is today a moral minefield, all contemporary fieldworkers are obliged to act as amateur bomb disposal experts. The question is, how to make them better at that job?

Some contributors put forward further ethical guidelines as a possible solution. The usual course here is to propose that the professional code be made more robust, detailed, responsive to contemporary concerns. The trouble is, as will now be very clear, that no code can specify what to do in every situation, as not every situation, even at a general level, is foreseeable. To this extent, the level of detail in a code verges on the irrelevant, and indeed is frequently misleading.

Moreover, as the profession wishes to practise and to display the highest standards of integrity, most codes are couched in near absolute terms, as though the ethical grounds on which they rest are of the firmest, and frequently with pretensions towards the timeless. The difficulty here is that all ethical codes, whatever their claims, fail to transcend the contexts of their production; on the contrary, they are products of their own time and circumstances, and need to be openly recognized as such. For instance, the 1971 'Principles of Professional Responsibility' produced by the American Anthropological Association (AAA), declared that members have to put the interests of the peoples they study first, and that clandestine research was taboo. However lofty-minded these principles might appear, they were at the same time the product of lobbying by anthropologists who disagreed with their government's use of their discipline in counterinsurgency operations. In the next decade, a different faction of anthropologists argued successfully for the ban to be softened.

These and other examples from the history of the AAA suggest strongly that internal debates which are apparently about ethics are often as much about political sniping from different sectors within the Association. Indeed Carolyn Fluehr-Lobban, in a review of these debates, goes so far as to state, 'A uniquely political history of the discipline can be discerned by examining closely the issues of ethics and professionalism in anthropology' (Fluehr-Lobban 1991a: 26). In other words, if you wish to understand the shifting alignments and power struggles within the profession's largest, most prestigious association, just follow the crooked path of their ethical wrangles. Here, ethics is not above politics, it is a key to it. Goodbye, absolutes.

If ethical codes are products of their time and place, then as committed anthropologists, we should expect cross-cultural comparison to reveal how peculiar each one is. In fact, the projected formulation of these codes can be so polemical that the anthropologists of some nations elect not to have one at all. In the 1990s German ethnologists, in an extremely enlightened moment, chose not to decide on a code because it would limit their ethical discussions, while an anthropological association in France used a workshop to broadcast its abhorrence of American-style ethical codes (Pels 1999: 101). The projected research of Dutch anthropologists is only subject to review if it places 'a demonstrable physical or psychological burden on its subjects' (Bosk and De Vries 2004: 259). And, as always, we need to attend to the silences as much as to what is stated. For instance, a comparison of three codes in biomedicine with those of the American and British anthropological associations showed that, unlike their biomedical counterparts, anthropologists tended to focus on the powerful leverage that commissioning agencies could exert over them, while quietly downplaying the strength of their own position over those they studied (Aagaard-Hansen and Johansen 2008: 19).

We can also query the effectiveness of any such codes. It might be consoling to the morally sensitive to know that their discipline has a code of ethics, but the important question is whether their professional association is prepared to implement it when necessary. The historical record is not reassuring. Anthropologists in interwar Germany had a well developed gentleman's code, but that did not prevent the majority of them later assisting the Nazi regime, and some of them participating in every phase of the Holocaust (Schafft 2007). Similarly David Price, in an exemplarily well-documented exposé of the AAA during the McCarthyite period, found the Association, bar rare exceptions, guilty of repeated inaction when some of its number were attacked by government agencies: 'instead it buried its head in the sand, ignoring anthropologists being fired, blacklisted, and taught the valuable lessons of self-censorship' (Price 2004: 69). If we cannot include British anthropology in this unfortunate list, that is most likely because this dimension of its political history is yet to be examined. The only indications MacClancy has found so far of such practice are the statements by the veteran anthropologists Ronnie Frankenberg that in postwar Britain Marxist anthropologists were banned from working in UK colonies, and by Peter Worsley that Evans-Pritchard prevented him from taking up a post because of his left-wing political beliefs (Worsley 2008).[5] In sum, it is difficult to laud professional codes of ethics in the Anglophone world when the actions of professional bodies and prestigious individuals there have been at times pusillanimous, if not downright subversive of radical, anti-government positions.

Codes of ethics and attempts to implement them can also have grievous consequences for the very disciplines they were designed to assist. For the whole process of ethical review and regulation is having a profound impact on research topic choices. At first, in the UK, this affected medical anthropologists wary of NHS barriers against working with patients who are all by definition 'vulnerable'. Now it has become a question of established anthropologists discouraging prospective research students from topics, however promising they might be, which require burdensome, impractical forms of clearance. Similarly, today, those in the higher ranks of UK university hierarchies remind their employees of their need to perform outstandingly in the Government's periodic research assessment exercises. Of course, ethically troublesome research may well not easily fit this bill. The insidious consequence is that both the tenured and the upcoming are pushed none too subtly away from ethically complex subjects. As Foucault recognized years ago, monitoring is not neutral; it is distorting.

Codes of ethics are reactive documents, co-produced by members of a professional association in response to a threat or crisis. The relative status of these regulations might undermine claims to ethical absolutes but does not affect the pressing nature of ethical considerations. Of course, the nature and style of these carefully wrought codifications are necessarily different from ethics as practised by all of us, every day. These daily moralities, to give them a term, are lived, embodied practices, employed and debated in a quotidian fashion, and whose fundamentals are rarely reflected upon in a sustained, critical manner. To a significant extent, it is misleading to call them 'personal ethics', as that term brushes aside the essentially social nature of these moralities, the continuing products of interaction between humans in communities, however constituted, fractured, or open they may be. In a related mode, Lynn Meskell and Peter Pels speak of 'embedded ethics', where morality, codified or not, is a pervasive dimension in the actions of all parties to the anthropological endeavour: anthropologists, their overseers, the studied, the media, the publics addressed, and so on (Meskell and Pels 2005). Here 'truth' is but an aspirational term, and endless negotiation the day-to-day reality.

In these shifting, dynamic contexts which characterize the contemporary situation, anthropologists and primatologists in the field have to juggle, at the very least, their own personal but socially encompassed ethics; professional codes of practice, however flawed; and the moralities of those studied, to the extent that they understand them. Perhaps the best that can thus be desired is that fledgling fieldworkers be trained to be as ethically aware as possible. And, given that they cannot be trained in every situation, because so many are unforeseeable, they can at least be schooled in the types of dilemmas they may well face, e.g. the local reactions to primatological research discussed by McLennan, the difficulty of leaving the online field highlighted by Miller.In these circumstances where moralities are multiple and all absolutes relative, claims to wear a badge of virtuous certainty, as though it conferred an aura of ethical superiority, are but pretentious postures, to be dismissed or researched. They are anathema. What is much harder, and more realistic, is for the would-be virtuous anthropologist to stake out an ever-negotiated claim as robust defender of the moral low ground. This is all we can claim.

Notes

1. See the video, http://sms.csx.cam.ac.uk/media/1125921. Accessed on 5 July 2011.
2. Chacolinks, an Oxford-based, international charitable organization, supports legal action in defence of Wichí land rights, against the threats of logging, deforestation and intensive cash-crop production. It is committed to raising awareness and letter-writing campaigns. In addition it provides funding to assist the setting up of small-scale projects to relieve poverty, and raise the standard of health among the Wichí (see www.chacolinks.org.uk). MacClancy admits to a special interest: he has been chairperson of Chacolinks since its founding.
3. http://blog.aaanet.org/2009/12/08/aaa-commission-releases-final-report-on-army-human-terrain-system/. Accessed on 2 May 2011.
4. The quotation is from the webpage cited in note 1.
5. See the video and transcript, http://sms.csx.cam.ac.uk/media/1116760;jsessionid=F59E0A1E28381B1292BF9EF49590B133. Accessed on 10 May 2011.

References

Aagard-Hansen, J. and M.V. Johansen. 2008. 'Research Ethics across Disciplines', *Anthropology Today* 24(3), June, 15–19.
Armbruster, H. and A. Laerke. (eds). 2008. *Taking Sides. Ethics, Politics and Fieldwork in Anthropology*. Oxford: Berghahn.
Boas, F. and G. Hunt. 1905. *Kwakiutl Texts*. (Publications of the Jesup North Pacific Expedition, vol. 3.) Leiden, Netherlands: Brill.
———. 1906. *Kwakiutl Texts – Second Series*. (Publications of the Jesup North Pacific Expedition, vol. 10). Leiden, Netherlands: Brill.
Boellstorff, T. 2008. *Coming of Age in Second Life: An Anthropologist Explores the Virtually Human*. Princeton: Princeton University Press.
Borofsky, R. 2005. *Yanomami. The Fierce Controversy and What We Can Learn From It*. Berkeley, CA: University of California Press.
Bosk, C.L. and R.G. De Vries. 2004. 'Bureaucracies of Mass Deception: Institutional Review Boards and the Ethics of Ethnographic Research', *Annals of the American Academy of Political and Social Sciences* 595, September, 249–63.
Bourgois, P. 1990. 'Confronting Anthropological Ethics: Ethnographic Lessons from Central America', *Journal of Peace Research* 27(1): 43–54.
Brosnan, S.F. 2012. 'Introduction to "Justice in Animals"', *Social Justice Research* 25: 109–19.
Caplan, P. 2003. 'Introduction', in P. Caplan (ed.), *The Ethics of Anthropology. Debates and Dilemmas*. London: Routledge, pp. 1–23.
Cefkin, M. (ed.). 2009. *Ethnography and the Corporate Encounter*. Oxford: Berghahn.
Collier, S.J. and A. Ong. 2005. 'Global Assemblages, Anthropological Problems', in A. Ong and S.J. Collier (eds), *Global Assemblages. Technology, Politics, and Ethics as Anthropological Problems*. Oxford: Blackwells, pp. 3–21.

Cowan, J.K., M.-B. Dembour and R.A. Wilson. (eds). 2001. *Culture and Rights. Anthropological Perspectives*. Cambridge: Cambridge University Press.

Elie, S. 2006. 'Anthropology, Post-colonial Thought and Positionality', *Studies in Social and Political Thought* 12, March, 53–72.

Eggerman, M. and C. Panter-Brick. 2011. 'Fieldwork as Research Process and Community Engagement: Experiences from the Gambia and Afghanistan', in J. MacClancy and A. Fuentes (eds), *Centralizing Fieldwork: Critical Perspectives from Primatology, Biological and Social Anthropology*. Oxford: Berghahn, pp. 137–56.

Faubion, J.D. 2011. *An Anthropology of Ethics*. Cambridge: Cambridge University Press.

Fluehr-Lobban, C. 1991a. 'Ethics and Anthropology 1890–2000', in C. Fluehr-Lobban (ed.), *Ethics and the Profession of Anthropology. Dialogue for Ethically Conscious Practice*. Walnut Creek, CA: Altamira, pp. 1–28. (ed.). 1991b. *Ethics and the Profession of Anthropology. Dialogue for Ethically Conscious Practice*. Walnut Creek, CA: Altamira.

Froment, A. 2011. 'Anthrobiological Surveys in the Field. Reflections on the Bioethics of Human Medical and DNA Surveys', in J. MacClancy and A. Fuentes (eds.), *Centralizing Fieldwork. Critical Perspectives from Primatology, Biological and Social Anthropology*. Oxford: Berghahn, pp. 186–99.

Fuentes, A. 2002. 'Monkeys, Humans, and Politics in the Mentawai islands: No Simple Solutions in a Complex World', in A. Fuentes and L.D. Wolfe (eds), *Primates Face to Face: The Conservation Implications of Human and Nonhuman Primate Interconnections*. Cambridge: Cambridge University Press, pp. 187–207.

Geismar, Haidy. 2009. 'Stone Men of Malekula. An Ethnography of an Ethnography', *Ethnos* 74 (2): 199–228.

Gonzalez, R. 2009. *American Counterinsurgency: Human Science and the Human Terrain*. Prickly Paradigm Press, no. 34. Chicago: University of Chicago Press.

Good, K. 1991. *Into the Heart: One Man's Pursuit of Love and Knowledge Among the Yanomama*. New York: Simon and Schuster.

Goody, J. 1995. *The Expansive Moment. Anthropology in Britain and Africa 1918–1970*. Cambridge: Cambridge University Press.

Gorer, Geoffrey. 1936. *Bali and Angkor. A 1930s Pleasure Trip looking at Life and Death*. London: Michael Joseph.

Guber, R. 2008. 'Committed or Scientific? The Southern Whereabouts of Social Anthropology and *Antropología Social* in 1960–70 Argentina', in A. Boskovic (ed.), *Other People's Anthropologies. Ethnographic Practice on the Margins*. Oxford: Berghahn, pp. 110–24.

Guha, R. 1999. *Savaging the Civilized: Verrier Elwin, his Trials, and India*. Chicago: University of Chicago Press.

Hale, C.R. 2007. 'In Praise of "Reckless Minds": Making a Case for Activist Anthropology', in L. Field and R.G. Fox (eds), *Anthropology Put to Work*. Oxford: Berg. pp. 103–28.

Howell, S. 1996. 'Introduction', in S. Howell (ed.), *The Ethnography of Moralities*. European Association of Social Anthropology, vol. 4. London: Routledge, pp. 1–24.

Jordan, A.T. 2010. 'The Importance of Business Anthropology: its Unique Contributions', *International Journal of Business Anthropology* 1(1): 15–25.

Kirtsoglou, E. 2004. *For the Love of Women: Gender, Identity and Same-sex Relations in a Greek Provincial Town*. London: Routledge.

Koepping, E. 1994. 'Trust and its Abuse in Long-term Fieldwork', *Anthropological Journal on European Cultures* 3(2), Special issue, 'Anthropology and Ethics, 99–116.

Kulick, D. and M. Wilson. (eds). 1995. *Taboo: Sex, Identity and Erotic Subjectivity in Anthropological Fieldwork*. London: Routledge.

Kummels, I. and M. Schäfer. 1994. 'Ethics in Visual Anthropology', *Anthropological Journal on European Cultures* 3(2), Special issue, 'Anthropology and Ethics, 117–31.

Lambek, M. 2010. 'Introduction', in M. Lambek (ed.). *Ordinary Ethics. Anthropology, Language, and Action.* New York: Fordham University Press.

Lawrence, P. 1964. *Road belong Cargo. A Study of the Cargo Movement in the Southern Madang District, New Guinea.* Manchester: Manchester University Press.

Layard, John. 1942. *Stone Men of Malekula.* London: Chatto & Windus.

Loizos, P. 1994. 'Confessions of a Vampire Ethnographer', *Anthropological Journal on European Cultures* 3(2), Special issue, 'Anthropology and Ethics, 39–53.

Lucas, G.R. Jr. 2009. *Anthropologists in Arms. The Ethics of Military Anthropology.* Lanham, Maryland: Altamira.

MacClancy, J. 1995. 'Brief Encounter: the Meeting, in Mass Observation, of British Surrealism and Popular Ethnography', *Journal of the Royal Anthropological Institute* 1(3), September, 495–512.

———. 2000. *The Decline of Carlism.* Basque Book Series. Reno, Nevada: University of Nevada Press, Reno.

———. 2011. 'Relating Relations', *Friends of the Pitt-Rivers Museum Newsletter,* December, p. 4.

Marks, J. 2010. 'Science, Samples and People', *Anthropology Today* 26(3), June, pp. 3–4.

McFate, M. 2007. 'Building Bridges, or Burning Heretics?', *Anthropology Today* 23(3), June, 21.

Meskell, L. and P. Pels. 2005. 'Introduction: Embedding Ethics', in L. Meskell and P. Pels (eds), *Embedding Ethics.* Oxford: Berg, pp. 1–26.

Mosse, D. 2005. *Cultivating Development: an Ethnography of Aid Policy and Practice.* London: Pluto.

———. 2006. 'Anti-social Anthropology? Objectivity, Objection, and the Ethnography of Public Policy and Professional Communities', *Journal of the Royal Anthropological Institute* 12(4), December, 935–56.

Network of Concerned Anthropologists. 2009. *The Counter-Counterinsurgency Manual.* Prickly Paradigm Press, no. 35. Chicago: University of Chicago Press.

Okely, J. 1987. 'Fieldwork up the M1: Policy and Political Aspects', in A. Jackson (ed.), *Anthropology at Home,* ASA Monographs 25, London: Tavistock, 53–73.

———. 1999. 'Writing Anthropology in Europe: an Example from Gypsy Research', *Folk* 41: 55–75.

Pels, P. 1999. 'Professions of Duplexity. A Prehistory of Ethical Codes in Anthropology', *Current Anthropology* 40(2), April, 101–36.

Pettigrew, J., S. Shneiderman and I. Harper. 2004. 'Relationships, Complicity and Representation', *Anthropology Today* 20(1): 20–25.

Pierce, J. and M. Bekoff. 2012. 'Wild Justice Redux: What We Know About Social Justice in Animals and Why It Matters', *Social Justice Research* 25: 122–39.

Price, D. 2004. *Threatening Anthropology. McCarthyism and the FBI's Surveillance of Activist Anthropologists.* Durham, NC: Duke University Press.

———. 2008. *Anthropological Intelligence. The Deployment and Neglect of American Anthropology in the Second World War.* Durham, NC: Duke University Press.

Price, R. and S. Price. 2003. *The Root of Roots or, How Afro-American Anthropology got its Start.* Chicago: Prickly Paradigm Press.

Ramos, A.R. 1990. 'Ethnology Brazilian Style', *Cultural Anthropology* 5 (4): 452–72.

Rynkiewich, M.A. and James P. Spradley. (eds). 1976. *Ethics and Anthropology. Dilemmas in the Field*. Hoboken, NJ: John Wiley and Sons.

Schafft, G.E. 2007. *From Racism to Genocide. Anthropology in the Third Reich*. Urbana, IL: University of Illinois Press.

Schell, L.M., J. Ravenscroft, M. Cole, A. Jacobs, J. Newman and Akwesasne Task Force on the Environment. 2005. 'Health Disparities and Toxicant Exposure of Akwesasne Mohawk Young Adults: a Partnership Approach to Research', *Environmental Health Perspectives* 113(12), December, 1826–32.

Schell, L.M., J. Ravenscroft, M. Gallo and M. Denham. 2007. 'Advancing Biocultural Models by Working with Communities: a Partnership Approach', *American Journal of Human Biology* 19: 511–24.

Schwegler, T. and M.G. Powell. 2008. 'Unruly Experts: Methods and Forms of Collaboration in the Anthropology of Public Policy', *Anthropology in Action* 15(2): 1–9.

Smith, L.T. 1999. *Decolonizing Methodologies. Research and Indigenous People*. London: Zed Books.

Speed, S. 2006. 'At the Crossroads of Human Rights and Anthropology: Toward a Critically Engaged Activist Research', *American Anthropologist* 108(1), March, 66–76.

Staehelin, I.M. 2000. 'Problems in Paradise: Sovereignty in the Pacific', *Cultural Survival Quarterly* 24(1), Spring. Also available at http://www.culturalsurvival.org/ourpublications/csq/article/decolonizing-methodologies-research-and-indigenous-peoples.   Accessed on 11 May 2011.

Stirrat, R. 2005. 'Ethics and Development', *Anthropology Today* 21(6), December, 19.

Sussman, R.W. and R.C. Cloninger. (eds). 2011. *Origins of Altruism and Cooperation*. Developments in Primatology: Progress and Prospects, 2011, Volume 36, Part 2. Basel: Springer.

Westermarck, E. 1906–1908. *The Origin and Development of the Moral Ideas,* 2 vols. London: Macmillan.

Wilson, C. 2001. 'Review of L.T. Smith 1999', *Social Policy Journal of New Zealand* 17, December, 214–17. Also available at http://www.msd.govt.nz/documents/about-msd-and-our-work/publications-resources/journals-and-magazines/social-policy-journal/spj17/17_pages214_217.pdf. Accessed on 11 May 2011.

Worsley, P. 2008. *An Academic Skating on Thin Ice*. Oxford: Berghahn.

Zigon, J. 2010. *Moralities. An Anthropological Perspective*. Oxford: Berg.

2

Questioning Ethics in Global Health

Melissa Parker and Tim Allen

Introduction

Twenty-five years ago it was a common occurrence for anthropological field-work to be undertaken without securing ethical clearance, even if it involved collecting blood, urine or stool samples and/or investigating sensitive issues. This rarely happens now. Anthropologists working in the arena of global health, for example, are supposed to secure ethical clearance from their universities and gate-keepers as well as relevant ethical boards based at hospitals or Ministries of Health and allied research institutions.[1] Indeed, there is sometimes an apparently endless series of procedures, both formal and informal. While it may be the case that most anthropologists would accept the need for clear ethical protocols as guidelines in certain circumstances, in general, the imposition of these procedures is viewed as little more than a set of irritating and time-consuming institutional hurdles. The regulations are sometimes treated with scorn and research proposals are submitted with the explicit intention of 'pulling the wool over the eyes' of ethics boards in the hope of not getting dragged into protracted discussions. Why are so many anthropologists scornful and dismissive of ethical clearance procedures? It is not as if they are disinterested in the ethical issues that emerge during fieldwork, or wish to undertake research which could endanger or harm the lives of their informants.

Pels (1999), Strathern (2000) and Caplan (2003) have highlighted how ethics has become closely associated with the politically conservative part of audit culture since the 1990s. Indeed, Caplan has pointed out that ideological resistance and resentment at the ever increasing volume of work that academics are asked to do, often at the expense of scholarship, has meant that securing ethical clearance has just become 'a public relations exercise aimed at keeping senior management off one's back'. There are other factors, too, that contribute to anthropological antipathy to the proliferation of ethical procedures, some of them specific to particular topics. A fundamental problem for anthropologists, however, is that the core anthropological method of participant observation may be viewed as 'unethical' by public health and medical ethics boards, because it is impossible to obtain informed consent from all those being researched. It is only then possible to obtain clearance by either pretending that participant observation is not going to occur, or pretending that insights emerging from participant observation will only be used if informed consent has been obtained from the relevant actors. Concerns also relate to the way in which anthropologists find ethical procedures being manipulated to control dissemination or discredit awkward information; to protect institutions and employees, rather than those people being studied; and, on occasion, to actually justify questionable methods. In other words, anthropologists have found that ethical procedures may have highly unethical qualities, and that their purported function seems to be at odds with how they are applied. In addition, there is even some anthropological scepticism about having a set of standard ethical guidelines. This, too, relates to the nature of anthropological research. Engaging so intimately in the lives of our informants, we find ourselves knowing secrets. Deciding what to do with that information can be far from straightforward, and is often beyond the remit of standardized rules. Surrendering to regulated ethics agendas does not let us off the hook – or at least it shouldn't do. Rather often we need to draw on our own moral compass.

The above issues are addressed in this chapter with reference to two case studies. The first is based on fieldwork undertaken in a clinical setting within a UK teaching hospital on sexual networks and the transmission of HIV/AIDS in the 1990s; and the second is based on fieldwork undertaken at selected sites in Tanzania and Uganda since 2005 on neglected tropical diseases. The case studies could not be more different from each other – not least because the study locations and the topics for research are completely different. So, too, are the political contexts in which the research occurred. Yet there are some striking similarities.

Both research projects involved working as part of a multi-disciplinary team with biological and social scientists on infectious diseases, and significantly perhaps, both research projects were soft-funded. The research on HIV/AIDS and sexual networks was funded by the Wellcome Trust and the research on neglected tropical diseases by the Bill and Melinda Gates Foundation. In terms of ethical clearance, the research on HIV/AIDS and sexual networks involved securing clearance from an ethics committee at the teaching hospital where the study was based, whereas the research on neglected tropical diseases involved an extensive paper trail including memorandums of understanding between a UK medical school and the Ministries of Health in Uganda and Tanzania. In addition, ethical clearance had to be secured from various other bodies, such as the Tanzanian Commission of Science and Technology. Together, these case studies highlight the multiple ways in which the political, social and economic context shapes contemporary understandings of ethical practice; and the importance of not only nurturing a critical, engaged and questioning approach to ethical procedures, but also, on occasion, a willingness to subvert, resist or ignore them.

Ethics and the Study of Sexual Networks and HIV/AIDS in London

To start with research exploring sexual networks and the transmission of sexually transmitted infections: this piece of work was undertaken in London by Parker from 1993 to 1996 (see Parker 2001 and Parker 2006 for details). It took place at a time when it was not at all clear how HIV would spread within the UK as there was very little understanding of the sexual links between those who were HIV positive and those who were HIV negative. Mathematical modelling suggested, however, that it was likely that if sexual mixing was limited to a point whereby those people who were HIV positive were mainly having unprotected sex with people who were part of a small, discrete grouping, then one would predict a sudden rise in the incidence of HIV, but the total number of people infected would be relatively small as the infection would be contained within a particular group. If sexual mixing was more diffuse and individuals who were HIV positive were having unprotected sex with a diverse array of people across groupings with people who were mainly free from HIV, then it would take longer for HIV to spread, but the total number of people infected would eventually be greater. The task, then, was to elicit detailed empirical information about sexual links and behaviour so that it would be possible to predict the ease with which HIV could spread through the population.

Ethical considerations guided the research protocol. Anti-retroviral therapies were few and relatively ineffective at the time. The absence of curative treatment underscored the reluctance to develop a UK wide system of partner notification whereby a person testing positive at an HIV clinic would be legally obliged to reveal the names and contact details of recent sexual contacts. A system of partner notification did, however, exist for another sexually transmitted infection: gonorrhoea. This disease is very infectious but, in contrast to HIV, it is easy to treat with antibiotics and not fatal.

Building on the existing system of partner notification for gonorrhoea, a research proposal was thus designed whereby patients diagnosed with gonorrhoea were asked for the names and contact details of all the sexual contacts they had had in the previous three months. These people were then invited to the clinic to be tested for gonorrhoea. They, too, were interviewed with a view to eliciting the names and contact details of all the other sexual contacts they had had in the previous three months. By tracking the spread of a highly infectious sexually transmitted disease in this way, it was hoped to build up a detailed picture of sexual networks in London. With gonorrhoea serving as a proxy for HIV, the research was also thought to provide much needed empirical information for those seeking to understand and contain the spread of HIV.

The proposed research was passed by the relevant ethics panel on the understanding that informed consent would be secured from all informants. However, within a few months of starting fieldwork, it became apparent that patients attending the clinic were far from enthusiastic about contributing to the research, and very few were willing to impart information enabling their sexual contacts to be identified or contacted. There were numerous reasons for their reluctance including widespread concern that discussion instigated by an anthropologist such as Parker with their sexual contacts about sex and sexuality would only serve to disrupt already fragile relationships.

Ironically, patients attending the clinic with HIV proved more amenable to contributing to research on sexual networks. Already on first name terms with many of the doctors responsible for their care, and familiar with the ethos of the clinic, they were willing to accept that every effort would be made to preserve anonymity and confidentiality. A protocol deviation was thus submitted to map out sexual networks through the transmission of gonorrhoea and HIV. Curiously, the ethical issues previously raised about tracking the spread of HIV were overlooked and the necessary research clearance was granted. All informants signed the informed consent form before their first interview but this was by no means the end of the story.

Numerous obstacles were put in Parker's path (mainly by relatively junior health professionals) to prevent research being undertaken in the way that she would have wished – including endeavours to banish her from the clinic on the grounds that the relationships she was developing with patients were 'unprofessional' and 'unethical' (see Parker 2001 for details). Health advisers within the clinic, for example, objected to the fact that she spoke to informants in an open-ended way in order to try and elicit their understandings of sex, sexuality, health and misfortune. This was viewed as unacceptable because it set aside the approach used by clinic staff, which emphasized the need to keep a distance from patients in order to relate to them in an 'objective' and 'professional' manner. There was a bigger agenda too: there were barely disguised efforts to use the language of ethics to prevent information being disseminated which might adversely affect future funding and the reputation of the clinic. The whole partner notification and follow-up system for gonorrhoea was in disarray. The efforts to banish Parker from the clinic in the early days of her research by suggesting that she was developing unethical and unprofessional relationships with patients was manifestly a way of trying to hide the fact that health advisers were struggling to systematically follow up and, where necessary, treat the contacts and contacts' contacts of patients diagnosed with this disease. Basically, this only happened on the relatively rare occasions that the patients themselves took the initiative.

As time passed, the attitude of the health advisers towards research on sexual networks and sexually transmitted infections began to change. This was partly because an easy-going and friendly relationship developed between them and Parker, but also because Parker came to share, and sympathize with, their frustrations – not least because she was unable to make much more headway than the staff themselves in persuading patients with gonorrhoea to talk about their sexual contacts. With respect to HIV/AIDS, however, things were rather different. The HIV patients in the clinic had a special status, and they were given many more opportunities to set their own agendas and make their own demands. Even so, Parker was instructed not to work on HIV networks in the clinic, but to do so, if she wanted to, in her own time. The expectation was that this would prove impossible for her. In the event, that was not so. But this raised other ethical issues, ones that Parker negotiated alone.

Some of these issues are encapsulated in the following example: Jack and Tom were two male prostitutes who lived together in South London.[2] They were also boyfriends and Parker spent a great deal of time talking to them both individually and together. In the course of the research they introduced her to one of their long-standing male clients, Nick. It soon became apparent that Jack and Tom were HIV positive while their client, Nick, was HIV negative. They had known each other for many years and their relationship was by no means just a commercial one. They went on holiday together and Nick, the client, clearly liked and valued them a great deal. One day, in the course of an interview with Nick, he revealed that he had recently re-written his will. He went on to say that if he should die before either Jack or Tom then they would inherit his three-bedroom flat in central London.

Nick also spoke about the fact that he was HIV negative and that he sometimes paid for unprotected anal sex with Jack, but that he did not worry about the risks as Jack had told him that he was HIV negative too. He trusted him as he had known him as a 'punter' for ten years. In fact, Jack was HIV positive. Only a few days prior to the conversation with Nick, Jack had talked to Parker about the fact that he always told his clients that he was HIV negative as he did not wish to scare them unnecessarily. He did not think it was a particularly big issue as he always had protected anal sex. While recounting this, he seemed to forget that on a different occasion he had mentioned that he sometimes sold unprotected anal sex as he was paid more for that kind of sex.

What should an anthropologist do in this kind of situation? Where does one's loyalty lie? Parker felt that she could not tell Nick that Jack was HIV positive as this would have been a betrayal of Jack's trust, but it seemed ethically wrong to do nothing. Nick was clearly putting himself at risk by having unprotected anal sex with Jack. The situation was complicated by the fact that both Nick and Jack had signed consent forms which clearly stated that all information revealed during the course of the research would be kept confidential, and there were no circumstances in which it would be passed on to other informants. Moreover, there was the possibility that one or other or both of them were not recounting events accurately.

After much reflection, Parker decided to quickly arrange another interview with Nick and use the occasion to sow seeds of doubt in his mind. In other words, when he asked her: 'How are you?', which he was very likely to do, she would respond: 'Fine … though I'm a bit concerned because I met someone today who thought their partner was HIV negative but actually I know they're not … It's such a shame that I am bound by rules of confidentiality and that I cannot say anything – I just wish people were more questioning of what they knew…'.

She did not think that there was anything else that could be done. They had both agreed to participate in the research on the understanding that all the information they revealed about their sexual behaviour and contacts would remain anonymous. It would have been a betrayal of their trust and confidence to renege on the agreement. This scenario had not been anticipated by Parker, the ethics committee at the hospital where she worked, or her informants, and there were no rules or guidelines to follow.

At this point, it also became apparent that the consent form served a useful purpose: it protected her from being drawn into a potentially complex legal suit.

If Nick had found out that he was HIV positive and that he had acquired this life-threatening infection from Jack, who would have been culpable? Parker certainly felt complicit. She was, after all, sitting on knowledge that Jack was HIV positive rather than HIV negative and yet she was choosing to remain silent. That said, he had agreed to participate in the research on the understanding that all information would be kept confidential. He had even signed a consent form agreeing to participate on these terms.

There have been many occasions since then when Parker has run through the details of the case and wondered if she responded appropriately. Did her own desire to develop a detailed picture of sexual networks lead her to justify her silence by hiding behind the security of a consent form? If she had explained the full implications of 'informed consent' more thoroughly (by emphasizing to every informant that it was not impossible for a scenario to arise whereby she became aware of their vulnerability to HIV, but would be unable to communicate it to them), then perhaps informants such as Nick would not have signed it. Perhaps, too, she lived in too relativistic a world. By defending herself to her imagined critics, she asked herself the rather rhetorical question: who was she to say that Nick should know the extent of his vulnerability to HIV? It was not as if he had never heard of HIV or as if he had no idea about how it was transmitted.

In sum, Parker had jumped through all the hoops required and completed countless forms. As far as the Wellcome Trust and the teaching hospital were concerned, she was 'ethically clean'. Yet, no amount of paperwork could ever have prepared her for the complex ethical challenges that emerged in the field. There were no guidelines to follow and she ended up drawing on her own understandings of the rationale for the research and personal morality to guide her through.

The process of doing this research also highlighted the fact that while ethics committees based at university teaching hospitals typically place a great deal of emphasis on securing informed consent from participants contributing to research on health issues, it is – in reality – extremely difficult to achieve. With respect to research on sexual networks and the transmission of sexually transmitted infections, it not only proved impossible to predict the full implications of participating in research, but it quickly became apparent that the notion of consent placed much too much respect for the wisdom of words on a bounded piece of paper and it proved extremely difficult to get people to engage with the information presented on the consent form. Indeed, there were countless occasions when Parker explained the rationale for the research to a potential informant, only for them to politely nod and sign the form with little more than a cursory glance. Even when she protested, and said: 'No! No! You must read it!' and 'feel free to ask any questions about the work', they would just politely smile and sign it without even glancing at it again.

Why? The reason is simple and straightforward: they did not choose to participate in the research because they had an academic interest in sexual networks or because they thought they would receive better clinical care at the hospital, but rather because of personal recommendations from friends that it was rather interest-

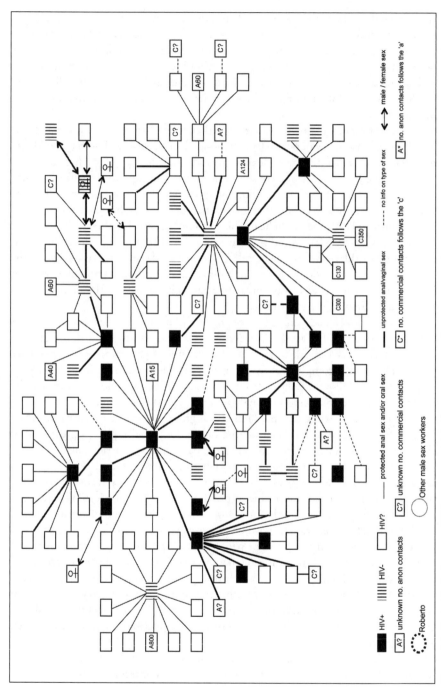

Figure 2.1. Sexual links between HIV positive and HIV negative men and women in London.

ing to meet this 'anthropology counsellor' who seemed to have infinite hours to sit and chat about all aspects of their lives. Perhaps, too, they knew better than Parker that it is impossible to guarantee confidentiality and anonymity when investigating a topic such as sexual networks. Thus, one of her informants looked at the network depicted in figure 2.1 and immediately worked out which one of the boxes depicted his place in the network. He then realized which one of the neighbouring boxes depicted his boyfriend and, realizing that the boyfriend had reported sixty anonymous sexual contacts in the previous year, declared: 'the dirty bugger … he never told me!' At this point, she whisked the piece of paper away from him, claiming that he was mistaken and that the network related to a study undertaken in a completely different place!

Ethics and Research on Neglected Tropical Diseases in East Africa

The second case study relates to research undertaken on neglected tropical diseases in Tanzania and Uganda since 2005. This research is part of a multi-disciplinary programme involving the mass distribution of drugs, free of charge, to millions of schoolchildren and adults living in predominantly rural areas where parasitic diseases such as schistosomiasis, lymphatic filariasis, onchocerciasis and soil-transmitted helminths are endemic. It involves collaborating with anthropologists, epidemiologists, statisticians and parasitologists from universities in the UK, Tanzania and Uganda as well as staff from the Ministries of Health in Tanzania and Uganda. The programme is part of an endeavour to control neglected tropical diseases in six countries in sub-Saharan Africa. In so doing, it hopes to contribute to the Millennium Development Goals by helping to 'make poverty history' and alleviating the suffering of 'the bottom billion'.

It is not straightforward to treat millions of economically poor people living in countries with weak infrastructures but it is anticipated that millions of schoolchildren and adults will have been treated for neglected tropical diseases in sub-Saharan Africa by 2015, aided and abetted by donations totalling more than one billion dollars from philanthropic organizations such as the Bill and Melinda Gates Foundation and the Carter Foundation, as well as bi-lateral agencies such as the UK Department for International Development and the United States Agency for International Development.

Anthropological assistance with this large programme of work primarily involves assessing local understandings and responses to the roll out of mass treatment. We have both spent more than a year undertaking ethnographic fieldwork at selected sites in Tanzania and Uganda since 2005 (for further details, see Parker et al. 2008; Parker and Allen 2011; Allen and Parker 2011; Parker et al. 2012; Parker and Allen 2013). This research falls broadly within the remit of monitoring and evaluation and, initially, presented few ethical difficulties.

In Tanzania, for example, our research proposal was presented as an addition to epidemiological research that had already been approved and clearance was provided by the National Institute for Medical Research (NIMR) and the Tanzanian

Commission of Science and Technology (COSTECH) with minimal amendments. In the field, it was possible to make a swift start: district officials were welcoming and numerous meetings were held at selected villages to explain the rationale for the research and the way in which it would be undertaken. Informed consent is not required when undertaking this kind of fieldwork in East Africa. Indeed, it would be impossible to acquire in any meaningful way as many adults have never been to school and cannot read or write. Moreover, nothing is more likely to jeopardize rapport while undertaking participant observation fieldwork than to request a signature on a slip of paper every time a person does or says something of interest. Nevertheless, the village meetings provided an invaluable opportunity to discuss the research and to answer queries and concerns.

Similarly, the fieldwork itself presented no exceptional difficulties: there was a regular flow of people seeking work as research assistants; numerous villagers requested money to help pay their children's school fees; sick villagers sought medical advice and so on. We did what we could, albeit discretely: we paid, and continue to pay, school fees for some of our informants; and we took a number of sick people to hospital and ensured that they were seen by doctors.

However, as the fieldwork progressed, it became apparent that there were a number of serious shortcomings with current strategies seeking to control neglected tropical diseases in Tanzania. In parts of Pangani and Muhesa districts, for example, our research revealed that by 2007 up to sixty-five per cent of adults were declining ivermectin and albendazole, the two drugs that were being distributed for the treatment of lymphatic filariasis. Follow-up research in 2011 revealed similarly low levels of drug uptake, even though this parasitic infection causes significant morbidity in this part of Tanzania (see Allen and Parker 2011 and Parker and Allen in press for details). In Ukerewe Island, Lake Victoria, research revealed widespread scepticism among adults about the merits of swallowing praziquantel, the free drug that was being distributed for the treatment of infection with *Schistosoma mansoni*. As a result, the uptake of drugs ranged from eighteen to seventy-four per cent at fourteen selected villages in 2007, with an overall average uptake of forty-four per cent among adults. Difficulties were also reported with the onchocerciasis control programme in Doma village, Morogoro region where Julie Hastings, a doctoral student at Brunel University, demonstrated that uptake among adults for ivermectin, the drug of choice for the treatment of onchocerciasis, fell from thirty-one per cent in 2004 to twenty-nine per cent in 2006 and seventeen per cent in 2007. These latter figures were derived by taking a twenty per cent random sample of households in each village, and interviewing one adult from each household.

At all sites, rumours circulated that endeavours to control tropical diseases such as schistosomiasis, onchocerciasis and lymphatic filariasis were a thinly veiled attempt by governments and international agencies to decimate politically weak and marginal populations by causing infertility, spontaneous abortions and even death. Concerns were also expressed that the drugs had gone 'bad' and were being dumped on the poorest of the poor by multi-national pharmaceutical companies.

These kinds of rumours are not specific to contemporary biomedical interventions on neglected tropical diseases; see, for example, research exploring rumours and resistance to tetanus vaccination campaigns in Cameroon (Feldman-Savelsberg et al. 2000); polio vaccination campaigns in Nigeria (Yahya 2007; Renne 2010); and public health endeavours to prevent the transmission of HIV/AIDS by distributing condoms in South Africa (Niehaus and Jonsson 2005). They have strong historical antecedents (White 2000) and often articulate local understandings of the workings of power and knowledge (Geissler and Pool 2006).

Concerned by the vehemence with which so many people resisted endeavours to control neglected tropical diseases, we spoke with health officials at a national and district level about the shortcomings of current policies. In the case of lymphatic filariasis, for example, it was clear that distributing the drugs ivermectin and albendazole, free of charge, to all adults irrespective of whether or not they were infected, and without providing detailed information about the aetiology, signs and symptoms of the disease, was creating enormous problems. Part of the confusion revolved around the fact that there is no Swahili word for lymphatic filariasis; but two biomedical signs of infection, swollen scrotums and swollen limbs, are locally understood as entirely different afflictions. These afflictions are called *mabusha* (swollen scrotums) and *matende* (swollen limbs) and they are perceived to have very different aetiologies. While it is recognized from a biomedical perspective that treatment with ivermectin and albendazole does not necessarily diminish the signs of infection, it is also the case that consumption of these drugs can prevent them from getting worse. Furthermore, it can prevent those who are infected, but asymptomatic, from developing visible signs of infection. Such facts were rarely known by staff employed at health centres, let alone those people living in villages with limited access to biomedical knowledge. Perhaps not surprisingly, the fact that swollen limbs and swollen scrotums rarely diminished in size served only to fuel anxieties that the drugs were part of a wider programme to reduce the rapid rate of population growth. If they had not been manufactured with the explicit intention of reducing fertility then it was argued that, in all likelihood, they had gone 'bad' and were being dumped on poor, powerless people.

In addition to the need to communicate more detailed information about the aetiology, signs and symptoms of lymphatic filariasis, as well as the rationale for mass treatment, there was a visible need for medical assistance for those suffering from *matende* (swollen limbs) as well as a need for supporting surgery for those suffering from *mabusha* (swollen scrotums). Without such support, it was hard to see how a convincing argument could be made that the government was genuinely committed to assisting those suffering from these afflictions.

The response by academics and government officials to these findings conveyed a great deal about the institutional pressures at work to ensure that biomedical interventions such as the control programmes for schistosomiasis, soil-transmitted helminths and lymphatic filariasis are constructed as successes, irrespective of the evidence. There are multiple ways in which this became manifest. At a district level, for example, officials who had been accommodating and helpful at the beginning of the research became unsettled by feedback suggesting that many villagers were rejecting free treatment and that the uptake of drugs had fallen below their targets of treating more than seventy-five per cent of the population. In one district, data documenting the uptake of drugs in Ministry of Health registers was suddenly placed in a locked cupboard (where previously it had been stored in dilapidated cardboard boxes on the top of a filing cabinet); and the person with the key went 'on safari' (travelling) for an unspecified period of time. We were also presented with summary statistics for the district suggesting that the uptake of drugs for lymphatic filariasis among adults exceeded the target of seventy-five per cent. Similarly, an official in a neighbouring district reported an uptake of drugs among adults of 100 per cent, clearly forgetting the fact that the Ministry of Health's protocol at the time advised pregnant women not to take the treatment.

At a national level, staff appeared edgy and concerned about the potentially negative ramifications of research detailing a low uptake of drugs for the treatment of lymphatic filariasis, but they politely thanked us for drawing their attention to difficulties with the control programme. In the same breath, they pointed out that our research clearance had been secured to work on schistosomiasis and soil-transmitted helminths, rather than lymphatic filariasis, and told us to submit a protocol deviation to COSTECH – the Tanzanian Commission for Science and Technology – before continuing with the work on lymphatic filariasis. We queried whether this was really necessary as the drug being used to treat soil-transmitted helminths, albendazole, was also one of the two drugs being used to treat lymphatic filariasis; and it would have been little short of impossible to investigate local understandings and responses to the roll out of drugs for soil-transmitted helminths without also investigating the roll-out of drugs for lymphatic filariasis. 'No! No!' came the response: it was very important to formally submit a protocol deviation, but it would not be a problem. In the event, it took the best part of a year to be officially told that the protocol deviation had been accepted. Although this might have been due to the slow pace of bureaucratic procedures, it was hard to avoid the conclusion that clearance procedures were being used to try and prevent the reporting of awkward information in the public domain.

The response by academics working with staff from the Ministry of Health also highlights the intense institutional pressures to continuously add to rhetorics of success, albeit in a different way. This has often been at the expense of seriously engaging with, and responding to, the difficulties arising at a local level. Thus, internal reports detailing difficulties with current control strategies and suggestions for change have been overlooked or set aside and requests have been made to avoid publication and discussion about more sensitive aspects of the research in public forums such as workshops and conferences. The underlying concern is that philanthropic agencies such as the Bill and Melinda Gates Foundation and bi-lateral agencies such as the

UK Department for International Development and the United States Agency for International Development will have no interest in continuing to fund strategies seeking to control neglected tropical diseases without evidence demonstrating that the selected strategies are effective. In addition, they are under no illusions that the withdrawal of funds would ensure that many academics and ministerial staff, who are currently employed on short-term contracts to carry out a specific piece of work, would lose their livelihoods. The stakes are high. The UK's Department for International Development alone has allocated more than £250 million for mass drug administration programmes with much of the money being distributed to a small number of institutions. In many respects, academics and policy makers in the arena of global health are caught between a rock and hard place; and it is little wonder that strategies such as delaying ethical clearance are used to control the type of information that is collected and placed in the public arena. Putatively objective research becomes an aspect of public relations in the constant scramble for funds by universities, ministries of health and research institutes. This can work against the interests of the very people they attempt to assist.

By way of illustration, we submitted a report based upon fieldwork undertaken in Tanga, Morogoro and Mwanza regions in Tanzania in 2007 to the funding body. It suggested that antipathy to mass drug administration was widespread and that the programme needed to be amended as a matter of urgency. However, while we were thanked for the report, we had a strong sense that it was being shelved and the advice ignored. In August 2008, there was an entirely predictable reaction to mass drug administration in the country in the form of violent riots. The trigger was the mass distribution of drugs in schools for the treatment of S. *haematobium,* which was occurring without the consent or indeed even the prior knowledge of parents. One of these riots occurred in Doma, Morogoro region and Julie Hastings, the doctoral student at Brunel University, who was observing the distribution of drugs at a village school, was rounded on by an angry group of parents. They threatened to kill her on the grounds that she was responsible for bringing the medicines that were poisoning their children. She took refuge in a school teacher's house and was later rescued by police from a nearby town under armed guard. Some teachers found distributing drugs elsewhere were not so lucky. They were beaten by angry mobs convinced that the mass distribution of drugs had sinister motives such as population control ((IRIN Humanitarian News and Analysis 2008; Daily News Online Edition 2008).

Mass drug administration was immediately halted and a consensus quickly arose among government officials and international policy makers that the riots were attributable to so-called radical Islamic groups attempting to undermine the government by actively spreading rumours to cast aspersions on the government treatment programme. While this interpretation of events highlighted one aspect of the unrest, it conveniently set aside a range of additional issues that we had raised in our research the previous year, including the risks and hazards of relying upon school teachers and village drug distributors to hand out treatment, insufficient and inadequate communication with target populations, and a chronic lack of social and biological monitoring.

Even before the riots had occurred, we had been asked to delay publication of our Tanzanian findings by a senior figure involved in mass drug administration, because of concerns that it might affect programme funding. However, rather than engaging urgently with our findings after the riots, the response was to try to downplay their significance. This was part of a broader process aimed at limiting bad publicity. For example, reports about the riots from the Tanzanian media on the internet were removed. Overall, it would be fair to say that sensitivities about criticism related to mass drug administration in the country were, if anything, exacerbated by what had happened. Responding to the pressure, we held back on publication. We also hoped that, whatever was said publically, improvements might be occurring on the ground, and that it would be best to carry out follow-up fieldwork after a few years to see if that was the case. However, in 2010, the WHO published its first global report on neglected tropical diseases, presenting a very optimistic picture of what had been achieved (WHO 2010). We felt compelled to write a response that mentioned some of the problems, including those leading to the riots in Tanzania (Allen and Parker 2011). We also expressed concern about the increasingly context free approach to mass drug administration being promoted as an idealized solution to alleviating poverty. The reaction was germane to our arguments here about ethics.

In a long paper published in *Parasites and Vectors*, Molyneux and Malecela, two of the key recipients of large grants to implement mass drug administration in Tanzania, wrote a defence of the largely context-free, vertical approach which they have been promoting (Molyneux and Malecela 2011). A substantial part of the paper comprises an attempt to discredit alternative points of view, including our own. However, it is striking that little attempt is made to engage with research suggesting that problems had arisen. In addition, the paper is cavalier with local details, including misnaming and mislocating the main official sentinel surveillance site in northern coastal Tanzania, and misrepresenting its findings – as well as our own. None of this appears to have been picked up by the reviewers. Indeed, in a later piece published in *The Lancet* (Molyneux et al. 2012), the authors claim that their paper in *Parasites and Vectors* had been 'factually verified' by the World Health Organization.

Such a defensive response was perhaps predictable. The sums of money involved in mass drug administration are large, and the competition to secure grants intense. However, it remains to be asked why credible medical journals would publish papers which make incorrect statements that could easily be checked. How is it possible to assert that the facts have been verified and that the reviewing process is rigorous? The answers to these questions relate to some of the arguments presented here about ethics. In the *Parasites and Vectors* paper, the authors repeatedly claim that those raising problems about mass drug administration are acting 'unethically'. They make this statement as if it is obvious, and incontrovertible. The point is that the evoking of ethical discourse by senior individuals in the arena of public health allows critical scrutiny of what is being claimed to be avoided. It connects a hegemonic discourse of biomedicine with vague, but emotive claims about ending the suffering of the poor. This makes recourse to a generalised sphere of moral probity, making close interrogation of evidence inappropriate.

Taking Ethics Seriously

The examples cited above illustrate the kind of difficulties encountered by anthropologists in the face of ethical procedures and discourses. They shed light on why so many anthropologists experience ethics as having little to do with acting morally or appropriately, and even less to do with the protection of vulnerable people. Indeed, there are occasions when ethics seems to be about the articulation of power and control, and even pose a threat to the discipline itself. However, these concerns should not deflect attention from the fact that serious ethical issues often arise during fieldwork – often with far-reaching, even life and death, ramifications. The example of Melissa Parker negotiating confidential information about HIV status is a case in point. The issues, in our experience, can be more pervasive and troubling where accountability is weakest, especially in Africa, where anthropologists often confront research protocols in the global heath arena that they themselves consider unethical, or at least ethically open to question. A few examples will suffice to make the point.

In the epidemiological cohort studies dealing with HIV/AIDS that Tim Allen has observed in Uganda, sero-discordant couples were not informed about their own or their partner's status, unless they specifically requested the information. This was to enable rates of infection between such couples to be monitored without external interference. In effect, the kind of issues raised in London for Parker about confidentiality were embedded in the research protocol itself, and effectively set aside as an issue. It seems reasonable to ask if such a protocol would have been ethically acceptable in the UK.

Another example relates to epidemiological research we observed which looked at the impact of supplementing children's diets with vitamin A capsules to reduce childhood morbidity and mortality in northern Ghana. A randomized control trial undertaken in the 1990s suggested that childhood morbidity and mortality could be significantly reduced if vitamin A capsules were handed out on a regular basis. Prior to the study, staff from the Ministry of Health stated that they would arrange for vitamin A capsules to be distributed, free of charge, through existing health services, if it could be shown that morbidity and mortality could be reduced by supplementing children's diets in this way. However, this did not happen, primarily because a trial monitoring the impact of insecticide-treated bednets on mortality and morbidity was being set up in the same place by the time an association between vitamin A supplementation and childhood morbidity and mortality was established. Key figures within Ghana argued that it would be unhelpful to alter the 'natural environment' by handing out vitamin A capsules as it would make it difficult to gauge how much any subsequent fall in mortality and morbidity was due to the widespread distribution of capsules, rather than to the distribution of bednets impregnated with insecticides. It seems reasonable to suppose that many children fell ill and even died of vitamin A deficiency that might have been saved. Was that ethical?

Finally, with respect to the programmes for neglected tropical disease control discussed above, we have been uncomfortable about the lack of engagement with target populations, not only because it has caused problems in terms of drug uptake, but also because it raised, for us, ethical issues in itself. To put in bluntly: what are the ethics of treating poor, marginal people in rural East Africa, when they have little or no understanding of what they are being treated for or when their understanding differs markedly from biomedical approaches? Similarly, what are the ethics of securing the co-operation of school teachers and village based drug distributors to administer treatment for neglected tropical diseases when the training they receive is so limited that they are confused as to which drug or combination of drugs to use for which disease? By way of illustration, a Ugandan school teacher from northwestern Uganda administered ivermectin to her pupils in 2008 without even knowing what the drug was for and without mentioning to the pupils' parents that such an exercise would be undertaken. Another teacher administered praziquantel and ivermectin to hundreds of school children at the same time, even though the Ugandan Ministry of Health guidelines (which are informed by protocols drawn up by the World Health Organization) stated, at the time, that the drugs should be given at two weekly intervals. The guidelines also recommend that praziquantel should be given on a full stomach, and invermectin on an empty stomach. Teachers have little, if any, control over the food children do or do not consume prior to treatment. In sum, the often haphazard approach to the distribution of drugs we observed on the ground raises an important question: is there an 'ethics for the rich' and an 'ethics for the poor'? It is unlikely that such procedures would be possible in London. Parents would be furious. There would also, surely, be legal implications.

Not surprisingly, perhaps, government officials and policy makers involved in mass drug administration respond to such points in a robust manner. The argument runs as follows: millions of school children and adults would not be treated for infections that cause significant morbidity, if procedures for distributing drugs had to be changed to a system whereby testing was mandatory and medical personnel were the only people authorized to treat adults and children. The drugs are 'safe' and 'efficacious' and, in the absence of a well-resourced infrastructure, surely it is better to treat millions of adults and children exposed to infection rather than continue with the current system whereby only a tiny fraction of those infected are treated at health centres and district hospitals?

It is not unusual for anthropologists to retreat from these kinds of arguments on the grounds that ethical principles do not travel easily across countries and cultures. However understandable this may be, it is perhaps helpful to reflect on the fact that, as we have indicated, the arguments cited above quickly become shrouded in 'ethics talk' to a point where key questions are ignored or poorly researched. With respect to neglected tropical diseases, it would be really useful, for example, to monitor the effects of treating multiple infections concurrently with adults and children who are immuno-compromised and/or malnourished. To overlook the concerns raised on the grounds that the drugs have been shown to be safe is misleading. They have, to our knowledge, only ever been tested on people who are thought to be relatively healthy and well-nourished.

Conclusion

There is widespread scepticism among anthropologists that ethical procedures do much to safeguard ethical practice in the field. This chapter sheds light on this scepticism. With reference to multi-disciplinary research undertaken on infectious diseases in the UK and East Africa, it suggests the following. First, ethics in the arena of global health has little to do with protecting the vulnerable (many of whom struggle with life-threatening illnesses) and much more to do with protecting the researcher and their funder. Second, ethics often ends up being manipulated and exploited to a point whereby the process of granting or rejecting research clearance becomes an explicit way of controlling the sort of information that is elicited from study populations and placed in the public arena. Third, the foregrounding of ethics in global health has created a space to use vague assertions of ethical criteria to seize the moral high ground, in order to discredit or sideline awkward facts. Fourth, emphasis on ethics protocols deflects attention from aspects of public health programmes which anthropologists are themselves likely to find unethical, and for which there are no mechanisms for holding those implementing them to account. The overall effect of these factors is to re-enforce the power of existing hierarchies.

This is not to suggest that ethics in the field does not matter. Ethics matter a great deal for anthropologists, a point that relates to our fifth conclusion. Securing ethical clearance through the multiple channels that are now necessary when undertaking ethnographic research with biomedics on health and disease can never fully prepare an anthropologist for the unexpected ethical dilemmas encountered in the field. In the sub-discipline of medical anthropology, it is not unusual for anthropologists to be left in the difficult position of taking decisions for which they need to apply their own moral standards. The imposition of more detailed or ever more stringent guidelines about the type of research that can and cannot be undertaken is not helpful. On the contrary, it is better to nurture a sceptical approach and to be alert to the possibility that institutions are more than capable of using ethical procedures in ways that are abusive. In such instances, there is a strong case for subverting or ignoring ethical procedures. Sometimes there is an ethical obligation on anthropologists to do so.

Notes

1.   Biomedical researchers and practitioners dominate these boards and it is not unusual for research clearance to be granted or rejected by people who have little or no understanding of anthropology. They may also embrace a rather different kind of ethics: an ethics grounded in the epistemology of science rather than the more open-ended, relativistic and less prescriptive approach common to anthropology.

2.   All names and identifying information have been changed to preserve anonymity.

References

Allen, T. and M. Parker. 2011. 'The "Other Diseases" of the Millennium Development Goals: Rhetoric and Reality of Free Drug Distribution to cure the Poor's Parasites', *Third World Quarterly* 32(1): 89–115.

Caplan, P. (ed.). 2003. *The Ethics of Anthropology: Debates and Dilemmas*. London: Routledge

Daily News Online Edition. 2008. 'Rowdy Mobs halt Bilharzia Vaccinations in Morogoro', 30 August, http://www.dailynews.co.tz/feature/?search=Rowdy+mob+Morogoro&searchtext=Search.

Feldman-Savelsberg, P., F. Ndonko and B. Schmidt-Ehry. 2000. 'Sterilizing Vaccines or the Politics of the Womb: Retrospective Study of a Rumor in Cameroon', *Medical Anthropology Quarterly* 14(2): 159–79.

Geissler, P.W. and R. Pool. 2006. 'Editorial: Popular Concerns about Medical Research Projects in sub-Saharan Africa – a Critical Voice in Debates about Medical Research Ethics', *Tropical Medicine and International Health* 11(7): 975–82.

IRIN, Humanitarian News and Analysis. 2008. 'TANZANIA: Vaccination Campaign treats Millions of Children', 2 September, http://www.irinnews.org/printreport. aspx?reportid=80123. Accessed on 4 April 2012.

Molyneux, D. and M. Malecela. 2011. 'Neglected Tropical Diseases and the Millennium Development Goals – Why the "Other Diseases" Matter: Reality Versus Rhetoric', *Parasites and Vectors* 4: 234.

Molyneux, D., M. Malecela, L. Savioli, A. Fenwick and P. Hotez. 2012. 'Will Increased Funding for NTDs Really Make Poverty History?' – Author's reply, *The Lancet* 379(9821): 1098–1100.

Niehaus, I. and G. Jonsson. 2005. 'Dr. Wouter Basson, Americans, and Wild Beasts: Men's Conspiracy Theories of HIV/AIDS in the South African Lowveld', *Medical Anthropology: Cross-Cultural Studies in Health and Illness* 24(2): 179–208.

Parker, M. 2001. 'Stuck in GUM: Life in a Clap Clinic', in D. Gellner and E. Hirsch (eds), *The Ethnography of Organisations: a Reader*. Oxford: Berg Press, pp. 137–56.

——————.2006. 'Core Groups and the Transmission of HIV: Learning from Male Prostitutes', *Journal of Biosocial Science* 38(1): 117–31.

Parker, M. and T. Allen. 2011. 'Does Mass Drug Administration for the Integrated Treatment of Neglected Tropical Diseases really work? Assessing Evidence for the Control of Schistosomiasis and Soil-transmitted Helminths in Uganda', *Health Research Policy and Systems* 9: 3.

——————.In press. 'Will Mass Drug Administration Eliminate Lymphatic Filariasis? Evidence from Northern Coastal Tanzania', *Journal of Biosocial Sciences*.

Parker, M., T. Allen and J. Hastings. 2008. 'Resisting Control of Neglected Tropical Diseases: Dilemmas in the Mass Treatment of Schistosomiasis and Soil-transmitted Helminths in Northwest Uganda', *Journal of Biosocial Science* 40(2): 161–81.

Parker, M., T. Allen, G. Pearson, N. Peach, R. Flynn and N. Rees. 2012. 'Border Parasites: Schistosomiasis Control among Uganda's Fisherfolk', *Journal of Eastern African Studies* 6(1): 97–122.

Pels, P. 1999. 'Professions of Duplexity: a Prehistory of Ethical Codes in Anthropology', *Current Anthropology* 40(2): 101–36.

Renne, E.P. 2010. *The Politics of Polio in Northern Nigeria*. Bloomington, IN: Indiana University Press.

Strathern, M. 2000. *Audit Cultures: Anthropological Studies in Accountability, Ethics and the Academy*. London and New York: Routledge.

White, L. 2000. *Speaking with Vampires: Rumor and History in Colonial Africa*. University of California Press.

Yahya, M. 2007. 'Polio Vaccines – "No thank you!" Barriers to Polio Eradication in northern Nigeria', *African Affairs* 106(423): 185–204.

World Health Organization (WHO). 2010. *Working to Overcome the Global Impact of Neglected Tropical Diseases*. Geneva: World Health Organization.

3

Ethical Issues in the Study and Conservation of an African Great Ape in an Unprotected, Human-Dominated Landscape in Western Uganda

Matthew R. McLennan and Catherine M. Hill

1. Introduction

Continuing human population growth in the tropics and the shrinkage, fragmentation and conversion of the natural habitats of nonhuman primates has meant that today primatology is increasingly conducted in human-dominated environments (Hill 2002; Paterson and Wallis 2005; Goulart et al. 2010; Moore et al. 2010; Campbell-Smith et al. 2011). Accordingly, prominent themes in applied primatology concern the conservation implications of human–nonhuman primate interactions and co-existence (Fuentes and Wolfe 2002; Riley 2007; Fuentes and Hockings 2010; Lee 2010), and the responses of primate species to human-driven habitat changes (Onderdonk and Chapman 2000; Chapman et al. 2003; Estrada 2006; Anderson et al. 2007; Isabirye-Basuta and Lwanga 2008; Asensio et al. 2009). Recent discussion in the literature regarding ethical aspects of primatological fieldwork has focused primarily on the impact of research on animals and their habitats, including concerns about habituating nonhuman primates (hereafter primates), risk of disease transmission, and the negative ecological impact of cutting trails and transects (Wallis and Lee 1999; Williamson and Feistner 2003; Goldsmith 2005;

Strier 2010). The ethics of working amid local human communities has received less attention (but see Wolfe 2005; Fedigan 2010). With the recognition that humans are an inescapable part of most environments inhabited by primates, and the inclusion of local people's wellbeing within current definitions of conservation (Bell 1987; Hulme and Murphree 2001), the ethical implications of field primatology require further consideration.

Field studies involve forging relationships with various groups of people including local residents and government officials (Wilson 1992). Since it is impossible for primatologists to carry out research without influencing the attitudes, behaviour and decision-making of such individuals to some degree, the implications of these relationships warrant careful attention. Whilst 'researcher influence' has long been recognized by social anthropologists in relation to the human groups they study (e.g., Kloos 1969; Wilson 1992), a similar effect has rarely been acknowledged by primatologist fieldworkers. It is imperative that primatologists, and other field biologists, consider their role in local social and political dynamics because these may have a direct impact on research and conservation.

In this chapter we describe some ethical issues experienced by the first author (M.M.) as a primatologist studying chimpanzee ecology outside a protected area in rural western Uganda. The research formed a component of a broader project headed by the second author (C.H.), which sought to examine human–wildlife interactions in Uganda within the context of the commercialization of rural production systems, land-use change and habitat degradation, set against the backdrop of the conservation of a high-profile, endangered large mammal, the chimpanzee.

Chimpanzees in Uganda

With approximately 5,000 chimpanzees, Uganda is an important country for the conservation of the eastern subspecies *Pan troglodytes schweinfurthii* (Plumptre et al. 2003). Chimpanzees inhabit the fragmented forests along the eastern edge of the Rift Valley in western Uganda, with the majority occurring within the larger national parks and forest reserves. In some regions chimpanzees also inhabit small unprotected forests, often along watercourses and in swampy valleys (Chapman et al. 2003; Isabirye-Basuta 2004; Reynolds et al. 2003; McLennan 2008). Uganda's deforestation rate is currently among the highest in Africa (2.6 per cent in 2000-2010 according to FAO [2011]), with most forest clearance taking place outside main forest blocks on private and communal land (MWLE 2002). Recent government initiatives to reduce rural poverty (e.g., the Plan for the Modernization of Agriculture; MAAIF/MFPED 2000), which promote cash cropping over subsistence farming and are funded by external agencies, have hastened increased conversion of unprotected forest and woodland to farmland (Figure 3.1). With ninety per cent of Ugandans reliant on wood fuels as their primary energy source (MWLE 2002), fuel wood production – in particular charcoal manufacture – is also a major contributor to deforestation outside of parks and reserves (Naughton-Treves et al. 2007). An additional pressure comes from unsustainable, often unlicensed, timber extraction.

Remaining chimpanzee habitat outside of protected areas is consequently severely threatened by current human activities (McLennan and Plumptre 2012).

Primates are not traditionally eaten in Uganda. With a growing human population and rapid conversion of unprotected forest, a situation has emerged in which chimpanzees outside of large protected habitats persist in shrinking forests surrounded by people, amid expanding agricultural land-use systems (McLennan 2008). However, chimpanzees can be troublesome neighbours. Where their home ranges encompass or border agricultural land, the apes readily incorporate cultivated crops into their diet (Hockings and McLennan 2012). Cutting wild food trees exacerbates this situation, leading to conflicts between apes and local farming communities (Hockings and Humle 2009). But crop-raiding is not always the main cause of conflict. Chimpanzees are large, potentially dangerous animals that occasionally attack humans. Although rare, the risk of attacks by chimpanzees – especially on children – increases whenever chimpanzees are forced into a close, competitive relationship with people, such as when forest is converted for agriculture (Wrangham 2001; Reynolds 2005; McLennan 2008; Hockings et al. 2010; McLennan and Hill 2010). As a result, chimpanzees are sometimes feared by local people (McLennan and Hill 2012).

Chimpanzees are classified as Endangered (IUCN 2010) and are therefore legally protected in Uganda. Laws often prohibit the use of traditional means

Figure 3.1. Tobacco growing on recently cleared forest land in Bulindi, in the Hoima District of western Uganda. Throughout this region, unprotected riverine forests inhabited by chimpanzees are being cleared to make way for tobacco cash-cropping (McLennan 2008).

of dealing with problem wildlife (e.g., hunting, trapping); however, local people often receive at best only limited support from government authorities (Hill 2004, 2005; Tumusiime and Svarstad 2011). This conflict situation is aggravated when protected wildlife is found outside of formally gazetted areas such as on private or communally-owned land. Should the wildlife species be perceived to have economic value (e.g., from ecotourism) then this adds a further layer of complexity as different stakeholders – from local farmers, to conservation organizations, government agencies, international researchers and private individuals – vie for a lead role in any future initiative.

Study Site

We conducted research in Hoima District, which forms part of the Bunyoro Kingdom of western Uganda. The District's human population totalled 343,480 at the most recent census in 2002, equivalent to 95.4 people per km². At 4.7 per cent, the average annual growth rate during 1991–2002 was high (the national figure is 3.2 per cent) and the population was projected to rise to 546,000 by 2012 (UBOS 2007). More than ninety per cent of the District population live in rural areas, of which seventy-four per cent depend on subsistence agriculture for their livelihoods. Farming is generally accomplished by hand with hoes and pangas (machetes), and using fire. Over ninety-five per cent of rural households use locally gathered firewood for cooking (UBOS 2007).

The northern part of Hoima lies between two major government forest reserves, Budongo and Bugoma forests, which both support important chimpanzee populations (Plumptre et al. 2003) (Figure 3.2). The intervening region is settled and cultivated but small forests inhabited by chimpanzees occur patchily along watercourses (McLennan 2008; McLennan and Plumptre 2012). Between May 2006 and January 2008, M.M. studied a population of chimpanzees in Bulindi in the northeast corner of the District (McLennan 2010a). Bulindi is situated approximately 25 km south of the southernmost fringe of Budongo Forest Reserve, where a chimpanzee research project has been ongoing since 1990 (Reynolds 2005; Babweteera et al. 2008) (Figure 3.2). Prior to our study, no foreign or national primatologists or social scientists had conducted research in Bulindi. However, personnel from a national non-government organization (NGO) made earlier exploratory visits to the site in response to reports of conflict between people and chimpanzees.

The habitat matrix in Bulindi comprises a mosaic of swampy riverine forest fragments and wooded grassland, intermixed with farmland and village areas. Eleven permanent villages are located within the 40 km² study area and most residents are native Banyoro (McLennan and Hill 2012). Forest fragments are small (the largest was approximately 50 ha) and unprotected. Locally, the forests are regarded as privately owned, but in most cases ownership is based on customary tenure and few households have formally registered land. Fragments are not owned by individuals or families in their entirety, but are instead partitioned into numerous portions, each belonging to a different individual or household. As many as 100 households claim ownership to parts of forest utilized by the chimpanzees. At the time of our study, private forests in Bulindi, as elsewhere in the District, were being extensively logged and converted to agricultural land (McLennan and Plumptre 2012). In Bulindi, the widespread sale and harvesting of trees for the commercial timber industry began several years prior to our research. While most timber cutters are hired by dealers and brought in to work from outside the District, some local men also make a living from pit-sawing. Linked to these land-use changes, chimpanzee behaviour was widely reported by residents to have undergone recent negative changes. The chimpanzees supplement their natural diet with agricultural crops such as sugar-

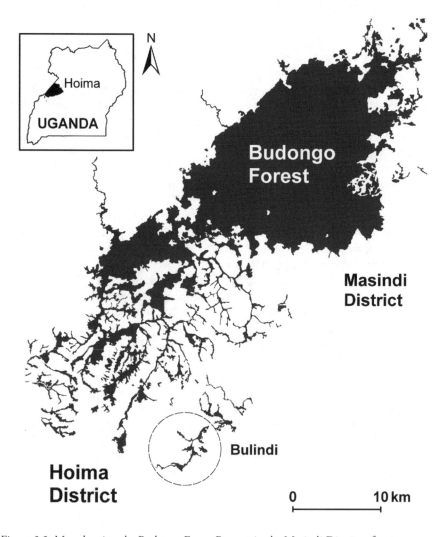

Figure 3.2. Map showing the Budongo Forest Reserve in the Masindi District of western Uganda and outlying riverine forests to the south and southwest. Grey areas represent forest. The study site at Bulindi in Hoima District is encircled.

cane, cocoa, guava, banana and papaya (McLennan 2010a) and were said to be entering village areas more often for food. In addition, the apes were reported to behave aggressively towards people when encountered, instead of running away. Accordingly, many villagers had come to view chimpanzees as worrisome agricultural pests (McLennan and Hill 2012). Harassment of the apes by people, including stone-throwing and chasing with dogs, occurred frequently during our study.

Research Aims

Research objectives were twofold: first, by studying chimpanzee ecology and interactions with people in this forest–farm ecotone, the research aimed to elucidate how these animals respond and adapt to habitat disturbance and fragmentation, and to increased contact with humans. This was to be achieved mainly through examining food availability, habitat use and diet, with human activities in and around forests and the nature of their interactions with apes also taken into account. The latter aspect was investigated via direct encounters with the chimpanzees (McLennan and Hill 2010) and through interviewing local residents (McLennan and Hill 2012). Second, because reports indicated rising levels of conflict between apes and farming communities outside protected areas and along borders of national parks and forest reserves (Wrangham 2001; JGI/UWA 2002; Reynolds et al. 2003), the research was intended to inform management strategies. Thus, while the research was designed as a theoretical study, it had intended conservation application. Although predominantly a study of primate ecology, the inclusion of interviews in data collection, as well as the agricultural setting, meant that frequent interactions with local people were expected. But while university ethics clearance was sought – and granted – in relation to interview methods and procedure, and treatment of human data generally, the possibility that by its very nature the study of a large protected mammal on unprotected land might be particularly sensitive and controversial, was not something we readily foresaw.

In this chapter the fieldwork experience of M.M. is presented as a case study to explore some ethical issues relating to the following:

1. The influence that the arrival of a primatologist and their subsequent research activities can have on local social processes and political dynamics. Specifically, the primatologist is considered here as a 'social actor' affecting what people say or do (Wilson 1992). We discuss this inadvertent 'researcher influence' in terms of its impact on both fieldwork and conservation.
2. The issue of consent when working with local communities. We examine this topic in relation to (i) the top-down process by which research clearance is obtained in Uganda, and (ii) the power relationship between a foreign researcher and rural, relatively powerless local people.
3. The distinction between research and conservation, and how these may become blurred during fieldwork. We consider the impact of conservation intervention on the social and political environment in which the researcher operates, and

on the researcher's interactions and standing with local people and government personnel.

4. Locally-employed field assistants and how their association with a research project can create a conflict of interest, affecting their relationships with members of their community.

5. Finally, we consider the thorny issue of whether, in certain circumstances, it is appropriate to expect impoverished rural communities to live amongst sometimes troublesome and potentially dangerous wildlife, including great apes.

2. The Arrival of a Primatologist: Local Social Processes and Political Dynamics

Here, we consider how the arrival of a primatologist in a region where no previous research had been done can generate unease among local villagers and local officials, potentially stimulating an increase in activities that adversely affect conservation. Ideally, before arriving at a new site a primatologist finds out as much as they can about the region in which they will conduct their research, including the local human culture. However, aspects of the local social and political environment that can directly impact fieldwork may become apparent only during the course of research. In this study, two such key aspects related to (i) the region's thriving timber industry, and (ii) local insecurities about land tenure and conservation projects.

Trees or Timber?

Prior to starting research in Hoima, we knew the District's small, unprotected forests were threatened by agricultural expansion, particularly cash cropping, and that recent habitat encroachment and degradation had reportedly given rise to conflict between farmers and chimpanzees (JGI/UWA 2002). Consequently, we anticipated a dynamic research environment and some forest clearance during the study. However, we were unaware that unprotected forests throughout the District were being targeted for timber production and that local forest owners were selling trees on their land. This extensive logging – mostly unlicensed – precipitates conversion of remaining natural forest because once large trees are removed the land is cleared for farming. In some cases, forest owners 'reforest' the land after logging by planting fast-growing exotic species such as pine or eucalyptus. At the time of our study, timber was big business regionally. However, the importance of the timber trade to local and District economies, and the broad spectrum of individuals benefitting from it – including forest owners, local leaders, businessmen, and representatives from various national agencies – became apparent only after many months of fieldwork.

Given this state of affairs, the arrival of a foreign scientist to conduct in-depth research about a legally-protected wildlife species in District forests might have provoked unease among some individuals, including in local government. At that time, Hoima District's small unprotected forests had avoided the close attention of conservation groups. While our research was not presented as a 'conservation project', by its very nature it might be expected to take a critical view of current forest management regionally. At the very least, officials might presume the study would draw attention to the presence of chimpanzees in unprotected forests in the District, which might stimulate conservation activities. Thus the arrival of a primatologist may have been viewed as a possible threat to the interests of certain powerful figures in Hoima.

Land Tenure Issues

Villagers in Bulindi also had cause to be wary about the research. As fieldwork progressed it became apparent that insecurity about land tenure was widespread among local residents; as noted above, only a minority of households had formally registered land. The 1998 Land Act recognized customary land ownership, which meant local households could claim legal ownership of natural forest on non-registered land (Government of Uganda 1998). Even so, many residents were evidently confused about legal rights to forest and forest produce on non-government land. For those households involved in unlicensed commercial timber cutting and charcoal burning, the unexpected arrival of a European scientist to work in local forests was perhaps especially concerning since such a figure may have been presumed to have legal authority and might attract unwanted attention to their activities.

Chimpanzee Conservation and Local Politics

Not only was land a sensitive issue, it transpired that chimpanzees were already a source of local controversy. Local people knew that these animals also occur in the large Budongo Forest Reserve in neighbouring Masindi District (see Figure 3.2), and some were aware of the apes' legal status. They also knew that foreigners visit Budongo because of the chimpanzees (for research and tourism purposes) and that local people's access to the reserve is restricted. Crucially, two years prior to our arrival in Hoima a man from a prominent family in Bulindi sought to develop a chimpanzee ecotourism project there. On an initial visit to Bulindi we were directed to speak with this man. He was enthusiastic about the research, perhaps because he supposed it would help attract interest and funds for his ecotourism project, which he claimed had the support of the wider community. In fact, it later emerged that his proposal was fiercely opposed by local councils because residents feared the forests would be gazetted as a reserve for chimpanzees and they would be forced off their land, or else lose access to forest resources.

At the start of M.M.'s fieldwork a series of village meetings was held to explain the purpose of his study, i.e. it was an academic research project that also aimed to provide relevant agencies and local people with practical information to aid management of the chimpanzees. The focus on chimpanzees, however, meant that in the eyes of many residents it had to be related to the unpopular ecotourism scheme. That M.M. had met with the man behind the scheme during his initial visit to Bulindi had not gone unnoticed. In spite of repeated public assertions that the study was unconnected with tourism, a lingering suspicion about the intentions of the research, and consequently a belief that it presented a risk to people's land and livelihood security, persisted. In fact, this suspicion was reinforced by subsequent events described below.

But M.M.'s arrival was not the sole cause of local anxiety: other outside agencies had also begun to show a close interest in the chimpanzees and the forests. Following reports of escalating habitat degradation and conflict between apes and farmers regionally (JGI/UWA 2002), the Uganda Wildlife Authority, as well as international, national and local NGOs, and other private individuals, came together to discuss solutions to the problem of chimpanzees in unprotected forest fragments in Hoima. Bulindi was among several sites identified for possible intervention. Nevertheless, at the start of our research no chimpanzee-focused conservation projects had yet been initiated in Bulindi or elsewhere in the District.

Several months into fieldwork, M.M. organized a public meeting to discuss the chimpanzee research in light of community concerns that had surfaced since its inception. It was well attended. Also present were members of a Hoima-based NGO – local partners of a national NGO – who unexpectedly used the occasion to announce their forthcoming project to conserve chimpanzees and forests regionally. This project included a renewed emphasis on ecotourism, but was independent of the earlier, opposed scheme. It was deliberately made to appear as if their programme was associated with M.M.'s research although, at that point, he was entirely unaware of their project plans. Inevitably, this reinforced local speculation that his research was a precursor to ecotourism development.

Following this meeting, the local NGO placed an announcement on local radio to publicize their imminent conservation project. Three days later, loggers arrived in Bulindi and began cutting trees with chainsaws in the heart of the chimpanzees' range. This may have been a coincidence. However, it is conceivable that the meeting was the catalyst for the logging since it seemingly demonstrated a link between the foreign researcher studying a protected animal in unprotected forest and the impending instigation of chimpanzee and forest conservation programmes regionally. It is tempting to speculate that the meeting prompted certain individuals, with an interest in forest exploitation rather than conservation, to act quickly to get the timber.

Similarly, in the context of local anxieties about land tenure and ownership of forest resources, it is not hard to understand why intensifying outside interest in chimpanzees and local forests led some residents to consider closely the cash value of forest resources on their land, and their immediate plans for that land. While forest owners across Hoima commonly arrange to have trees cut for money, timber dealers also approach owners directly, offering cash for particular trees. These processes were already underway when M.M. began fieldwork at Bulindi – evidence of recent, extensive logging in the forest fragments was widespread (for example, most large mahoganies had been removed). However, according to M.M.'s local field assistants the timber cutting that followed the initiation of research differed from previous logging in speed and intensity. It appeared that some forest owners felt compelled to convert trees into cash immediately, believing they would soon be prevented from doing so. There may also have been a perception that once trees are cut and the land placed under cultivation, it cannot be gazetted. Thus by drawing attention to a conservation situation through research – or in the case of the local NGO, through public statements about future intervention – the Bulindi example illustrates how, in some circumstances, the conservation situation may inadvertently be made worse.

3. Research Permission and Local Consent

Given these circumstances it is reasonable to ask: was permission to conduct the research obtained locally? There can be little doubt that some residents in Bulindi would have preferred not to have a foreign researcher working in the forest on their land (though this was not immediately apparent). So why did they not refuse? The answer lies partly in the top-down procedure by which scientists typically gain research approval, but it may also reflect a perceived power imbalance between a foreign researcher and relatively powerless rural farmers.

In Uganda, the first step towards obtaining research clearance is to submit a research proposal to the Uganda National Council for Science and Technology and other relevant departments in central government. Once this has been accepted, fees are paid and researchers receive an official letter of endorsement to be presented to district government officers and, if appropriate, to Subcounty, parish and village-level officials too. At each administrative tier the senior official wrote M.M. a letter of support requesting that the relevant official at the level below grant him permission to work locally and provide him with any assistance needed. This process culminated with a series of meetings organized by local village leaders in Bulindi at which he introduced himself to residents and explained about the research. On paper this procedure is presented as a process by which a researcher seeks permission at different administrative levels, from top to bottom, but the reality is that once research approval is granted at the top, and fees paid, officials and villagers at lower political tiers are obliged to assist.

One aspect of the research involved surveying forest patches to answer questions about the influence of forest composition and food availability on chimpanzee diet and habitat use (McLennan and Plumptre 2012). The sampling regime entailed cutting narrow transect lines within forests along which vegetation plots were established, and fixing numbered aluminium tags to food trees monitored for fruit production (White and Edwards 2000). Permission was sought from multiple individual forest owners of five main forest fragments, and consent was given without exception. However, it later transpired that several forest owners were unwittingly missed from this process owing to difficulties establishing ownership of all parts of the forest: individuals sometimes falsely claimed ownership or exaggerated the area of forest belonging to them, or else neglected to mention additional owners.

Vegetation surveys proved to be a particularly enduring source of suspicion and contention despite their purpose being explained both at public meetings and in conversation with individual farmers. Each time the explanation was apparently accepted. However, the transect lines were regarded by some as a way of dividing up the land – an activity associated with government surveys. The numbered tags on trees were considered a claim to ownership, especially if tagged trees had timber value. People observed that these research activities seemingly had little to do with chimpanzees. Rumours abounded about what this European researcher and his team – which included locally-employed field assistants – were really doing inside the forests (for example, perhaps he was bio-prospecting or looking for oil?). Attempts to address these concerns directly met with polite acquiescence: people said there was no problem. When M.M. asked his field assistants why certain individuals who were reportedly unhappy about the research had given permission for him to be on their land, the answer was: how could they refuse? As a *muzungu* ('white person' in current usage) he was presumed to have money and influence. Indeed, he employed a number of people locally, drove a personal vehicle and carried expensive-looking equipment. Moreover, he was known to communicate with powerful people in local government and had arrived in Bulindi with documents of authorization from central government. Consequently, local people may have felt powerless to refuse consent.

4. Research versus Conservation – Blurring of Boundaries?
Role Conflict and Personal Ethics

Although research and conservation are technically different activities, for researchers studying endangered wildlife the boundaries between the two are easily blurred. By definition, research into endangered species and threatened habitats has inherent conservation application, as was true of the study described here. One rationale behind such research is to provide data that can guide policy makers, government departments and conservation organizations. But there may also be occasions when fieldworkers face difficult choices and must make decisions directly pertaining to a conservation situation.

Primatologists often have considerable empathy for their study animals and concern for their wellbeing (Vitale 2011). Consequently, a departure from an exclusive role as a researcher may arise out of a sense of responsibility towards animals and their habitat, but may also be motivated by a corresponding desire to help local human communities with whom the primatologist also interacts. Owing to the enormous challenges to conservation throughout the tropics, and the continual human incursion into primate habitats, it is often impossible for primatologists to conduct their research and not be exposed to difficult conservation problems. This is especially true in human-dominated landscapes where the interests of people and wildlife so obviously conflict, often to the detriment of both animal and human safety and wellbeing. In such circumstances a position of research objectivity can be hard to maintain and out of a sense of personal ethics a researcher may feel morally bound to address conservation issues directly, even if this compromises research.

Intervention and its Impact on Fieldwork and Conservation

In Uganda it is illegal to cut timber in natural forests by hand using a chainsaw (Kambugu et al. 2010). Even so, the use of chainsaws was widespread in Hoima District during our study. The logging that followed the instigation of research in Bulindi was initially restricted to one forest fragment but quickly spread to others as growing numbers of forest owners arranged to sell trees. From a research perspective, the situation became increasingly intolerable: these were small forests and it was difficult to avoid logging teams. The men were cutting timber illegally and were clearly wary of M.M., making for an uncomfortable working environment. At times timber cutters hid from him and his field assistants. Furthermore, aspects of the research were compromised when trees being monitored for a phenology study were cut or crushed, or when entire vegetation plots were obliterated by the crowns of felled trees. Each day new large trees were cut, many of which were chimpanzee food trees (Figure 3.3). For example, the main tree species targeted for timber was *Antiaris toxicaria*, the fruits of which formed an important part of the chimpanzee diet during some months (McLennan and Plumptre 2012). Yet while M.M. suspected his presence was inadvertently contributing to the worsening degradation of the chimpanzee's habitat, it was difficult to confirm this unequivocally.

Figure 3.3. A felled *Antiaris toxicaria* tree in open, heavily-logged forest in Bulindi. Note the absence of large trees. *Antiaris* fruits were among the most important fruits for chimpanzees in some months (McLennan and Plumptre 2012).

This situation presented a major ethical dilemma. As a foreign visitor to Bulindi, M.M. was keen to gain the goodwill of residents and was mindful of the fact that these were not government forests. There seemed little that M.M. could do – or even should do – to address the escalating deforestation. A forest owner's decision to sell or cut trees was considered a private matter locally. Finally, following an incident in which a chimpanzee attacked and hospitalized a local child, M.M. decided to raise the issue at the District headquarters and also with local residents. Although attacks on children by wild chimpanzees have been documented at several sites where people and apes coexist (Wrangham et al. 2000; Kamenya 2002; Reynolds 2005; Hockings et al. 2010), none had occurred previously in Bulindi. According to local reports, chimpanzees had crossed the main Hoima–Masindi road from the direction of a forest patch in which men were felling timber with a chainsaw, when they encountered a group of children at a well. A four-year old child was grabbed and badly bitten by a chimpanzee. It is uncertain whether stress from the noise of the machines was a causal factor in this case; chimpanzees were heard reacting with evident agitation to the sound of chainsaws on previous occasions (i.e., by engaging in prolonged bouts of vocalizing and drumming, possibly intended to intimidate loggers). Even so, residents suggested the children may have provoked the apes, for example by throwing stones. Whatever the cause, following this incident M.M. decided it was personally unethical to ignore the events that were unfolding. The choice was simple: abandon the research or address the logging problem, despite the potential knock-on effect that it might have on the study. Accordingly, he approached forest owners and local councillors to discuss the possible consequences of the rapid deforestation on the behaviour of the chimpanzees. He suggested that the cutting of food trees and frequent harassment of the apes by people were likely causal factors explaining the reported rise in chimpanzee crop-raiding and confrontational behaviour. Many residents blamed the logging on allegedly corrupt local forest rangers and other officials. Several forest owners also claimed that forestry personnel advised them to clear natural forest and re-plant with exotic pine or eucalyptus. Thereafter M.M. reported the matter to the District Chairman, who agreed to look into it. The logging continued unabated, however. Eventually, M.M. contacted a senior forestry official whose responsibilities included law enforcement around the Budongo Forest Reserve in neighbouring Masindi District. As a result, after four months of continuous logging, a team of armed forest guards travelled to Bulindi, arrested two hired (non-local) timber cutters and confiscated a chainsaw.

What effect did this intervention have on fieldwork and the interactions between the primatologist and the local community? Firstly, mechanized logging in Bulindi ceased immediately. The respite was short-lived, however: the chainsaws were soon replaced by an increase in manual pit-sawing, a time-consuming but less detectable method of cutting timber. Nevertheless, logging was now often conducted in parts of forest away from the main areas of research activity, or at times when M.M. and his assistants were unlikely to be in the forest (for example, on weekends or evenings). As a result, the disruptive effect of logging on research was reduced and forest work became more relaxed. Secondly, the act of tree felling – previously a private matter – and its environmental impact became a much-talked about public issue. Thirdly, although M.M. was not present when the loggers were arrested, his involvement in the incident was plain. In addition to his role as a foreign researcher he now inevitably acquired a second role: that of a law enforcement agent, apparently able to call in powerful people. (Residents noted that the forest guards came from outside the District.) Perhaps surprisingly, his relationship with most residents did not appear to be negatively affected. Rather, the quality of the interactions changed. Increasingly, he was obliged to discuss with local people issues relating to management of the forests, the chimpanzees, and other 'problem wildlife' (e.g., baboons), and his involvement in community affairs intensified. As an increasingly visible member of the social milieu he was now expected to attend village meetings and share opinions on matters unrelated to the chimpanzee research, with the growing expectation that he might have an important role to play in the future fortunes of community members.

Residents in Bulindi acknowledge that forests provide them with important resources (e.g., firewood, building and craft materials), and many also recognize the ecological benefits of forests, for example climate regulation (McLennan 2010a). Forest owners commonly claimed they did not wish to cut their forest but needed money for basic commodities and to pay school fees. Seeking a solution, M.M. arranged a series of meetings in villages within the chimpanzees' range, together with representatives from a national NGO that work with local communities around Budongo Forest Reserve. The purpose was to explore the potential for a future project with the twin aims of (i) providing local households with economic alternatives to selling trees and clearing forest, and (ii) conserving chimpanzee habitat through sustainable forest management. While most villagers expressed support for this proposal and acknowledged that timber cutting had become excessive, others – namely timber dealers, pit-sawyers, and charcoal producers – were angered at the interference by an outsider and the potential threat to their livelihoods. Following these meetings, certain individuals attempted to encourage opposition to the proposal by stoking up local insecurities about land loss to chimpanzee and conservation projects. Furthermore, there was widespread concern that particular families would benefit from such projects at the expense of others. Consequently, the 'chimpanzee project' became a divisive topic locally. In the eyes of local people, M.M. was now someone with a far more clearly defined interest in the future of the forests, the chimpanzees and local residents. Yet his purpose, as it was now understood locally, was a clear departure from his formal, proclaimed role as a primatologist researcher.

With his involvement in forestry and conservation issues in Bulindi, M.M.'s dealings with District officials inevitably increased. Officials, perhaps under pressure to clarify their positions, publicly vowed to stamp out illegal timber cutting in the forests and voiced support for the development of community forestry projects locally. As a result, timber production at Bulindi was periodically (but always fleetingly) halted by District forestry personnel; however, pit-sawyers and timber dealers complained they had been instructed to stop cutting or else move to other forests because their activities were interfering with the muzungu's research. It later transpired that an allegation was made to the District wildlife authorities that M.M. was involved in the illegal trade of infant chimpanzees. Although the source of the allegation is unknown, it may have been politically motivated.

5. Field Assistants – A Conflict of Interests

The practice of employing local people to assist with research activities is widespread in primatology fieldwork. Such individuals are familiar with the local landscape and may have particular knowledge of the resources within it (e.g., plants) and/or the habits of study animals. Additionally, they provide feedback to their communities about research projects (and are often a valuable source of 'inside information' for researchers about local attitudes and activities), and may act as local ambassadors for the animals. At Bulindi, three local men who displayed interest in the research and the chimpanzees were trained as full-time field assistants (Figure 3.4). These men proved to be excellent assistants and the research benefitted greatly from their involvement. However, their association with the project plainly affected their standing within their community, causing a shift in their relationships with other residents in ways that were both positive and negative. Firstly, the men's status rose, partly because they were working with a supposedly 'powerful' foreign researcher but also because they were now considered authori-

Figure 3.4. Local field assistants at work in the forest at Bulindi.

ties about chimpanzees and forest issues. Furthermore, the men's use of research equipment, such as binoculars and GPS receivers, marked them out as specialists in their community.

It is commonly supposed that employing local people will be viewed favourably by the wider community. This may indeed be the case where employment opportunities are wide-reaching and research projects contribute significantly to local economies (e.g., Kasenene and Ross 2008; Strier 2010). However, small-scale projects (such as this one) offer economic benefits to only a small minority. In Bulindi, the field assistants' employment provoked jealousy and resentment among some community members.[1] For example, they were rumoured to be paid huge sums of money. Moreover, through their association with the foreign researcher some residents may have viewed the field assistants as party to whatever the 'true' purpose of the research was. They too became subjects of gossip and speculation (e.g., they were rumoured to use magic to calm the chimpanzees).

Most troubling, however, was the perceived association of the chimpanzee research with law enforcement, and the effect this had on relationships between the field assistants and local persons involved in activities known or suspected to be illegal. Regardless of the presence of M.M., some residents modified their behaviour in front of the assistants, for example by refraining from harassing chimpanzees (e.g., with dogs) or avoiding hunting in forest areas where the field assistants were working. When the logging became a matter of public debate the assistants found themselves at the centre of this controversy. Several times pit-sawyers and timber dealers came to argue with them at the parish trading centre. A locally-stationed forest ranger directed timber dealers to speak with the assistants to find out whether or not it was 'safe' to cut, or if an arrangement could be made so that logging could be conducted freely. The field assistants were offered money in exchange for information about the research schedule. Because of this situation they were given the opportunity to stop working, but they did not wish to do so. They were therefore instructed to remind others in their community that their purpose was to assist in the study of chimpanzees, and that M.M. was happy to answer any concerns regarding the research; on the other hand, inquiries pertaining to permission to cut timber needed to be directed to the relevant District authorities. This position had limited effect, however, since prevailing local opinion was that the authorities did not oppose the cutting.

6. Can People Live Alongside Chimpanzees?

In Uganda, expanding rural human populations and forest clearance for agriculture has meant that great apes are coming into ever-closer contact with farming communities (Reynolds 2005; Madden 2006; McLennan 2008; Tumusiime and Svarstad 2011; McLennan and Hill 2012). A similar process of habitat conversion is taking place over much of equatorial Africa. Thus, unless hunted, some populations of great apes increasingly inhabit human-dominated and degraded environments (Hockings and Humle 2009). From a conservation perspective this begs the question: is long-term co-existence between chimpanzees and people in agricultural landscapes achievable? (Figure 3.5)

Chimpanzees are an ecologically and behaviourally flexible species. They appear able to adapt to moderate levels of habitat disturbance, including farm–forest mosaics, at least in the short-term (Hockings et al. 2009; Hockings and McLennan 2012). Although relatively harmonious relationships between humans and sympatric chimpanzees have been reported at some West African sites (Dunnett et al. 1970; Leciak et al. 2005; Yamakoshi 2005; Hockings and Sousa 2011), wherever human population densities are sufficiently high, and where humans exert unrestrained and unsustainable pressure on forest land and resources, competition and conflict between apes and people is inevitable (Wrangham 2001; Reynolds et al. 2003; McLennan 2008; Hockings and Humle 2009; McLennan 2010b). In some regions tolerance of chimpanzees persists due to totemic beliefs held locally (Yamakoshi 2005). However, human cultural beliefs are liable to change in accordance with prevailing socio-economic circumstances and other external influences, as is increasingly the case in parts of Asia where traditionally primates have enjoyed a degree of tolerance not always extended to their relatives in other geographical regions (Priston and McLennan 2012). Consequently, the long-term survival of ape populations in densely populated agricultural landscapes is doubtful without intervention.

Figure 3.5. Adult male chimpanzees in Bulindi.

In Bulindi, low-level crop-raiding of domestic fruits by chimpanzees was often tolerated (McLennan and Hill 2012), but when cash crops such as sugarcane were damaged some farmers took steps to protect their livelihoods, for example through trapping or leaving out poisoned fruits. Furthermore, some of the adult male chimpanzees had developed the habit of charging and pursuing people (McLennan and Hill 2010, 2012). Aggressive behaviour towards humans by great apes, including physical attacks, engenders fear and hostility and is unlikely to be tolerated by local communities in the long-term (Wrangham 2001; Madden 2006; Hockings et al. 2010). In recognition of these problems, prevention and mitigation of ape–human conflicts is increasingly a focus of applied research (Hockings and Humle 2009; Hockings and McLennan 2012).

Chimpanzees are disappearing rapidly across equatorial Africa (Caldecott and Miles 2005). While small, outlying populations in unprotected habitats can sometimes play a role in maintaining gene flow between fragmented forest blocks and protected areas (McLennan 2008), in most instances their conservation will be of lesser immediate priority relative to that of larger populations occupying less disturbed habitat (Plumptre et al. 2010). Even so, negative interactions between apes and farming communities threaten to undermine local support for chimpanzee conservation in and around protected areas (Wrangham 2001; Reynolds 2005). In Uganda cases of chimpanzees attacking people have been reported in the national press (Rwebembera 2004; Tenywa 2006), and occasionally these stories surface in the international media (Smith and Marsh 2003). Conflict between impoverished farming communities and 'problem' apes in village areas therefore also has the potential to adversely affect national and international public support for the conservation of the species. For this reason, it would be short-sighted to disregard populations inhabiting agricultural landscapes. A second justification for intervention is a moral one: it is unethical to ignore the plight of these animals where they face persecution, and inevitably, extirpation. Equally, government authorities and conservation agencies have a responsibility to intervene if a legally protected species such as chimpanzees poses a threat to local people's safety and livelihoods, even when this occurs entirely outside protected areas.

The Bulindi example illustrates the formidable challenges to wildlife and forest conservation outside protected areas in Uganda. Clearly, the economic benefits to local people of maintaining natural forest on their land and living alongside large mammals such as chimpanzees must outweigh the costs substantially (Hill 2002; Nelson 2007). Worryingly, studies indicate that where forest is cut for farming and chimpanzees are forced to live amid expanding human populations, attacks by the apes on people – which may include predation on children – are a grimly predictable, if rare, occurrence (Wrangham et al. 2000; Reynolds 2005; McLennan 2008; Hockings et al. 2010).[2] This begs a second, more controversial question: is it appropriate to conserve chimpanzees in such circumstances? In essence we are asking impoverished rural communities to live cheek by jowl with an animal that potentially threatens their safety and which, in most instances, is not perceived in the local culture to have the same intrinsic value that the international conservation and scientific community assigns it (McLennan and Hill 2012). As conservationists we need to be careful not to fall into the trap of assuming that because something is done in the name of conservation it is automatically morally right, as expounded by Brockington (2004: 414) who states 'The good of conservation is such a powerful "myth" that it dulls our expectations of ill effects.'

7. Discussion

This chapter examines how the arrival of a foreign primatologist to study chimpanzees on private and communal land in western Uganda had a destabilizing effect on the local social and political environment, igniting prevailing insecurities about loss of land and control of forest resources to conservation projects. There was a strong indication that M.M's research and the concomitant interest from other outside agencies concerned with chimpanzee conservation, inadvertently precipitated increased levels of habitat degradation as local forest owners, business people and officials sought to profit from timber, apparently believing their access to forest land and resources might be curtailed in the future. Thereafter, via a series of social processes and events that saw the primatologist become ever more entrenched in socio-political dynamics locally, his formal role as an impartial observer became that of a 'partisan' conservationist. In doing so he became a key actor, influencing the ecological, conservation and social landscape which he had gone to Uganda to study as a researcher.

The issue of consent when working with local communities is perhaps frequently overlooked in primatology fieldwork. Wilson (1992) points out the importance of gaining informed consent from the actual people participating in fieldwork rather than from officials and/or local leaders. However, as described here, this may be difficult to achieve in practise due to the top-down manner in which research permission is granted. This has obvious ethical implications. Whilst the presence of foreign researchers can generate interest, excitement, and some employment opportunities locally, tangible benefits to local communities may appear limited – especially in short-term studies or during the early stages of longer-term projects. Conversely, perceived threats to local interests, through protection of animals and habitat and scrutiny of people's activities (some of which may be illegal), may seem all too apparent. Yet rural people in primate habitat countries may have little real power to refuse consent. Thus, although permission may appear to be granted at the grassroots level, as it was in this study, the research may in fact be viewed as an unwanted imposition by some members of the local community.

The ethical dimensions of the fieldwork reported here were undoubtedly intensified by a particular combination of local social and political factors, but many of the issues raised in this chapter are broadly pertinent across a range of environments where primates and other wildlife are studied. However, ethical aspects of primatology fieldwork are seldom discussed in the literature. Unlike in the social sciences, it is not in the primatologists' disciplinary heritage to regard themselves as 'social actors' affecting local social and political processes. As humans continue to penetrate and alter virtually all primate habitats, few primatologists conduct fieldwork outside a social sphere that includes important and complex interactions with local human communities and political figures, with implications for people, primates and their environments. Indeed, many primatologists are directly involved in community-based conservation activities at their field sites, either directly through their participation in projects or through their dealings with government and non-government agencies (see, for example, Wrangham and Ross [2008] and papers therein). At the same time, it is not uncommon for research projects to work closely with government authorities in matters of law enforcement, particularly within protected areas (e.g., Struhsaker 1997). The fact is that primate fieldworkers are often expected to be conservation-active, though they may have no specific training in implementing conservation or development initiatives or in managing community relations.

Policy reforms and intervention which promote local responsibility for wildlife and habitat management, and improved public education about chimpanzee behaviour, will go some way to reducing human–great ape conflicts. But the reality is that the long-term requirements of large mammals such as chimpanzees in forest–farm landscapes may be incompatible with the short-term needs of humans in densely populated regions such as Hoima District, where pressure on dwindling forest land and resources is set to intensify, and where current socio-political factors do not favour sustainable natural resource management on private or communal land. We acknowledge that some primatologists and conservationists may view this statement as unacceptable or even morally inexcusable. However, it should be recognized that the idea of putting wildlife needs above those of impoverished human beings is equally incomprehensible and morally reprehensible to many people, particularly those who currently live alongside 'troublesome' animals. This is not because they are ill-educated or misinformed, but because their experiences, and thus understandings and perceptions of the situation, are very different to those of outsiders. The challenge remains as to how best to develop strategies and institutional structures to facilitate effective co-existence between people and great apes. Shying away from these controversies and ethical dilemmas is not a practical solution to mitigating people–ape conflict or developing effective, long-term great ape conservation. Rather, a full and candid exploration of the issues, by all stakeholders, is the way forward.

Conclusions

The aim of this chapter was not to offer solutions to the particular ethical problems that we experienced during our research in Hoima District, Uganda. However, we believe it is vital that primatologists are open about the dilemmas, hurdles and pitfalls encountered during the course of their fieldwork. Not only will this enable future researchers and conservation practitioners to anticipate similar challenges in the field, it will aid the development of comprehensive ethical guidelines for conducting primatological studies in increasingly human-dominated landscapes (see also Fedigan 2010). Through doing so the hope must be that our research, much of which is applied, will better assist conservation goals and also be of greater benefit to local human communities.

Acknowledgements

Permission to conduct the research was granted by the President's Office, the Uganda National Council for Science and Technology (UNCST), and the Uganda Wildlife Authority (UWA). The help of the following government officers and organizations in Hoima District is gratefully acknowledged: District Environment Officer, District Chairman, Kyabigambire Subcounty Chairman, District Forest Services, National Forest Authority, and Uganda Wildlife Authority. This research would not have been possible without the participation and hospitality of numerous residents of Bulindi. Fieldwork was conducted with the help of the late Dan Balemesa, Gerald Sunday Mayanda, Tom Sabiiti, Moses Ssemahunge and Jane Stokoe. We thank the following non-government organizations in Uganda for support: the Jane Goodall Institute, the Budongo Conservation Field Station, and the Chimpanzee Sanctuary and Wildlife Conservation Trust. Figure 2 is based on a vegetation map courtesy of Nadine Laporte of the Woods Hole Research Center's Africa Program (Protected Area Watch Project) and WCS-Kampala. This research was funded by an ESRC/ NERC interdisciplinary studentship to Matthew McLennan, and a Leverhulme Trust award to Catherine Hill and Katherine Homewood (Project reference: F/00 382/F). The manuscript was greatly improved by comments from Kim Hockings.

Notes

1. During research with people living on the southern edge of the Budongo Forest Reserve (1992–1996) several informants pointed out that jealousy of another's good fortune, or their apparent assuming of a status or degree of importance, is a cause of dissent and conflict between neighbours in this part of Uganda (Hill, unpublished data). This perception is borne out by Beattie in his ethnography of the Banyoro, where he makes the point that social relationships between Banyoro people 'were and probably still are pervaded by the idiom of "inequality"' (Beattie 1971: 8), which influences the way in which people think about themselves and others.
2. Attacks understandably generate fear and hostility towards chimpanzees, and may trigger retaliatory killings. In such circumstances it may be difficult for a researcher to condemn such behaviour or to appear sympathetic towards the animals (see Wrangham 2001).

References

Anderson, J., J.M. Rowcliffe and G. Cowlishaw. 2007. 'Does the Matrix Matter? A Forest Primate in a Complex Agricultural Landscape', *Biological Conservation* 135: 212–22.
Asensio, N., et al. 2009. 'Conservation Value of Landscape Supplementation for Howler Monkeys living in Forest Patches', *Biotropica* 41: 768–73.

Babweteera, F., V. Reynolds and K. Zuberbühler. 2008. 'Conservation and Research in the Budongo Forest Reserve, Masindi District, Western Uganda', in R. Wrangham and E. Ross (eds), *Science and Conservation in African Forests: The Benefits of Long-term Research*. Cambridge: Cambridge University Press, pp. 145–57.

Beattie, J. 1971. *The Nyoro State*. London: Oxford University Press.

Bell, R. 1987. 'Conservation with a Human Face: Conflict and Reconciliation in African Land Use Planning', in D. Anderson and R. Grove (eds), *Conservation in Africa: People, Policies and Practice*. Cambridge: Cambridge University Press, pp. 79–101.

Brockington, D. 2004. 'Community Conservation, Inequality and Injustice: Myths of Power in Protected Area Management', *Conservation and Society* 2: 411–32.

Caldecott, J. and L. Miles. (eds). 2005. *World Atlas of Great Apes and their Conservation*. Berkeley: University of California Press.

Campbell-Smith, G., et al. 2011. 'Apes in Space: Saving an Imperilled Orangutan Population in Sumatra', *PLoS ONE* 6: e17210.

Chapman, C.A., et al. 2003. 'Primate Survival in Community-owned Forest Fragments: Are Metapopulation Models useful amidst Intensive Use?', in L.K. Marsh (ed.), *Primates in Fragments: Ecology and Conservation*. New York: Kluwer Academic/Plenum Publishers, pp. 63–78.

Dunnett, S., J. van Orshoven and H. Albrecht. 1970. 'Peaceful Co-existence between Chimpanzee and Man in West Africa', *Bijdragen tot de Dierkunde* 40: 148–53.

Estrada, A. 2006. 'Human and Non-human Primate Co-existence in the Neotropics: A Preliminary View of some Agricultural Practices as a Complement for Primate Conservation', *Ecological and Environmental Anthropology* 2: 17–29.

Food and Agriculture Organization of the United Nations (FAO). 2011. 'State of the World's Forests 2011'. Rome: Food and Agriculture Organization of the United Nations.

Fedigan, L.M. 2010. 'Ethical Issues faced by Field Primatologists: Asking the Relevant Questions', *American Journal of Primatology* 72: 754–71.

Fuentes, A. and K.J. Hockings. 2010. 'The Ethnoprimatological Approach in Primatology', *American Journal of Primatology* 72: 841–47.

Fuentes, A. and L.D. Wolfe. (eds). 2002. *Primates Face to Face: The Conservation Implications of Human–nonhuman Primate Interconnections*. Cambridge: Cambridge University Press.

Goldsmith, M.L. 2005. 'Habituating Primates for Field Study: Ethical Considerations for African Great Apes', in T.R. Turner (ed.), *Biological Anthropology and Ethics*. Albany: State University of New York Press, pp. 49–64.

Goulart, V.D.L.R., C.P. Teixeira and R.J. Young. 2010. 'Analysis of Callouts made in Relation to Wild Urban Marmosets (*Callithrix penicillata*) and their Implications for Urban Species Management', *European Journal of Wildlife Research* 56: 641–49.

Government of Uganda. 1998. 'The Land Act', *The Uganda Gazette* No.41, vol. XCI, Acts Supplement No.11. Entebbe: Uganda Publishing and Printing Corporation.

Hill, C.M. 2002. 'Primate Conservation: Ethical Issues and Debates', *American Anthropologist* 104: 1184–94.

———. 2004. 'Farmers' Perspectives of Conflict at the Wildlife–Agriculture Boundary: Some Lessons learned from African Subsistence Farmers', *Human Dimensions of Wildlife* 9: 279–86.

———. 2005. 'People, Crops, and Primates: A Conflict of Interests', in J.D. Paterson and J. Wallis (eds), *Commensalism and Conflict: The Human-Primate Interface*. Norman, Oklahoma: American Society of Primatologists, pp. 41–59.

Hockings, K.J., J.R. Anderson and T. Matsuzawa. 2009. 'Use of Wild and Cultivated Foods by Chimpanzees at Bossou, Republic of Guinea: Feeding Dynamics in a Human–Influenced Environment', *American Journal of Primatology* 71: 636–46.

Hockings, K. and T. Humle. 2009. 'Best Practice Guidelines for the Prevention and Mitigation of Conflict Between Humans and Great Apes'. Gland, Switzerland: IUCN/SSC Primate Specialist Group.

Hockings, K.J. and M.R. McLennan. 2012. 'From Forest to Farm: Systematic Review of Cultivar Feeding by Chimpanzees – Management Implications for Wildlife in Anthropogenic Landscapes', *PLoS ONE* 7: e33391.

Hockings, K.J. and C. Sousa. 2011. 'Human–Chimpanzee Sympatry and Interactions in Cantanhez National Park, Guinea-Bissau: Current Research and Future Directions', *Primate Conservation*, 26.

Hockings, K.J., et al. 2010. 'Attacks on Local Persons by Chimpanzees in Bossou, Republic of Guinea: Long-term Perspectives', *American Journal of Primatology* 72: 887–96.

Hulme, D. and M. Murphree. 2001. 'Community Conservation in Africa: An Introduction', in D. Hulme and M. Murphree (eds), *African Wildlife and Livelihoods: The Promise and Performance of Community Conservation*. Oxford: Heinemann, James Currey, pp. 1–8.

International Union for Conservation of Nature (IUCN). 2010. 'IUCN Red List of Threatened Species'. Version 2010.4. Website: http://www.iucnredlist.org.

Isabirye-Basuta, G. 2004. 'The Status and Distribution of Primates in Mubende-Toro Woodlands and Forests', *African Journal of Ecology* 42(suppl. 1): 84–86.

Isabirye-Basuta, G. and J.S. Lwanga. 2008. 'Primate Populations and their Interactions with Changing Habitats', *International Journal of Primatology* 29: 35–48.

Jane Goodall Institute and Uganda Wildlife Authority (JGI/UWA). 2002. 'Investigation into the Human–Chimpanzee Conflict in Hoima District'. Unpublished report.

Kambugu, R.K., A.Y. Banana and G. Odokonyero. 2010. 'Chainsaw Milling in Uganda', *ETFRN News* (Newsletter of the European Tropical Forest Research Network) 52: 194–202.

Kamenya, S. 2002. 'Human Baby killed by Gombe Chimpanzee', *Pan Africa News* 9(2): 26.

Kasenene, J.M. and E.A. Ross. 2008. 'Community Benefits from Long-term Research Programs: A Case Study from Kibale National Park, Uganda', in R. Wrangham and E. Ross (eds), *Science and Conservation in African Forests: The Benefits of Long-term Research*. Cambridge, Cambridge University Press, pp. 99–114.

Kloos, P. 1969. 'Role Conflicts in Social Fieldwork', *Current Anthropology* 10: 509–23.

Leciak, E., A. Hladik and C.M. Hladik. 2005. 'Le palmier à huile (*Elaeis guineensis*) et les noyaux de biodiversité des forêts-galeries de Guinée maritime: à propos du commensalisme de l'homme et du chimpanzé', *Revue d'Ecologie (La Terre et la Vie)* 60: 179–84.

Lee, P.C. 2010. 'Sharing Space: Can Ethnoprimatology contribute to the Survival of Non-human Primates in Human-Dominated Globalized Landscapes?', *American Journal of Primatology* 72: 925–31.

MAAIF/MFPED. 2000. 'Plan for Modernisation of Agriculture: Eradicating Poverty in Uganda'. Kampala: Ministry of Agriculture, Animal Industry and Fisheries & Ministry of Finance, Planning and Economic Development.

Madden, F. 2006. 'Gorillas in the Garden: Human–Wildlife Conflict at Bwindi Impenetrable National Park', *Policy Matters* 14: 180–90.

McLennan, M.R. 2008. 'Beleaguered Chimpanzees in the Agricultural District of Hoima, Western Uganda', *Primate Conservation* 23: 45–54.

_____. 2010a. 'Chimpanzee Ecology and Interactions with People in an Unprotected Human-dominated Landscape at Bulindi, Western Uganda', Ph.D. dissertation. Oxford: Oxford Brookes University.

_____. 2010b. 'Case Study of an Unusual Human–Chimpanzee Conflict at Bulindi, Uganda', *Pan Africa News* 17: 1–4.

McLennan, M.R. and C.M. Hill. 2010. 'Chimpanzee Responses to Researchers in a Disturbed Forest–Farm Mosaic at Bulindi, Western Uganda', *American Journal of Primatology* 72: 907–18.

McLennan, M.R. and C.M. Hill. 2012. 'Troublesome Neighbours: Changing Attitudes towards Chimpanzees (*Pan troglodytes*) in a Human-Dominated Landscape in Uganda', *Journal for Nature Conservation* 20: 219–27.

McLennan, M.R. and A.J. Plumptre. 2012. 'Protected Apes, Unprotected Forest: Composition, Structure and Diversity of Riverine Forest Fragments and their Conservation Value in Uganda', *Tropical Conservation Science* 5: 79–103.

Ministry of Water, Lands and Environment (MWLE). 2002. 'The National Forest Plan'. Kampala, Uganda: Ministry of Water, Lands and Environment.

Moore, R.S., K.A.I. Nekaris and C. Eschmann. 2010. 'Habitat Use by Western purple-faced langurs *Trachypithecus vetulus nestor* (Colobinae) in a Fragmented Suburban Landscape', *Endangered Species Research* 12: 227–34.

Naughton-Treves, L., D.M. Kammen and C.A. Chapman. 2007. 'Burning Biodiversity: Woody Biomass Use by Commercial and Subsistence Groups in Western Uganda's Forests', *Biological Conservation* 134: 232–41.

Nelson, F. 2007. 'Are Large Mammal Declines in Africa Inevitable?', *African Journal of Ecology* 46: 3–4.

Onderdonk, D.A. and C.A. Chapman. 2000. 'Coping with Forest Fragmentation: The Primates of Kibale National Park, Uganda', *International Journal of Primatology* 21: 587–611.

Paterson, J.D. and J. Wallis (eds). 2005. *Commensalism and Conflict: The Human–Primate Interface*. Special Topics in Primatology, Volume 4. Norman, Oklahoma: American Society of Primatologists.

Plumptre, A.J., D. Cox and S. Mugume. 2003. 'The Status of Chimpanzees in Uganda'. Albertine Rift Technical Report Series 2. New York: Wildlife Conservation Society.

Plumptre, A.J, et al. 2010. 'Eastern Chimpanzee (*Pan troglodytes schweinfurthii*) Status Survey and Conservation Action Plan 2010–2020'. Gland, Switzerland: IUCN.

Priston, N.E.C. and M.R. McLennan. 2012. 'Managing Humans, Managing Macaques: Human–Macaque Conflict in Asia and Africa', in S. Radhakrishna, M. Huffman and A. Sinha (eds), *The Macaque Connection: Cooperation and Conflict between Humans and Macaques*. New York: Springer, pp. 225–50.

Reynolds, V. 2005. *The Chimpanzees of the Budongo Forest: Ecology, Behaviour and Conservation*. Oxford: Oxford University Press.

Reynolds, V., J. Wallis and R. Kyamanywa. 2003. 'Fragments, Sugar, and Chimpanzees in Masindi District, Western Uganda', in L.K. Marsh (ed.), *Primates in Fragments: Ecology and Conservation*. New York: Kluwer Academic/Plenum Publishers, pp. 309–20.

Riley, E.P. 2007. 'The Human–Macaque Interface: Conservation Implications of Current and Future Overlap and Conflict in Lore Lindu National Park, Sulawesi, Indonesia', *American Anthropologist* 109: 473–84.

Rwebembera, W. 2004. 'I Was Beaten By a Chimp', *New Vision*, 11 May 2004.

Smith, L. and S. Marsh. 2003. 'Chimps Eat Children in War of Survival', *The Times Online*, 31 December 2003. Website: http://www.timesonline.co.uk

Strier, K.B. 2010. 'Long-term Field Studies: Positive Impacts and Unintended Consequences', *American Journal of Primatology* 72: 772–78.

Struhsaker, T.T. 1997. *Ecology of an African Rainforest: Logging in Kibale and the Conflict between Conservation and Exploitation*. Gainesville: University Press of Florida.

Tenywa, G. 2006. 'When Chimps Kill', *Sunday Vision*, 18 June 2006.

Tumusiime, D.M. and H. Svarstad. 2011. 'A Local Counter-narrative on the Conservation of Mountain Gorillas', *Forum for Development Studies* 38: 239–65.

Uganda Bureau of Statistics (UBOS). 2007. 'Hoima District 2002 Population and Housing Census Analytical Report'. Kampala: Uganda Bureau of Statistics.

Vitale, A. 2011. 'Primatology between Feelings and Science: a Personal Experience Perspective', *American Journal of Primatology* 73: 214–19.

Wallis, J. and D.R. Lee. 1999. 'Primate Conservation: The Prevention of Disease Transmission', *International Journal of Primatology* 20: 803–26.

White, L. and A. Edwards. 2000. 'Vegetation Inventory and Description', in L. White and A. Edwards (eds), *Conservation Research in the African Rain Forests: A Technical Handbook*. New York: Wildlife Conservation Society, pp. 115–51.

Williamson, E.A. and A.T.C. Feistner. 2003. 'Habituating Primates: Processes, Techniques, Variables and Ethics', in J.M. Setchell and D.J. Curtis (eds), *Field and Laboratory Methods in Primatology: A Practical Guide*. Cambridge: Cambridge University Press, pp. 25–39.

Wilson, K. 1992. 'Thinking about the Ethics of Fieldwork', in S. Devereux and J. Hoddinott (eds), *Fieldwork in Developing Countries*. London: Harvester Wheatsheaf, pp. 179–99.

Wolfe, L.D. 2005. 'Field Primatologists: Duties, Rights and Obligations', in T.R. Turner (ed.), *Biological Anthropology and Ethics*. Albany: State University of New York Press, pp. 15–26.

Wrangham, R.W. 2001. 'Moral Decisions about Wild Chimpanzees', in B.B. Beck, T.S. Stoinski, M. Hutchins, T.L. Maple, B. Norton, A. Rowan, E.F. Stevens and A. Arluke (eds), *Great Apes and Humans: The Ethics of Coexistence*. Washington: Smithsonian Institution Press, pp. 230–44.

Wrangham, R.W. and E. Ross (eds). 2008. *Science and Conservation in African Forests: The Benefits of Long-Term Research*. Cambridge: Cambridge University Press.

Wrangham, R.W. et al. 2000. 'Chimpanzee Predation and the Ecology of Microbial Exchange', *Microbial Ecology in Health and Disease* 12: 186–88.

Yamakoshi, G. 2005. 'What is Happening on the Border between Humans and Chimpanzees? Wildlife Conservation in West African Rural Landscapes', in K. Hiramatsu (ed.), *Coexistence with Nature in a 'Glocalizing' World: Field Science Perspectives*. Kyoto: Kyoto University, pp. 91–97.

4

Are Observational Field Studies of Wild Primates Really Noninvasive?

Karen B. Strier

Introduction

Contemporary field primatologists, like other biological anthropologists, have become increasingly self-conscious about the ethical implications of their research (e.g., Turner 2004; Fedigan 2010; MacKinnon and Riley 2010). This is especially, but not exclusively, the case for those of us who work with threatened or endangered species because of the tensions between conservation and scientific priorities that inevitably arise. Concerns about our potential impact on the animals we seek to simultaneously study and save can create ethical dilemmas, only some of which can be anticipated and therefore resolved in advance. Others arise unpredictably or emerge as problems only gradually over the course of a long-term study. For example, based on assessments of the risks and benefits to the animals and the research, all field researchers routinely make methodological decisions about whether or not to handle our study animals to mark or measure them and about whether to manipulate their social or physical environments for practical or experimental purposes. By contrast, dilemmas over whether to intervene on behalf of an ill or injured animal are more likely to arise unpredictably and to involve special considerations that must be evaluated on a case-by-case basis, however 'hands-off' a particular project's protocol may be (Fedigan 2010).

Ultimately, efforts to balance research and conservation interests can lead to far-reaching policies that affect the protection of primates and their habitats, both of which can be jeopardized by the presence of researchers, the methods we employ, and the visitors that the researchers and our discoveries attract (Strier 2010a). Chimpanzees and gorillas, for example, are particularly vulnerable to human infectious respiratory diseases because of their biological similarities to us. Infectious diseases can be transmitted by field researchers, whose observational studies bring them into close proximity with habituated primates, as well as by ecotourists, whose donations provide critical revenue for conservation but may be predicated on the prospects of viewing the primates close-up (e.g., Goldsmith 2004; Boesch 2008; Pusey et al. 2008). Weighing the health risks that humans pose against the potential benefits we can provide to these primates is a controversial topic that has generated much debate (e.g., Goldberg 2008; Köndgen et al. 2008; Walsh 2008).

Although few primates are as susceptible to infection from human pathogens as the African apes, many other primates, and especially the macaques, often live in close contact with humans and human refuse and are therefore also negatively affected by exposure to human diseases (e.g., Fuentes 2006; Engel et al. 2008). But even the most reclusive primates are potentially vulnerable to other more subtle kinds of risks as a direct or indirect result of the field studies conducted on them. Consider, for example, the position of wild primates that have been habituated by researchers for observational studies. Habituation is usually regarded as successful when the animals notice but do not react to the presence of an observer, who can then begin to collect the close behavioural observations that many research questions require. Yet, wild primates that have grown too accustomed to the proximity of benign researchers may then be in greater danger from hunters and poachers than those that have not lost their wariness toward humans as a result of their habituation.

The ethical implications of habituating wild primates in areas where their long-term safety cannot be reasonably assured apply as much to new researchers embarking on new field studies as they do to experienced researchers renewing their long-term funding and permits (Wolfe 2004). In all cases, the potential trade-offs between the risks associated with subjecting the primates to the consequences of habituation should be weighed against the improved protection that researchers and their discoveries may be able to provide.

Previously, I employed a risk analysis approach (e.g., Travis et al. 2008) to examine some of the unexpected consequences that my long-term field study of the critically endangered northern muriqui (*Brachyteles hypoxanthus*) has had on the animals, their habitat, and the local human community in southeastern Brazil (Strier 2010b). Here, I extend these reflections, which are based on my experience with the muriquis, to consider more specifically some of the ways in which the ethical landscape of a long-term field study can shift as the research questions and the animals change over time.

Background to the Field Study

The northern muriqui project of Caratinga began with a two-month pilot study in 1982 and a fourteen-month study for my doctoral dissertation from 1983–1984. I focused on one of the two muriqui groups (Matão group) inhabiting the privately-owned forest fragment at Fazenda Montes Claros, in Caratinga, Minas

Gerais, Brazil (Strier 1999). In 2001, this 965 hectare forest was transformed into a federally protected, private reserve known as the Reserve Particular Patrimonio Natural-Feliciano Miguel Abdala, or RPPN-FMA (Castro 2001). By 2003, we were systematically monitoring the entire population of what has grown to be more than 300 individuals distributed among four mixed-sex groups (the Matão group, the second original group, known as Jaó group, which split twice to create two additional groups; Strier and Boubli 2006; Strier et al. 2006). As of June 2012, the project was beginning its fourth decade, corresponding to the fourth generation in the Matão muriquis' lives, and it had provided training for over forty-five Brazilian students (Strier and Mendes 2009, 2012). More than 400 individual muriquis have been monitored over the years, and over 300 of them are currently (as of June 2012) alive in the population. Thus, some members of the original Matão group have been followed by researchers on a near daily basis for nearly a third of a century; others have spent nearly every day of their lives accompanied by human observers.

From the outset, my unwavering mantra has been a strict adherence to the use of noninvasive methods of observation. With one notable exception, we have stuck to this stance even though doing so meant frustrating delays in data collection and some agonizing compromises about the kinds of research that we would not pursue based on assessments of the potentially negative impact of the research on the animals. The critically endangered status of the northern muriqui made it difficult to justify taking even the most minimal risks, such as capturing them to mark them for identification or to take measurements or blood samples, or using vocal play-backs or radio collars to expedite our ability to locate them. Instead, we have relied on our ability to find, follow, individually identify, and observe the muriquis in order to learn about their dietary, ranging, grouping, and social patterns (Strier 1999). We also relied on analyses of the fresh dung samples we collected during different phases of the project to investigate their parasites, hormones, and molecular genetics (e.g., Stuart et al. 1993; Strier and Ziegler 1994; Chaves et al. 2006, 2011; Fagundes et al. 2008; Strier et al. 2011). The decision not to capture the muriquis was particularly influential because it contributed to an excruciating delay in our studies of their genetics, which could have been pursued long ago if we had opted to obtain blood samples instead of faecal samples for analyses. Never handling or sedating the animals has also precluded the collection of morphometric data from this population, despite the value of these data for comparative analyses.

The sole exception to our hands-off policy occurred in November 1992, when we rescued a four-month old infant female who was found alone and dazed on the forest floor. She was carried to the research house and nourished overnight, and then returned to her mother in the forest the next morning (Nogueira et al. 1994). The infant, who we had previously named Princesa, was still fully dependent on her mother at that time, and she would have certainly died without our intervention. Instead, she has contributed to the growth of this population and to the recovery of the species' numbers through her own survival and the offspring she has since produced (Strier 1999, 2007).

Was our intervention justified on compassionate or conservationist grounds, or did we disrupt the process of natural selection that would have eliminated Princesa's genes from the population (Dietz 2000)? There is no doubt that the only reason it was even possible to save this female infant of a critically endangered species in the wild was because observers were present and familiar with the individual muriquis as a result of the long-term study. Nor is there any doubt that this single intervention altered not only Princesa's fate, but also her mother's life history and the population's composition. Yet, there is no dispute that our intervention was a deviation from an otherwise strictly noninvasive research policy, however positive the intentions and effects of the intervention may have been.

It is even more difficult, however, to assess the effects of the long-term observational field study on the muriquis. Like the philosophical question about the sound of a tree falling when no one hears it, we cannot describe how the monkeys behave unless we are able to observe them. Thus, we can only speculate about how this observational study might impact the muriquis on a daily basis or how it may have altered this population of muriquis, many of whom have lived their entire lives under our scrutiny.

Phases of Observational Field Studies

Like many other long-term field studies, the northern muriqui project can be divided into discrete phases according to the main objectives and types of questions appropriate at different times (Figure 4.1). The duration and particular components

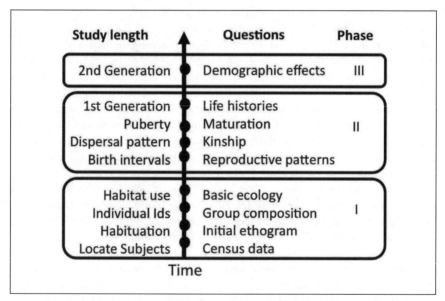

Figure 4.1. Chronological phases of long-term observational field studies. (Modified from Fig. 3 in Strier 2002)

of each of these phases vary widely across studies as a result of the differences in the histories and ecologies of study sites and species, as well as the differences in the particular research objectives pursued and the methodological approaches applied.

Phase I: Basic Natural Histories

All field studies of wild primates pass through a sequence of phases that begins with locating a suitable study site where the study subjects are known to occur and where the collection of the kind of data being sought is presumed to be feasible. I was fortunate that the muriqui population at what became my long-term study site was already known to the scientists and conservationists who arranged my initial two-month visit in1982. I was also fortunate that the owner of the forest, Senhor Feliciano Miguel Abdala, understood the conservation importance of his land and the muriquis, and had already made a commitment to the ongoing protection of both (Strier 2000). In addition, he appreciated the value of the research I proposed, and welcomed me when I returned the next year, and then the next, and then was joined by a series of students who came to participate on the project thereafter (Strier 2007).

I chose the twenty-three-member Matão group as my study subjects because the core of their home range was more convenient to the research house than the Jaó group's home range, which was situated in the northern part of the forest some distance away. A one-lane dirt road, just wide enough for a truck, also traversed the main valley used by the Matão group and connected the Fazenda's coffee fields and pastures. Local farmers walked this road daily on their way to and from the fields, and the muriquis crossed it in several spots where large trees with connecting canopies provided arboreal pathways. The Matão muriquis had ample opportunities to see people along this road, and although they were initially much more elusive when I tried to follow them into the forest, the Matão group's greater familiarity with humans made them less wary than the more isolated Jaó group. The road also provided a convenient starting point from which to search for the muriquis if I didn't know their location, and from which I could sometimes observe them in full view, where they could also gain some familiarity with me at a distance.

Following the standards of the time, my goal was to be able to accompany my study group throughout the forest on a daily basis, making systematic observations on the feeding, ranging, and social behaviour of all individuals so that I could evaluate quantitatively whether these monkeys conformed to or deviated from predictions based on comparative models of primate behavioural ecology at the time. In order to collect these data, I would need to be able to find and follow the muriquis, and then observe how they behaved by monitoring what they ate, where and how far they travelled, and how individual group members interacted with one another and with the other muriquis in the population that they might encounter during their daily routine. Gaining their trust was a first essential step toward beginning the process of systematic data collection; learning how to identify each of the individuals in my study group was the second.

Habituation

To make close behavioural observations of wild primates requires gaining the animals' trust so that they tolerate the proximity of observers. It is an exhilarating, almost spiritual, experience to succeed in this process of crossing the human-animal boundary, as anyone who has habituated a wild animal knows. Yet, the length of time required to cross this threshold probably reflects less on an observer's perseverance or skills than it does on the prior history of the primates with humans. I was fortunate because the muriquis had not been hunted for decades at this site, and, as mentioned previously, my chosen study group also had regular visual and auditory contact with the local people who lived and worked in the fields surrounding the forest. Although completely naïve primates may exhibit great curiosity and even approach to investigate novel researchers or their cameras (Morgan and Sanz 2003), the more common scenario is one in which primates have been the targets of hunters or poachers, and have therefore learned to fear and flee from humans. Prior negative experience with humans can make it difficult, if not impossible, to habituate primates for research, and is an important factor to consider in addition to the ethics of attempting to do so.

Provisioning was once a fairly common practice because the lure of food could help to overcome the primates' innate or learned wariness, bringing them into the open where their social interactions, magnified by their common attraction to the food, could be observed sooner than they might be otherwise. Potential negative impacts of provisioning include altering the diets, habitat use, and overall ecological behaviour of the animals, and creating larger feeding parties where levels of competition may exceed those that occur in response to naturally occurring foods (Asquith 1989; Hill 1999; Nash 2004; Wolfe 2004). Although interest in primate ecological adaptations has made provisioning much rarer in recent years, food platforms are still often used to evaluate cognitive abilities and foraging decisions in some primate field studies (e.g., Janson and DiBitteti 1997; Janson 2007; Garber et al. 2009). Careful research design and consideration of the appropriateness of particular species can minimize the negative impacts of provisioning for field experiments, which have remained outside the scope of the muriqui project due to conservation concerns.

Despite the obvious importance of habituation for obtaining observational data on primates, our assumptions about the noninvasiveness of habituation are much less transparent. In the short term, habituated primates who tolerate observers may be protected by the presence of researchers. This passive protection works not only against hunters who are unlikely to approach when researchers are near, but also against natural predators or food competitors, whose wariness of humans often results in their keeping their distance (Isbell and Young 1993; Matsuda and Izawa 2008). In the long term, however, being protected against the threat of predation or from competition with their own or other species may not be ideal. For example, increased levels of survival can lead to high rates of population growth, resulting in over-crowding or declines in the populations of other species with which they compete. Thus, although the quintupling of the muriqui's population size since 1982 is good news if it signifies the recovery of a healthy population (Strier and Mendes

2012), we have no way of knowing if the muriquis' population growth has been responsible for a recent decline in the population of the sympatric brown howler monkey (*Alouatta guariba*), whose diet overlaps extensively with that of muriquis (Almeida-Silva et al. 2005). It is possible that the howler monkey population declined due to unrelated factors, resulting in competitive release that permitted the muriqui population to grow. But, it is also possible that the increase in muriqui numbers, perhaps due to their high survivorship in the company of human chaperones, led to higher levels of indirect competition with the less competitive howler monkeys over food (Dias and Strier 2000).

Individual Identification

The value of distinguishing the behaviour of primates at the level of individuals lies initially in the comparative questions that can be addressed between and within different age-sex classes, and ultimately with the insights that emerge from whatever patterns may occur in the variation. Thus, for example, the activity budgets and diets of females can be compared with those of males, as well as examined according to their individual attributes, such as age or social rank. Theoretical advances in behavioural ecology typically rely on testing predicted relationships, such as those between diet quality and female rank; systematic data on individuals are necessary to characterize this behavioural variation and to evaluate the patterns it exhibits.

Like many primates, northern muriquis have individual hair and facial coloration patterns that make it possible to distinguish them by their natural markings. In species with fewer or more subtle physical differences, distinguishing individuals may require the use of artificial markings, such as beaded-collars, tattoos, or ear notching, which are typically applied to captured and sedated animals, who are then subsequently released. With the muriquis, however, it was easy enough to observe the physical details that distinguished one individual from the next. I drew caricatures of their features to keep them straight in my mind until each muriqui became as recognizable as a familiar human face might be.

This practice of sketching the muriquis' features continues to be a highly effective method that we use when training the new students who join the project each year and must learn to recognize increasingly more individuals than I had to teach myself at the outset, when the study population was much smaller. We now also use high-quality photographs to reinforce the drawings that the new students make during the eight-week annual training periods they spend under the tutelage of their predecessors from the previous year.

The muriquis' recognizable physical features made it possible for me to collect behavioural data on them as individuals from the outset, and to begin to accumulate individual life history data on them early on. Indeed, the transmission of the individual identifications to project personnel from year to year is perhaps the most critical – and most vulnerable – step in insuring the continuity of the long-term project. Any funding lapses or mishaps during this process could result in confusion and even potentially some irrevocable losses of the unique life history data being collected and maintained.

The decision to rely on the monkeys' natural markings continues to be predicated on the noninvasive approach that I adopted early on, but is this decision still justified now that the continuity of a long-term database, instead of just a doctoral dissertation, is at stake? One missed year or faulty training period could jeopardize our ability to re-identify individuals whose prior histories were known. Indeed, the scientific and conservation value of these individual life history data makes it much more difficult to dismiss the use of more invasive methods that would permit us to mark the animals and gain the insurance that more permanent identification records would provide. An alternative position, however, and the one I still hold, is that the risks of disruption in the long-term life history data are far outweighed by concerns about the potential risks we might be imposing if we opted to mark them for security.

Phase II: The First Generation: Life Histories

In addition to the basic behavioural and ecological data around which the initial studies were designed, the first phase of the project also yielded some clues about the muriquis' reproductive and dispersal patterns, although these patterns still required many additional years to document. Like other primates, muriquis have slow life histories, and the only way to decipher these was to monitor individuals and document when they passed through each of the main developmental milestones.

As successive cohorts of infants were weaned and their mothers resumed copulating and ultimately gave birth again, it became possible to calculate their average birth interval, which has been roughly three years throughout the study (Strier and Mendes 2012). By 1988, three of the four females but neither of the two males who were present as infants in 1982 had emigrated from the study group. Although two females immigrated into the study group in 1983, it was not until this first known cohort of natal infants of both sexes approached puberty that the indications of female-biased dispersal and male philopatry in these animals could be confirmed (Strier 1990). By 1989, the one female from the original natal cohort who had remained in her natal group gave birth to her first infant, providing the first insight into female age at first reproduction in this species (Strier 1991).

Sample sizes for dispersal patterns and life history traits have increased over the years as the size of the study population has grown (e.g., Strier and Mendes 2012), but even by the early 1990s, the dispersal and life history data were generating new questions about the hormonal mechanisms underlying female dispersal and regulating the reproductive biology of both females and males. We pursued these questions with the use of noninvasive faecal steroid assays, which permitted us to measure hormone concentrations from the muriquis' dung.

We began with a subset of adult females with prior reproductive experience, and on a near daily basis we collected fresh faecal samples as they landed on the forest floor throughout the day. With proper preservation, estradiol and progesterone could be extracted from the faeces and their concentrations measured. Eventually, we had sampled enough females over sufficiently extended periods of time to describe the post-partum resumption of their ovarian cycles and cycle lengths, the periovulatory period (or the days on which ovulation was most likely to occur), the variation in cycling estradiol levels among fertile and infertile females and in the number of cycles before conception for fertile females, and gestation length based on hormonal indications of pregnancy and the birthdates of the infants conceived (Strier and Ziegler 1997, 2005; Strier et al. 2003). We then moved onto males, whose cortisol but not testosterone levels exhibited seasonal fluctuations (Strier et al. 1999), and to young females who evidently dispersed prior to the onset of puberty and became sexually active at the same time as they experienced their first ovarian cycles (Strier and Ziegler 2000).

Convention required us to validate the faecal hormone assays, which we did during a brief study involving collections of faecal and urine samples from two female muriquis housed at the Rio de Janeiro Primate Center (Ziegler et al. 1997). However, it was the ability to glean so much information about the physiological regulation of reproduction in wild muriquis that made the faecal hormone study so exciting.

Obtaining the fresh faecal samples from targeted individuals at frequent intervals was an arduous task, and the extraction and analyses of the hormones were both expensive and time-consuming, independent of whether the processing was done in the US, as was initially the procedure, or in the field station's laboratory, as occurred during the last few years once our extraction techniques improved (Strier 2010b). Yet, despite the costs and effort, the hormone study was a major component of the muriqui project for more than a decade. Although other field primatologists were also conducting faecal steroid studies of other species elsewhere, the development and application of novel, explicitly noninvasive methods for investigating the hormonal correlates of reproduction and fertility in a critically endangered primate in the wild generated a great deal of positive attention and contributed much to our ongoing conservation efforts. The study also yielded many new insights that continue to inform other aspects of the long-term research today.

Nonetheless, after more than a decade of systematic collections on different subsets of individuals in the Matão group, I decided to bring the hormone component of the project to a halt. One reason for this decision was that limited funding and time for the analyses had generated a backlog of samples that took priority over any new collections we made. Even more compelling, however, was my nagging perception that the muriquis might benefit from a break in the intensity of observations that the collection of fresh faecal material had required. Typically, the muriquis whose faeces were scheduled to be collected on a particular day were located and observed until they defecated, which could happen anytime from a few minutes to several hours after observations began. So, in contrast to our systematic methods of behavioural sampling, which had not involved following a focal subject for more than ten continuous minutes, during the hormone study some muriquis might be under close observations for far more extended periods of time.

Although there were no behavioural – or hormonal – indications that the muriquis were ever stressed by this attention, they had nevertheless begun to exhibit what appeared to me to be a new level of disregard to our presence. Not only were they now approaching us more closely while they were in the trees, but they were also beginning to extend their tolerance of the close proximity of observers when they were on the ground; by 2005 this close proximity was occurring at notably higher frequencies and in more diverse contexts than it had in the past. Although these behavioural changes in the muriquis may have been entirely unrelated to the hormone study, by terminating it we could avoid monitoring individuals as intensively for such extended periods or at such close range. In fact, we established the maintenance of no less than a ten-meter distance between observers and muriquis as the project's norm.

Phase III: The Second Generation: Phenotypic Plasticity

There are many possible explanations for why the Matão muriquis' use of the ground was increasing, with perhaps the most likely one being related to the increase in the size and density of both this group and the rest of the muriqui population (Tabacow et al. 2009). Understanding how primates adjust their behaviour in response to demographic and ecological fluctuations is critical to evaluating their adaptive potentials, and is therefore as relevant to conservation concerns as it is to evolutionary theories (Struhsaker 2008; Strier 2009, 2011; Fuentes 2010). While comparative studies of different populations of the same species can offer important insights into this phenotypic plasticity in primate behaviour (reviewed in Chapman and Rothman 2009), long-term studies of particular populations are uniquely suited to provide insights into the mechanisms that underlie this plasticity in primate behavioural responses (Strier 2009, 2011). Thus, within the first fifteen years of the study, the Matão group had tripled in size, but instead of increasing their daily travel distances to meet the greater feeding requirements of their larger group, the muriquis shifted their pattern of association from one in which the entire group travelled as a cohesive unit, to one involving smaller, more fluid associations among group members who collectively exploited a larger total home range than they had when the group was so much smaller (Dias and Strier 2003).

The twenty-fold increase in the frequency with which the muriquis engaged in terrestrial substrate use over a twenty-two-year period might represent a similar type of behavioural adjustment to increasing demographic pressures in this isolated forest fragment (Strier and Ives 2012). If the population has expanded to the forest's carrying capacity, then there would have been limited or no available habitat into which the growing Matão group could expand. The group's increased use of terrestrial substrates could therefore reflect an expansion of their vertical niche that was driven by ecological necessity under conditions of increasingly high population densities compared to those of the past. And, once the use of the ground became established for essential feeding, it could easily have expanded into what now appears to be a terrestrial 'tradition' based on the diversity of nonessential activities now also conducted on the ground and the spread of this behaviour along established social networks (Tabacow et al. 2009).

More alarming, however, is the possibility that the adaptive expansion of the muriqui's vertical niche and its subsequent establishment as a local tradition could be leading the muriquis' into an ecological or evolutionary trap, or a behavioral decision, in this case associated with their use of the ground, that is maladaptive under current conditions and could lead to their extinction (Schlaepfer et al. 2002; Robertson and Hutto 2006). Whatever role the long-term project has played in enabling the muriqui population's growth also makes the project at least partially responsible for the ecological necessity thought to have driven the increase in essential terrestrial feeding that now occurs in all of the groups. Likewise, our long-term observations, especially of the Matão group, may have contributed to a relaxation of their preference for the safety of the trees, and therefore further facilitated the extension of their nonessential terrestrial tradition.

We will never know whether this muriqui population would have grown as much if the long-term field study had never been initiated or maintained, or whether, even had they reached their current densities, the muriquis would have begun using the ground to the extent that they do now if they had not had years to observe us on the ground, without either of our species coming to any harm in one another's presence. Nonetheless, their current use of the ground exposes the muriquis to terrestrial predators and pathogens, such as parasites in the dung they can only encounter on the ground. And, even if our presence inhibits predators from attacking, we do not yet know how often the muriquis now descend to the ground when no researchers are with them to serve as buffers, or whether current demographic conditions would permit them to make different behavioural adjustments if we were not present (Figure 4.2).

Final Reflections

It is greatly satisfying to know that the muriquis in our study population are still thriving, and that the future of the forest these muriquis inhabit is now secure.

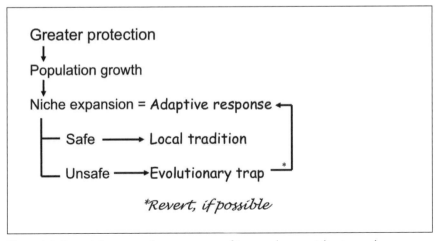

Figure 4.2. Potential causes and consequences of increased terrestriality in northern muriquis.

It is also tremendously satisfying to acknowledge how much we have been able to learn about the behaviour one of the world's most critically endangered primates through an observational study alone. Yet, as I hope I have conveyed in this essay, I suspect that we may be deluding ourselves if we assume that our observational field studies are entirely noninvasive.

If 'noninvasive' implies a complete absence of deleterious effects on the animals, then it is probably fair to say that our observational approach has been much less invasive than some of the other methods practiced by other types of field ecologists. For example, king penguin chicks that were banded with flipper tags suffered greatly reduced survival rates (Gauthier-Clerc et al. 2004). Similarly, the long-standing practice of clipping the toes of amphibians to mark them as individuals has been shown to negatively affect recapture rates, and by inference, the animals' survival (McCarthy and Parris 2008). Importantly, it took decades to demonstrate the negative effects of toe-clipping because small sample sizes prevented robust statistical comparisons (May 2004).

Small sample sizes are a concern in most primate field studies, and there are no studies on the effects of marking primates comparable to those on birds and amphibians. But, even the effects of observational studies can be difficult to document because of limitations in our comparative perspectives. For example, until recently, nearly everything that was known about wild northern muriquis came from our studies on the Matão group, representing an N=1. It has only been more recently, as our research has expanded to include other groups in this population and as other research groups have launched other studies on other populations of this species elsewhere, that we can begin to consider how differences in factors such as levels of habituation (Mourthé et al. 2007) or habitat disturbances (Silva Júnior et al. 2009) might be affecting the muriquis' behaviour.

The scarcity of comparative perspectives on how other groups and populations of northern muriquis behave has reinforced my decision, initially based on their critically endangered status, to exclude even the most benign of field experiments from our objectives. Among more familiar species such as chimpanzees, which have been studied for decades at multiple field sites, it can be confidently asserted that the study subjects 'responded to our playback stimuli in adaptive ways' based on an assessment of the ethical implications of a field experiment (Herbinger et al. 2009: 1396). Yet, despite nearly three decades of field observations, I do not think that we know enough about the range of northern muriqui behaviour patterns to evaluate what an adaptive response from them would be. I wonder, though, whether we can learn enough about a wild primate from observational studies alone to be able to evaluate our impact and the effects of our research on them.

Acknowledgements

I am grateful to Jeremy MacClancy and Agustin Fuentes for inviting me to participate in their conference, *Ethics in the Field: Contemporary Challenges*, held at Oxford Brookes University in April 2009, and for inviting me to contribute a version of my paper to this volume. The research described in this chapter has been funded by a variety of sources: National Science Foundation (BNS 8305322, BCS 8619442, BCS 8958298, BCS 9414129, BCS 0621788, BCS 0921013), National Geographic Society, Liz Claiborne and Art Ortenberg Foundation, Fulbright Foundation, Sigma Xi Grants-in-Aid, Grant #213 from the Joseph Henry Fund of the NAS, World Wildlife Fund, L.S.B. Leakey Foundation, Chicago Zoological Society, Lincoln Park Zoo Neotropic Fund, Center for Research on Endangered Species (CRES), Rutherford Foundation, Primate Action Fund, Margot Marsh Biodiversity Foundation, Conservation International, the Graduate School of the University of Wisconsin-Madison, and a Hilldale Professorship and a Vilas Professorship from the University of Wisconsin-Madison. I also wish to thank the many students who have contributed to the long-term field study (in alphabetical order) through June 2012: L. Arnedo, M.L. Assunção, N. Bejar, J.P. Boubli, P. Silva Campos, T. Cardosa, A. Carvalho, D. Carvalho, C. Cäsar, A.Z. Coli, C.G. Costa, P. Coutinho, L. Dib, Leo G. Dias, Luiz G. Dias, D.S. Ferraz, A. Ferreira, J. Fidelis, A.R.G. Freire Filho, J. Gomes, D. Guedes, V.O. Guimarães, R. Hack, M.F. Iurck, M. Kaizer, M. Lima, M. Maciel, I. Inforzato Martins, W.P. Martins, F.D.C. Mendes, I.M. Mourthé, F. Neri, M. Nery, S. Neto, C.P. Nogueira, A. Odalia Rímoli, A. Oliva, L. Oliveira, F.P. Paim, C.B. Possamai, R.C. Printes, J. Rímoli, S.S. Rocha, R.C. Romanini, B.G.M. da Silva, J.C. da Silva, V. Souza, D.V. Slomp, F.P. Tabacow, W. Teixeira, M. Tokudo, K. Tolentino, and E.M. Veado. I thank Drs. Célio Valle, César Ades, Gustavo Fonseca, and Sérgio L. Mendes for serving as my Brazilian sponsors at different times over the years. The field study has been conducted with permission from Brazilian authorities and in compliance with all Brazilian and US regulations.

References

Almeida-Silva, B., A.A. Cunha, J.P. Boubli, S.L. Mendes and K.B. Strier. 2005. 'Population Density and Vertical Stratification of Four Primate Species at the Estação Biológica de Caratinga/RPPN-FMA, Minas Gerais, Brazil', *Neotropical Primates* 13 (Supplement): 25–29.

Asquith, P.J. 1989. 'Provisioning and the Study of Free-Ranging Primates: History, Effects, and Prospects', *American Journal of Physical Anthropology* 32(Suppl10): 129–58.

Boesch, C. 2008. 'Why Do Chimpanzees Die in the Forest? The Challenges of Understanding and Controlling for Wild Ape Health', *American Journal of Primatology* 70(8): 722–26.

Castro, M.I. 2001. 'RPPN Feliciano Miguel Abdala – A Protected Area for the Northern Muriqui', *Neotropical Primates* 9(3): 128–29.

Chapman, C.A. and J.M. Rothman. 2009. 'Within-Species Differences in Primate Social Structure: Evolution of Plasticity and Phylogenetic Constraints', *Primates* 50(1): 12–22.

Chaves, P.B., C.S. Alvarenga, C.B.Possamai, L.G. Dias, J.P. Boubli, K.B. Strier, S.L. Mendes and V. Fagundes. 2011. 'Genetic Diversity and Population History of a Critically Endangered Primate, the Northern Muriqui (*Brachyteles hypoxanthus*)', *PLoS One,* 6, e20722.

Chaves, P.B., M.F. Paes, S.L. Mendes, K.B. Strier, I.D. Louro and V. Fagundes. 2006. 'Non-invasive Genetic Sampling of Endangered Muriqui (Primates, Atelidae): Efficiency of Fecal DNA Extraction', *Genetics and Molecular Biology* 29: 750–754.

da Silva Junior, W.M., J.A. Alves Meira-Neto, F.M. da Silva Carmo, F. Rodrigues de Melo, L. Santana Moreira, E. Ferreira Barbosa, L.G. Dias and C.A. da Silva Peres. 2009. 'Habitat Quality of the Woolly Spider Monkey (*Brachyteles hypoxanthus*)', *Folia Primatologia* 80(4): 295–308.

Dias, L.G. and K.B. Strier. 2000. 'Agonistic Encounters between Muriquis, *Brachyteles arachnoides hypoxanthus* (Primates, Cebidae), and Other Animals at the Estação Biológica de Caratinga, Minas Gerais, Brazil', *Neotropical Primates* 8: 138–41.

————. 2003. 'Effects of Group Size on Ranging Patterns in *Brachyteles arachnoides hypoxanthus*', *International Journal of Primatology* 24: 209–21.

Dietz, J.M. 2000. 'Book Review', *Quarterly Review of Biology* 75(1): 84.

Engel, G.A., M. Pizarro, E. Shaw, J. Cortes, A. Fuentes, P. Barry, N. Lerche, R. Grant, D. Cohn and L. Jones-Engel. 2008. 'Unique Pattern of Enzootic Primate Viruses in Gibraltar Macaques', *Emergent Infectious Diseases* 14(7): 1112–15.

Fagundes, V., M.F. Paes, P.B. Chaves, S.L. Mendes, C.B. Possamai, J.P. Boubli and K.B. Strier. 2008. 'Genetic Structure in Two Northern Muriqui Populations (*Brachyteles hypoxanthus*, Primates, Atelidae) as Inferred from Fecal DNA', *Genetics and Molecular Biology* 31: 166–71.

Fedigan, L.M. 2010. 'Ethical Issues Faced By Field Primatologists: Asking the Relevant Questions', *American Journal of Primatology* 72(9): 754–71.

Fuentes A. 2006. 'Human Culture and Monkey Behavior: Assessing the Contexts of Potential Pathogen Transmission Between Macaques and Humans', *American Journal of Primatology* 68(9): 880–96.

————. 2010. 'Social Systems and Socioecology – Understanding the Evolution Of Primate Behavior', in C.J. Campbell, A. Fuentes, K.C. MacKinnon, S.K. Bearder and R. Stumpf (eds), *Primates in Perspective*, 2nd edition, New York: Oxford University Press, pp. 500–11.

Garber, P.A., J.C. Bicca-Marques and M.A.O. Azevedo-Lopes. 2009. 'Primate Cognition: Integrating Social and Ecological Information in Decision-Making', in P.A. Garber, A. Estrada, J.C. Bicca-Marques, E.W. Heymann and K.B. Strier (eds), *South American Primates: Comparative Perspective sin the Study of Behavior, Ecology, and Conservation.* New York: Springer, pp. 365–85.

Gauthier-Clerc, M., J.P. Gendner, C.A. Ribic, W.R. Fraser, E.J. Woehler, S. Descamps, C. Gilly, C. Le Bohec and Y. Le Maho. 2004. 'Long-Term Effects of Flipper Bands on Penguins', *Proceedings of the Royal Society B Biological Sciences* 271 (Suppl 6): S423–26.

Goldberg, T.L. 2008. 'Commentary on "Pandemic Human Viruses Cause Decline of Endangered Great Apes", by Köndgen et al., 2008, Current Biology 18: 260-264', *American Journal of Primatology* 70(8): 716–18.

Goldsmith, M.L. 2004. 'Habituating Primates for Field Study: Ethical Considerations for African Great Apes', in T.R. Turner (ed.), *Biological Anthropology and Ethics: From Repatriation to Genetics.* Albany: State University of New York Press, pp. 49–64.

Herbinger, I., S. Papworth, C. Boesch and K. Zuberbühler. 2009. 'Vocal, Gestural and Locomotor Responses of Wild Chimpanzees to Familiar and Unfamiliar Intruders: A Playback Study', *Animal Behaviour* 78(6): 1389–96.

Hill, D.A. 1999. 'Effects of Provisioning on the Social Behaviour of Japanese and Rhesus Macaques', *Primates* 40: 187–98.

Isbell, L.A. and T.P. Young. 1993. 'Human Presence Reduces Predation in a Free-Ranging Vervet Monkey Population in Kenya', *Animal Behaviour* 45: 1233–35.

Janson, C.H. 2007. 'Experimental Evidence for Route Integration and Strategic Planning in Wild Capuchin Monkeys', *Animal Cognition* 10(3): 341–56.

Janson, C.H. and M.S. Di Bitetti. 1997. 'Experimental Analysis of Food Detection in Capuchin Monkeys: Effects of Distance, Travel Speed, and Resource Size', *Behavioral Ecology and Sociobiology* 41: 17–24.

Köndgen, S, H. Kuhl, P.K. N'Goran, P.D. Walsh, S. Schenk, N. Ernst, R. Biek, P. Formenty, K. Matz-Rensing, B. Schweiger et al. 2008. 'Pandemic Human Viruses Cause Decline of Endangered Great Apes', *Current Biology* 18(4): 260–64.

MacKinnon, K.C. and E. Riley. 2010. 'Field Primatology of Today: Current Ethical Issues', *American Journal of Primatology* 72(9): 749–53.

Matsuda, I. and K. Izawa. 2008. 'Predation of Wild Spider Monkeys at La Macarena, Colombia', *Primates* 49: 65–68.

May, R.M. 2004. 'Ecology: Ethics and Amphibians', *Nature* 431(7007): 403.

McCarthy, M.A. and K.M. Parris. 2008. 'Optimal Marking of Threatened Species to Balance Benefits of Information with Impacts of Marking', *Conservation Biology* 22(6): 1506–12.

Morgan, D. and C. Sanz. 2003. 'Naive Encounters with Chimpanzees in the Goualougo Triangle, Republic of Congo', *International Journal of Primatology* 24: 369–81.

Mourthé, I.M., D. Guedes, J. Fidelis, J.P. Boubli, S.L. Mendes and K.B. Strier. 2007. 'Ground Use by Northern Muriquis (Brachyteles hypoxanthus)', *American Journal of Primatology* 69(6): 706–12.

Nash, L.T. 2004. 'Studies of Primates in the Field and in Captivity: Similarities and Differences in Ethical Concerns', in T.R. Turner (ed.), *Biological Anthropology and Ethics: From Repatriation to Genetics*. Albany: State University of New York Press, pp. 27–48.

Nogueira, C.P., A.R. Carvalho, L. Oliveira, E.M. Veado and K.B. Strier. 1994. 'Recovery and Release of an Infant Muriqui, *Brachyteles arachnoides*, at the Caratinga Biological Station, Minas Gerais, Brazil', *Neotropical Primates* 2: 3–5.

Pusey, A.E., M.L. Wilson and D.A. Collins. 2008. 'Human Impacts, Disease Risk, and Population Dynamics in the Chimpanzees of Gombe National Park, Tanzania', *American Journal of Primatology* 70(8): 738–44.

Robertson, B.A. and R.L. Hutto. 2006. 'A Framework for Understanding Ecological Traps and an Evaluation of Existing Evidence', *Ecology* 87(5): 1075–85.

Schlaepfer, M.A., M.C. Runge and P.W. Sherman. 2002. 'Ecological and Evolutionary Traps', *Trends in Ecology and Evolution* 17(19): 474–80.

Strier, K.B. 1990. 'New World Primates, New Frontiers: Insights from the Woolly Spider Monkey, or Muriqui (*Brachyteles arachnoides*)', *International Journal of Primatology* 11: 7–19.

———. 1991. 'Demography and Conservation in an Endangered Primate, *Brachyteles arachnoides*', *Conservation Biology* 5: 214–18.

———. 1999. *Faces in the Forest: The Endangered Muriqui Monkeys of Brazil*. Cambridge, MA: Harvard University Press.

———. 2000. 'An American Primatologist Abroad in Brazil', in S.C. Strum and L.M. Fedigan (eds), *Primate Encounters: Models of Science, Gender, and Society*. Chicago: University of Chicago Press, pp. 194–207.

———. 2003. 'Primatology Comes of Age', 2002 AAPA Luncheon Address, *Yearbook of Physical Anthropology* 122: 2–13.

———. 2007. *Faces na Floresta*. Rio de Janeiro: Preserve Muriqui.

———. 2009. 'Seeing the Forest Through the Seeds: Mechanisms of Primate Behavioral Diversity from Individuals to Populations and Beyond', *Current Anthropology* 50: 213–28.

————.2010a. 'Conservation', in C.J. Campbell, A. Fuentes, K.C. MacKinnon, S.K. Bearder and R. Stumpf (eds), *Primates in Perspective, 2nd edition*. New York: Oxford University Press, pp. 664–75.

————.2010b. 'Long-Term Field Studies: Positive Impacts and Unintended Consequences', *American Journal of Primatology* 72(9): 772–78.

————.2011. 'Social Plasticity and Demographic Variation in Primates', in R.W. Sussman and C.R. Cloninger (eds), *Origins of Altruism and Cooperation*. New York: Springer Science+Business Media, LLC, pp. 179–92.

Strier, K.B. and J.P. Boubli. 2006. 'A History of Long-Term Research and Conservation of Northern Muriquis (*Brachyteles Hypoxanthus*) at the Estação Biológica de Caratinga/ RPPN-FMA', *Primate Conservation* 20: 53–63.

Strier, K.B., J.P. Boubli, C.B. Possamai and S.L. Mendes. 2006. 'Population Demography of Northern Muriquis (*Brachyteles Hypoxanthus*) at the Estação Biológica de Caratinga/ Reserva Particular do Patrimônio Natural-Feliciano Miguel Abdala, Minas Gerais, Brazil', *American Journal of Physical Anthropology* 130(2): 227–37.

Strier, K.B., Chaves, S.L. Mendes, V. Fagundes and A. Di Fiore. 2011. 'Low Paternity Skew in a Patrilocal, Egalitarian Primate', *Proceedings of the National Academy of Sciences USA* 108(47): 18915–919.

Strier, K.B. and A.R. Ives. 2012. 'Unexpected Demography in the Recovery of an Endangered Primate Population', *PLoS One* 7(9): e44407.

Strier, K.B., J.W. Lynch and T.E. Ziegler. 2003. 'Hormonal Changes During the Mating and Conception Seasons of Wild Northern Muriquis (*Brachyteles arachnoides hypoxanthus*)', *American Journal of Primatology* 61: 85–99.

Strier, K.B. and S.L. Mendes. 2009. 'Long-Term Field Studies of South American Primates', in P.A. Garber, A. Estrada, J.C. Bicca-Marques, E. Heymann and K.B. Strier (eds), *South American Primates: Comparative Perspectives in the Study of Behavior, Ecology, and Conservation*. New York: Springer, pp. 139–55.

————.2012. 'The Northern Muriqui (*Brachyteles hypoxanthus*): Lessons on Behavioral Plasticity and Population Dynamics from a Critically Endangered Primate', in P.M. Kappeler and D. Watts (eds), *Long-Term Studies of Primates*. Heidelberg: Springer-Verlag, pp. 125–40.

Strier, K.B. and T.E. Ziegler. 1994. 'Insights into Ovarian Function in Wild Muriqui Monkeys (*Brachyteles arachnoides*)', *American Journal of Primatology* 32(1): 31–40.

————.1997. 'Behavioral and Endocrine Characteristics of the Reproductive Cycle in Wild Muriqui Monkeys, *Brachyteles arachnoides*', *American Journal of Primatology* 42: 299–310.

————.2000. 'Lack of Pubertal Influences on Female Dispersal in Muriqui Monkeys, *Brachyteles arachnoides*', *Animal Behaivour* 59: 849–60.

————.2005. 'Variation in the Resumption of Cycling and Conception by Fecal Androgen and Estradiol Levels in Female Muriquis (*Brachyteles hypoxanthus*)', *American Journal of Primatology* 67: 69–81.

Strier, K.B., T.E. Ziegler and D. Wittwer. 1999. 'Seasonality in Fecal Testosterone and Cortisol Levels in Wild Male Muriquis (*Brachyteles arachnoides*)', *Hormones and Behavior* 35: 125–34.

Struhsaker, T.T. 2008. 'Demographic Variability in Monkeys: Implications for Theory and Conservation', *International Journal of Primatology* 29(1): 19–34.

Stuart, M.D., K.B. Strier and S.M. Pierberg. 1993. 'A Coprological Survey of Parasites of Wild Muriquis, *Brachyteles arachnoides*, and Brown Howling Monkeys, *Alouatta fusca*', *Journal of the Helminthological Society of Washington* 60: 111–15.

Tabacow, F.P., S.L. Mendes and K.B. Strier. 2009. 'Spread of a Terrestrial Tradition in an Arboreal Primate', *American Anthropologist* 111: 238–49.

Travis, D.A., E.V. Lonsdorf, T. Mlengeya and J. Raphael. 2008. 'A Science-Based Approach to Managing Disease Risks for Ape Conservation', *American Journal of Primatology* 70(8): 745–50.

Turner, T.R. (ed.). 2004. *Biological Anthropology and Ethics: From Repatriation to Genetic Identity*. Albany, NY: State University of New York Press.

Walsh, P.D. 2008. 'A Rant on Infectious Disease and Ape Research Priorities', *American Journal of Primatology* 70(8): 719–21.

Wolfe, L.D. 2004. 'Field Primatologists: Duties, Rights, and Obligations', in T.R. Turner (ed.), *Biological Anthropology and Ethics: From Repatriation to Genetics*. Albany: State University of New York Press, pp. 15–26.

Ziegler, T.E., C.V. Santos, A. Pissinatti and K.B. Strier. 1997. 'Steroid Excretion During the Ovarian Cycle in Captive and Wild Muriquis, *Brachyteles arachnoides*', *American Journal of Primatology* 42: 311–21.

5

Complex and Heterogeneous Ethical Structures in Field Primatology

Nobuyuki Kutsukake

Field ethics – a moral compass for decision making during fieldwork – is currently a necessitated but unstructured topic in primatology. Field primatologists are likely to confront ethical issues in relationships with local people and communities, governmental authorities, colleagues, funding agencies, the public, and the mass media (Eudey 2002; Fuentes and Wolfe 2002; Goldsmith 2005; Nash 2004; Ross et al. 2008; Turner 2004; Williamson and Feistner 2003; Wolfe 2005; Fedigan 2010; Garber et al. 2010; MacKinnon and Riley 2010; Malone et al. 2010; Strier 2010). In the 'Anthropocene' era (Crutzen 2002), in which the impact of human activity can never be ignored, this ethical discussion is particularly important in the domain of primate conservation because most primate species are at risk of extinction. Primatologists need to act as anthropologists during fieldwork because primatologists working in the field are basically 'aliens' who live in a different community with a different culture. Some of the ethical challenges encountered by primatologists are common to those faced in other domains of anthropological research (Turner 2004), although a critical difference is that primatologists do not address the ethical problems pertaining to human rights and informed consent (exceptions can be found in ethnoprimatologal approaches: Fuentes and Hockings 2010; Lee 2010; Nekaris et al. 2010). Ethical challenges for field primatologists also differ from those facing researchers on captive primates, in which animal welfare, enrichment, husbandry, and guidelines about the use of animals in experiments (3Rs: refinement, reduction, and replacement) have been intensively discussed (Nash 2004).

Field primatologists have been aware of the potential importance of ethical issues, although formal discussions on this topic have started only recently (Fedigan 2010). For example, Bearder et al. (2003) published an excellent A to Z dictionary of field primatology. Although 'Ethics' does not appear on this list (the topic after 'Embassy' is 'Excess-baggage'!), the following relevant cautions can be found within various topics.

Language training

The fact that you are trying to embrace what is in many ways the essence of a local culture will make people more accepting of you. Better yet, try learning a song in the local language. In many places, if you can sing a song, your hosts will be pleased, and your fieldwork will progress even more smoothly. (p. 316)

Other people

Many filed sites have more than one researcher, plus other staff. You must be able to live and work co-operatively in crowded, difficult conditions, with different characters. This can be one of the best parts of the whole experience but, equally, it can also be the worst! Remember too that other researchers may come after you, and how you act will affect their success as well as your own. (p. 317)

Understanding other cultures (cited in part by this author)

Perhaps the most vital key to success is to be aware of the knowledge and customs of local people. You will make slow progress if you fail to observe rituals of etiquette and politeness that are normal in an area, so listen, learn, and behave accordingly.

It is advisable to spend a few days visiting village elders and important officials at the start, to enable them to understand why you are there, and to listen to their advice.

Remember to adjust your pace of life and try to be at least as calm and as patient as the people you meet.

Local assistants/informers/translators/friends are invaluable for cultural information, and you will learn a huge amount about other people just by sitting down to talk—one of the best things about fieldwork. (pp. 320–21)

In this chapter, I attempt to provide an overview of the historical and current status of field ethics in primatology in order to stimulate future discussion on this topic. Consistent with previous articles, I will describe and analyse ethical issues that derive from my personal field experiences and perspective (e.g., Eudey 2002; Wolfe 2005; Strier et al. 2006). (Figure 5.1) However, I will also adopt a slightly different approach by focusing on the overall framework and structure of ethical problems in field primatology. I first review the history of ethical incidents in field primatology and explain why it has been difficult to discuss field ethics. Because of limitations in space and in access to relevant information, I acknowledge that this chapter is not comprehensive. However, a re-examination of past ethical issues makes it obvious that primatologists need a more formal platform from which to promote discussion of ethical problems. In the latter part of this discussion, I will explain the ethical structure of problems confronted by Japanese primatologists in relation to endemic primates, Japanese macaques, *Macaca fuscata*. This case will highlight the fact that a simple ethical structure does not necessarily resolve issues; instead, each ethical challenge is characterized by uniquely difficult ethical considerations, irrespective of the complexity of its structure.

Ethics in Field Primatology

This section provides a brief review of three aspects of field ethics in primatology, namely, why it is difficult to (a) follow, (b) define, and (c) unify field ethics in primatology.

Following the Ethical Principles of Primatology in Field Settings

Ultimately, the aim of field research among wild primates can be summarized in terms of the following three issues.

Figure 5.1. The author in the field in Borneo.

[i]   *Scientific understanding*: To promote our understanding of primates in the context of basic science. Primatologists are interested in understanding wild primates from anthropological, ecological, or evolutionary biological perspectives. Thus, exerting artificial influences on and altering the behaviour and ecology of primates is not desirable.

[ii]   *Primate conservation*: To provide benefits to our study subjects with regard to conservation considerations. It is unacceptable to harm or threaten primate populations.

[iii] *Relationships with the local community*: Providing benefits to the local community is particularly important in the context of conservation because the local community plays a critical role in community-based conservation. Disturbing and violating the social systems of local communities, including their values, economy, traditions, and culture, is not desirable. It is not acceptable to exploit local communities and people in a unidirectional fashion.

At first glance, the ethical principles underpinning field research appear to be easy to follow in that they seem to involve doing what looks good and not doing what looks bad. However, one soon discovers that following this rule is difficult because good and bad are not always mutually exclusive in practice.

[i] Scientific Understanding

Despite our interest in the scientific understanding of 'normal' wild primates, research activity inevitably affects normative environmental and primate characteristics. This effect becomes exaggerated when researchers have habituated primates to their presence (Williamson and Feistner 2003; Goldsmith 2005). Habituated wild primates tolerate the presence of researchers, but this does not mean that wild primates behave in purely normal ways. Caution about the effect of observers is noted in the standard textbook of animal behaviour (Martin and Bateson 1990). More critically, however, the environment the researchers create can alter primate behaviour in more direct ways. For example, a male chimpanzee was reported to use objects brought by humans in agonistic displays, thereby raising his dominance rank (Goodall 1986). Also, if contact between humans and great apes results in disease transmission (Wallis and Lee 1999; Woodford et al. 2002; Köndgen et al. 2008), it is impossible to collect data on purely natural demographic parameters.

The effects of human presence can manifest themselves in indirect ways. Human presence in the field affects the behaviour of predators and, as a result, reduces the mortality of primates (Isbell and Young 1993; Williamson and Feistner 2003). Because unhabituated individuals avoid researchers, these individuals might avoid immigrating to the habituated group, or the habituated group might win inter-group conflicts simply because of the presence of researchers (Goldsmith 2005; Williamson and Feistner 2003). Therefore, it is impossible to conduct field research on the completely normal behaviour and ecology of wild primates.

[ii] Primate Conservation

Currently, most primate populations face conservation and management problems because of habitat destruction, bush-meat trading, and risks of disease. The activities of primatologists can inadvertently harm primates. Given that disease is one of the main factors contributing to the decline of great ape populations, fieldworkers are required to consider the risks to great apes of disease transmission. Once primates are habituated to humans, they do not fear them and may approach human areas, which might lead directly to the initiation of crop damage (Williamson and Feistner 2003; Hockings and Humle 2009). Provisioning has been used to habituate wild primates (Asquith 1989; explained below), but this might accelerate learning about human food and ultimately precipitate crop damage or attacks on humans to steal food. The habituated individuals might also be more likely to be hunted by poachers (Williamson and Feistner 2003; Wolfe 2005), although it is known that the presence of researchers decreases the risks of poaching (Köndgen et al. 2008; Campbell et al. 2011). Wolfe (2005) claimed that primatologists might have to bear responsibility for habituation because of these potential risks. Primatologists are often involved in the establishment of ecotourism as an approach to conservation. Ecotourism is certainly a better option than the destruction of habitats for cultivation, but it is also known that ecotourism negatively affects wild primates (e.g., Butynski 2001; Treves and Brandon 2005; Berman et al. 2007; Macfie and Williamson 2010).

[iii] Relationships with Local Communities

Asymmetrical relationships between researchers and local communities can have a great effect on the latter. Indeed, the establishment of national parks for the conservation of primates forces local people to leave their native areas (Wright 1992; Eudey 2002). Field primatologists usually hire local research assistants, and it is highly possible that economic differences between researchers and local people will change local economic patterns. Although primatologists in field settings are responsible for providing education about conserving primates and the ecosystem, such education usually adopts a top-down approach (educating rather than sharing), which might alter the culture of the local community.

Thus, it is not always possible to separate the good from the bad in the field activities conducted by primatologists. In such situations, primatologists need to carefully consider the benefits and costs associated with their decisions and must find an ethical compromise.

How have primatologists coped with these ethical challenges thus far? In the next section, I consider why such ethical issues in field primatology have not been discussed.

Discussing Ethics in Field Primatology

I surveyed the reports of previous examples of ethical challenges contained in academic publications. Although this investigation was unavoidably less than comprehensive, it did produce the overall finding that only a few academic peer-reviewed journals (primatological, other anthropological, and conservational) mentioned ethical issues. This is reasonable, given that the primary function of these journals is to publish scientific research. However, I did find several journal papers mentioning ethical issues. *Ecological and Environmental Anthropology* (2006, Volume 2) published a special issue on human–primate relationships (Fuentes 2006; Strier et al. 2006), and the *American Journal of Primatology* (2008, Volume 70, Issue 8) published a series of commentaries by primatologists concerning disease transmission between humans and great apes. Recently, the *American Journal of Primatology* (2010, Volume 72, Issue 9 and 10) published special issues on ethical issues on field primatology and ethnoprimatology. These articles might reflect that recently attention has been paid to ethical issues in field primatology, possibly indicating a change in the field towards publishing articles about ethical issues in peer-reviewed journals.

Currently, it is impossible to analyse ethical issues in field primatology because of the lack of sufficiently detailed records (i.e., about the discussions or processes by which ethics decisions were reached). This represents an unfortunate situation for succeeding generations of primatologists who are required to learn field ethics. Thus, one promising approach involves examining previous ethical incidents by collecting data and interviewing primatologists, thereby enabling subsequent generations to learn from these archives. I encountered one example in which discussions about ethical issues could be extracted from published reports. In 1981, when Japanese primatologists observed two neighbouring groups of wild chimpanzees in the Mahale Mountains of Tanzania, males in one group encountered a mother–infant pair from the neighbouring group, resulting in a male gang attack on the pair. Dr Mariko Hasegawa and her research assistant intervened in this gang attack and prevented the potential infanticide (Nishida and Hiraiwa-Hasegawa 1985).

The account of this event in the academic publication (Nishida and Hiraiwa-Hasegawa 1985) was as follows:

> The encounter lasted for two hr … until the mother–son pair fled north from the M-group because the observers intervened between them. (p. 4)
>
> All of us (four people) feared that the mother and son would be killed if left alone. Therefore, three of us chased the adult males away and surrounded the mother and son, forming a tight-knit barrier against the aggressors. Although the mother and son were completely encircled by the humans, they were not at all frightened! Strangely the excitement of the aggressors very rapidly dwindled, once we had prohibited them from attacking. (p. 10)

This description does not clarify how the decision to intervene was reached. Dr Hasegawa was subsequently interviewed for a popular book regarding female primatologists and primates (Jahme 2000), where the aftermath of the incident was described in greater detail:

> When Birute Galdikas heard how Mariko had put a stop to the murder of two wild chimps, she made a point of writing to Mariko's supervisor, saying that she thought she had done the right thing in saving the lives ... but other Western scientists ... were critical, arguing that she should have remained detached and calmly observed the incident. (p. 155, cited in part)

This is one case in which we can glimpse the details of an ethically challenging incident. My purpose in citing this incident is not to discuss whether researchers should have intervened in the intraspecific killing, but rather to focus on highlighting the possibility that ethical challenges might be accessible to analysis through intensive literature searches and personal interviews. Needless to say, it is important to assess the reliability of the descriptions contained in non-peer-reviewed books. It is likely that ethical discussions also occurred in other contexts, such as whether to vaccinate great apes in response to disease risk (Goodall 1986; Ryan et al. 2011), to shoot wild chimpanzees for humanitarian reasons when a polio-like disease was becoming widespread (Goodall 1986), to relocate a primate group (Strum 1987), to establish a national park (Eudey 2002; Wright 1992), and so on.

As noted above, we have only fragmentary records of the ethical challenges faced in field primatology. Why have ethical issues not been identified and discussed in field primatology? In addition to the aforementioned reluctance of peer-reviewed research journals to include articles about ethical issues, several reasons can be proposed. First, primatology is still a young discipline relative to other areas of anthropology; thus, it might not have reached the stage at which ethical issues can be considered from an historical perspective. The other side of this fact is that the current generation of field primatologists are in a good position to start archiving those reports because it is still possible to interview members of the founder generation of primatologists and collect first-person reports of ethical challenges. Second, detailed records of sensitive ethical issues can be used as fodder for scandals, and aggressive competition among colleagues can result in conflicts among relevant groups. Such scandals, if widely known, might hinder research activities (e.g., research permission and funding might be withheld). Consequently, knowledge of ethical issues might have emerged in the form of gossip orally exchanged among primatologists at universities or conferences rather than in the form of written documentation. Third, discussions about ethics have not been considered a legitimate academic activity thus far. Therefore, primatologists facing severe academic competition (particularly the case for the younger generations) might not have the time and energy to devote to recording and analysing these ethical issues, as they are obliged to concentrate on their scientific outputs (i.e., publication). Finally, and related to the previous points, field primatologists lack the formal methods to record episodes of ethical issues. In researching into biological and cultural anthropology, the mass media has enthusiastically addressed any suspected ethical violations (e.g., Turner 2004), thus providing an opportunity to shed light on the details and importance of ethical issues. However, a brief examination suggests that there has been no such incidents in field primatology which have attracted the attention of the mass media. This may be because there have been no such ethical violations in field primatology, but also may be that the mass media may not be interested in the potential ethical violations in field primatology compared to those in the fields of biological and cultural anthropology.

Unifying Field Ethics in Primatology

I have given possible reasons to explain field primatology's neglect of formal consideration of ethical issues. In this section, I suggest an additional important factor relevant to field primatology (and other areas of anthropology): the difficulty of unifying and negotiating among different ethical perspectives. Thus far, I have used the term 'ethics' vaguely. Of course, ethical sensibilities often differ among researchers, between a researcher and other people involved in field research activities, and among different groups with different interests. More formally, at least three kinds of field ethics should be considered:

(i) *Personal ethics*: The ethical and moral decisions reached by each researcher as an individual. This is affected by personal values, culture, nationality, religion, individual careers, and so on.

(ii) *Professional ethics*: Given that primatologists are educated and trained to be specialists, field primatologists are expected to and should behave in a responsible way as professional scientists. The most explicit guidelines that primatologists are expected to follow are the ethical codes and guidelines established by academic societies, such as those promulgated by the *American* Anthropological *Association* (AAA), the American Association of Physical Anthropologists (AAPA), and the International Primatological Society (IPS).

(iii) *Community ethics*: Currently, most field primatologists come from developed countries and conduct fieldwork with endemic primates in developing countries (Africa, South America, and Asia). In such cases, it is common for local communities/people at the field sites to differ from the primatologists in terms of history, culture, social system, religion, and values. In the context of conservation, differences in the concepts pertaining to the relationships between humans and animals or the environment should be considered (Sicotte and Uwengeli 2002; Loudon et al. 2006).

These classifications indicate that the ethics involved in field primatology involve multiple levels that might differ with regard to what is considered to comprise an ethical or moral decision. On some occasions, primatologists might need to follow local community ethics despite differences between these values and their own personal or professional ethics. Similarly, a primatologist's behaviour might be regarded as ethical in the context of personal and professional ethics but as unethical in the context of community ethics. Thus, it is difficult to unify the different ethical systems, and disagreements among these divergent perspectives must be negotiated.

Even the aforementioned classification of multilayered ethical considerations presents too simplified a picture because each level also has heterogeneous components. Personal ethics vary because the beliefs of each person reflect the unique background of that individual. Professional ethics are frequently general and include only the most common considerations. Thus, primatologists might face decisions that the more general ethical codes do not cover. Community ethics are often characterized by differences in the interests and ethics of local governments and local communities. The typical outcome of such heterogeneous and asymmetrical ethical structures is the neglect of the interests of minor stakeholders, which in most cases means local people. This neglect frequently occurs despite the ability of local people to directly address primate conservation issues. Such multiple and heterogeneous ethical structures result in an increasing number of stakeholders and an increasing necessity for negotiation, rendering the unification of ethical guidelines in field primatology difficult.

The Unique Ethical Structure of Japanese Primate Research

Thus far, I have briefly reviewed the ethical structure of field primatology and have suggested that complex and heterogeneous ethical structures complicate approaches to ethical challenges. However, a simple ethical structure does not necessarily result in easy solutions either and might lead to another dimension of difficulties. In what follows, I will provide an example of this by discussing the ethical and social problems related to Japanese macaques and to field studies on this species conducted by Japanese primatologists.

Based on the advantages associated with studying an endemic primate species (i.e., Japanese macaques), Japanese primatology had independent origins from that of Western countries, soon after the Second World War. Early Japanese primatology was characterized by original approaches, such as anthropomorphism, provisioning, individual identification, and long-term study (Asquith 1986, 1989, 2000; Takasaki 2000; Kutsukake 2011). It has been said that the concept of nature held by Japanese people, involving an intimate connection to nature and more ambiguous boundaries between other animals and humans, differs from that held in Western countries; and these differences have a bearing on the original approaches adopted by early Japanese primatology (Asquith 1986, 2000; Kutsukake 2011).

Japanese primatologists have studied Japanese macaques in multiple field sites for over sixty years (Nakagawa et al. 2010). In addition to these intensive research activities, Japanese primatologists have also been involved in management and conservation problems relating to Japanese macaques. Of these problems, crop damage and the associated economic losses have emerged as among the most intense, causing much conflict between humans and Japanese macaques (Sprague 2002; Knight 2003). Farmers and primatologists work together in an effort to prevent crop damage by proposing effective ways to defend farms (Sprague and Iwasaki 2006). The simplest way to reduce crop damage – also the most unpalatable for primatologists – involves culling Japanese macaques as agricultural pests. In the early 2000s, the number of individuals hunted exceeded 10,000 (Sprague and Iwasaki 2006). However this culling was not based on scientific planning: no detailed population census across the whole of Japan had been conducted, and thus, the number of groups or individuals in each region remained unknown. This is a serious problem, given that macaque populations in the western areas of Japan are at risk of disappearing even though they are not endangered as a species and have been expanding in their geographical distribution (Watanabe and Muroyama 2004).

An additional problem, with which I have personal familiarity, is provisioning. During the earlier days of Japanese primatology, provisioning was regularly used to habituate wild Japanese macaques. However, it soon became clear that provisioning had serious effects on the population, such as rapid population growth and artificial alterations of natural behaviour (Asquith 1989). One dilemma involves the difficulty of stopping provisioning after it has started, given the rapid population growth and the possibility that individuals depending on provisioned food might begin to damage crops. As a graduate student in the late 1990s, I studied provisioned groups of Japanese macaques at Shiga heights in Nagano prefecture. The staff of the Jigokudani Monkey Park have provisioned groups in this area since the 1960s for purposes of tourism. Japanese macaques living in this field site are known throughout the world as 'snow monkeys', and the images of Japanese macaques in the hot spring attract numerous visitors from abroad to the monkey park, contributing to the local economy. These groups show the typical sequellae of provisioning, such as rapid population growth and related problems. Nagano prefecture is one of the areas suffering most severe crop damage caused by Japanese macaques. In this context, local attitudes towards Japanese macaques were not benign. During my observation of Japanese macaques, it was not rare for local people to approach me and ask, 'If you have time to study Japanese macaques, why don't you think of something to stop their bad behaviour and crop damage?' It was highly likely that large groups of macaques would approach human areas and damage crops if provisioning ceased. Therefore, provisioning represents the second-best option for allowing monkeys to remain in mountain areas.

A committee was organized by local people and elder Japanese primatologists to plan for the future of the provisioned groups. The committee discussed proposals for addressing this dilemma and decided to implant a drug that would suppress oestrous expression in most of the adult females in order to control population growth, and to capture individuals in these groups to send abroad to zoos and other captive facilities. Although I was not a member of this committee, I heard that it engaged in many discussions about whether the artificial manipulation of the group structure and demography of wild primates was acceptable, given that this approach went against the concept of nature held by Japanese people. It should also be noted that these strategies do not fundamentally solve the problems of provisioning *per se*, but are rather temporary solutions that avoid the immediate costs of provisioning.

These represent only a sample of the social problems relating to Japanese macaques. Additional problems involve the ongoing hybridization between Japanese macaques and newly introduced rhesus macaques, *Macaca mulatta,* or Taiwanese macaques, *Macaca cyclopis*; the removal of these hybrid individuals; the stable supply of Japanese macaques as experimental animals; and so on. The ethical structure of these complicated problems is unique in that the local community and Japanese primatologists originate from the same country, are relatively symmetrical in terms of economic and political perspectives, and have much in common (e.g., the concept of nature, the sense of values, economic status, and so on). It is also easier for Japanese primatologists to engage in life-time commitments to particular field sites than it is for primatologists studying abroad. Thus, community and personal ethical considerations were characterized by many areas of agreement, and unifying the ethical structure was relatively simple. Nonetheless, the complexity of the problems relating to Japanese macaques indicates that even a simple ethical structure involving relatively few and relatively homogenous stakeholders does not always result in solutions that are easy to develop and to implement; rather, a different dimension of difficulty seems to characterize such a simple ethical structure. Although the top-down approach to conservation strategies based on immense economic power has often been employed with regard to primate conservation in developing countries, such an approach might be less useful in solving the problems relating to Japanese macaques. A bottom-up approach, characterized by mutual communication and negotiation, has also been adopted for the community-based conservation of primates in developing countries. In the case of problems concerning Japanese macaques, a bottom-up approach combined with a limited/minor top-down approach is preferred because of the relative symmetries among stakeholders. This is in order to achieve a realistic compromise and negotiated solution. Concerning the situation of Japanese macaques, if such a well-balanced combination can be achieved, it will be a unique case of ethical negotiation in field primatology.

Acknowledgements

Many thanks to Jeremy MacClancy for inviting me to the stimulating conference 'Ethics in the Field: Contemporary Challenges to Anthropology'. I would like to thank Jeremy MacClancy and Agustin Fuentes for editing the book, the participants of the conference for their discussion, and Mariko Hasegawa and Keiko K Fujisawa for constructive discussion and support. This study was financially supported by the Japan Society for Promotion of Science, Hayama Center for Advanced Studies at the Graduate University for Advanced Studies, PRESTO at JST, and the Japan Foundation.

References

Asquith, P.J. 1986. 'Anthropomorphism and the Japanese and Western Traditions in Primatology', in J.G. Else and P.C. Lee (eds), *Primate Ontogeny, Cognition and Social Behavior*. Cambridge: *Cambridge* University Press, pp. 61–71.

———. 1989. 'Provisioning and the Study of Free-ranging Primates: History, Effects and Prospects', *Yearbook of Physical Anthropology* 32: 129–58.

———. 2000. 'Negotiating Science: Internationalization and Japanese Primatology', in S. Strum and L.M. Fedigan (eds), *Primate Encounters: Models of Science, Gender, and Society*. Chicago, Ill.: The University of Chicago Press, pp. 165–83.

Bearder, S.K., K.A.I. Nekaris, D.J. Curtis, L. Dew and J.M. Setchell. 2003. 'Tips from the Bush: an A-Z of Suggestions for Successful Fieldwork', in J.M. Setchell and D.J. Curtis (eds), *Field and Laboratory Methods for Primatologists*. Cambridge: *Cambridge* University Press, pp. 309–23.

Berman, C.M., J.H. Li, H. Ogawa, C. Ionica and H.B. Yin. 2007. '*Primate Tourism, Range Restriction, and Infant Risk among Macaca thibetana at Mt. Huangshan, China*', *International Journal of Primatology* 28: 1123–41.

Butynski, T.M. 2001. 'Africa's Great Apes', in B. Beck, S. Stoinski, M. Hutchins, T. Maple, B. Norton, A. Rowan, E. Stevens and A. Arluke (eds), *Great Apes and Humans. The Ethics of Coexistence*. Washington, D.C: Smithsonian Institution Press, pp. 3–56.

Campbell, G., H. Kuehl, A. Diarrassouba, P,K. N'Goran and C. Boesch. 2011. 'Long-term Research Sites as Refugia for Threatened and Over-harvested Species', *Biology Letters* 7: 723–26.

Crutzen, P.J. 2002. '*Geology of Mankind*', *Nature* 415: 23.

Eudey, A.A. 2002. 'The Primatologist as Minority Advocate', in A. Fuentes and L.D. Wolfe (eds), *Primates Face to Face*: *Conservation Implications of Human-Nonhuman Primate Interconnections*. Cambridge: *Cambridge* University Press, pp. 277–87.

Fedigan, L.M. 2010. 'Ethical Issues faced by Field Primatologists: Asking the Relevant Questions', *American Journal of Primatology* 72: 754–71.

Fuentes, A. 2006. 'Human-nonhuman Primate Interconnections and their Relevance to Anthropology', *Ecological and Environmental Anthropology* 2: 1–11.

Fuentes, A. and K.J. Hockings. 2010. 'The Ethnoprimatological Approach in Primatology', *American Journal of Primatology* 72: 841–47.

Fuentes, A. and L.D. Wolfe. 2002. *Primates Face to Face*: *Conservation Implications of Human-Nonhuman Primate Interconnections*. Cambridge: *Cambridge* University Press.

Garber, P.A., A. Molina and R.L. Molina. 2010. 'Putting the Community back in Community Ecology and Education: the Role of Field Schools and Private Reserves in the Ethical Training of Primatologists', *American Journal of Primatology* 72: 785–93.

Goldsmith, M.L. 2005. '*Habituating* Primates for Field Study: *Ethical* Considerations for African Great Apes', in T.R. Turner (ed.), *Biological Anthropology and Ethics: From Repatriation to Genetic Identity*. Albany: State University of New York Press, pp. 49–64.

Goodall, J. 1986. *The Chimpanzees of Gombe*: *Patterns of Behavior*. The Belknap Press of Harvard University Press.

Hockings, K. and T. Humle. 2009. *Best Practice Guidelines for the Prevention and Mitigation of Conflict between Humans and Great Apes*. Gland, Switzerland: IUCN/SSC Primate Specialist Group (PSG).

Isbell, L.A. and *T.P. Young. 1993.* 'Human Presence reduces Leopard Predation in a Freeranging *Population of Vervet Monkeys (Cercopithecus aethiops)*', *Animal Behaviour* 45: 1233–35.

Jahme, C. 2000. *Beauty and the Beasts: Woman, Ape, and Evolutions*. London: Virago.

Knight, J. 2003. *Waiting for Wolves in Japan: an Anthropological Study of People-Wildlife Relations*. Oxford: Oxford University Press.

Köndgen, S., H. Kühl, P.K. N'Goran, P.D. Walsh, S.Schenk, N. Ernst, R. Biek, P. Formenty, K. Mätz-Rensing, B. Schweiger, S. Junglen, H. Ellerbrok, A. Nitsche, T. Briese, W.I. Lipkin, G. Pauli, C. Boesch and F.H. Leendertz. 2008. 'Pandemic Human Viruses cause Decline of Endangered Great Apes', *Current Biology* 18: 260–64.

Kutsukake, N. 2011. 'Lost in Translation: Field Primatology, Culture, and Interdisciplinary Approaches', in J. MacClancy and A. Fuentes (eds), *Centralizing Fieldwork: Critical*

Perspectives from Primatology, Biological Anthropology and Social Anthropology. Oxford and New York: Berghahn, pp. 104–20.

Lee, P.C. 2010. 'Sharing Space: Can Ethnoprimatology Contribute to the Survival of Non-human Primates in Human-dominated Globalized Landscapes?', *American Journal of Primatology* 72: 925–31.

Loudon, J.E., M.L. Sauther, K.D. Fish, M. Hunter-Ishikawa and J.I. Youssouf. 2006. 'One Reserve, Three Primates: Applying a Holistic Approach to understand the Interconnections among Ring-tailed Lemurs (*Lemur catta*), Verreaux's Sifaka (*Propithecus verreauxi*), and Humans (*Homo sapiens*) at Beza Mahafaly Special Reserve, Madagascar', *Ecological and Environmental Anthropology* 2: 54–74.

Macfie, E.J. and E.A. Williamson. 2010. *Best Practice Guidelines for Great Ape Tourism.* Gland, Switzerland: IUCN/SSC Primate Specialist Group (PSG).

MacKinnon, K.C. and E.P. Riley. 2010. 'Field Primatology of Today: Current Ethical Issues', *American Journal of Primatology* 72: 749–53.

Malone, N.M., A. Fuentes and F.J. White. 2010. 'Ethics Commentary: Subjects of Knowledge and Control in Field Primatology', *American Journal of Primatology* 72: 779–84.

Martin, P. and P. Bateson. 1990. *Measuring Behaviour, an Introductory Guide.* Cambridge: *Cambridge* University Press.

Nakagawa, N., M. Nakamichi and H. Sugiura. 2010. *The Japanese Macaques.* Tokyo: Springer.

Nash, L.T. 2004. 'Studies of Primates in the Field and in Captivity: Similarities and Differences in Ethical Concerns', in T.R. Turner (ed.), *Biological Anthropology and Ethics: from Repatriation to Genetic Identity.* Albany: State University of New York Press, pp. 27–48.

Nekaris, K.A., C.R. Shepherd, C.R. Starr and V. Nijman. 2010. 'Exploring Cultural Drivers for Wildlife Trade via an Ethnoprimatological Approach: a Case Study of Slender and Slow Lorises (Loris and Nycticebus) in South and Southeast Asia', *American Journal of Primatology* 72: 877–86.

Nishida, T. and M. Hiraiwa-Hasegawa. 1985. 'Responses to a Stranger Mother-son Pair in the Wild Chimpanzee: a Case Report', *Primates* 26: 1–13.

Ross, S.R., K.E. Lukas, E.V. Lonsdorf, T.S. Stoinski, B. Hare, R. Shumaker and J. Goodall. 2008. '*Inappropriate Use and Portrayal of Chimpanzees*', *Science* 319: 1487.

Ryan, S.J. and P.D. Walsh. 2011. 'Consequences of Non-intervention for Infectious Disease in African Great Apes', *PLoS One* e29030.

Sicotte, P. and P. Uwengeli. 2002. 'Reflections on the Concept of Nature and Gorillas in Rwanda: Implications for Conservation', in A. Fuentes and L.D. Wolfe (eds), *Primates Face to Face: Conservation Implications of Human-Nonhuman Primate Interconnections.* Cambridge: Cambridge University Press, pp. 163–82.

Sprague, D. 2002. 'Monkeys in the Backyard: Encroaching Wildlife and Rural Communities in Japan', in A. Fuentes and L.D. Wolfe (eds), *Primates Face to Face: Conservation Implications of Human-Nonhuman Primate Interconnections.* Cambridge: Cambridge University Press, pp. 254–72.

Sprague, D. and N. Iwasaki. 2006. 'Coexistence and Exclusion between Humans and Monkeys in Japan: Is either really Possible?', *Ecological and Environmental Anthropology* 2: 30–43.

Strier, K.B. 2010. 'Long-term Field Studies: Positive Impacts and Unintended Consequences', *American Journal of Primatology* 72: 772–78.

Strier, K.B., J.P. Boubli, F.B. Pontual and S.L. Mendes. 2006. '*Human Dimensions of Northern Muriqui Conservation Efforts*', *Ecological and Environmental Anthropology* 2: 44–53.

Strum, S.C. 1987. Almost Human. New York: Random House.

Takasaki, H. 2000. 'Traditions of the Kyoto School of Field Primatology in Japan', in S. Strum and L.M. Fedigan (eds), *Primate Encounters: Models of Science, Gender, and Society*. Chicago, Ill.: The University of Chicago Press, pp. 151–64.

Treves, A. and K. Brandon. 2005. 'Tourist impacts on the Behavior of Black Howling Monkeys (*Alouatta pigra*) at Lamanai, Belize', in J. Paterson and J. Wallis (eds), *Commensalism and Conflict: The Human-Primate Interface*. Special Topics in Primatology. Norman, OK: American Society of Primatologists, pp. 146–67.

Turner, T.R. 2004. *Biological Anthropology and Ethics: from Repatriation to Genetic Identity.* Albany: State University of New York Press.

Wallis, J. and D.R. Lee. 1999. 'Primate Conservation: the Prevention of Disease Transmission', *International Journal of Primatology* 20:8 03–26.

Watanabe, K. and Y. Muroyama. 2004. 'Recent Expansion of the Range of Japanese Macaques, and Associated Management Problems', in J. Paterson and J. Wallis (eds), *Commensalism and Conflict: The Human-Primate Interface*. Special Topics in Primatology. Norman, OK: American Society of Primatologists, pp. 313–31.

Williamson, E.A. and A.T.C. Feistner. 2003. *'Habituating Primates: Processes, Techniques, Variables and Ethics', in* J.M. Setchell and D.J. Curtis (eds), *Field and Laboratory Methods for Primatologists*. Cambridge: *Cambridge* University Press, pp. 25–39.

Wolfe, L.D. 2005. 'Field Primatologists: Duties, Rights, and Obligations', in T.R. Turner (ed.), *Biological Anthropology and Ethics: from Repatriation to Genetic Identity*. Albany: State University of New York Press, pp. 15–26.

Woodford, M.H., T. Butynski and W.B. Karesh. 2002. 'Habituating the Great Apes: the Disease Risks', *Oryx* 36: 153–60.

Wright, P.C. 1992. 'Primate Ecology, Rainforest Conservation, and Economic Development: Building a National Park in Madagascar', *Evolutionary Anthropology* 1: 25–33.

6

Contemporary Ethical Issues in Field Primatology

Katherine C. MacKinnon and Erin P. Riley

Introduction

In general, primatologists adhere to a set of principles outlined in resolutions and policy statements on the ethical treatment of nonhuman primates, particularly in captivity and biomedical contexts. For primatologists who do fieldwork, the issues can be more obfuscated, and we often find ourselves immersed in matters such as primate health concerns (e.g., bidirectional transmission of pathogens between humans and nonhuman primates living in the same environments), and the conservation/management of wild primate populations (e.g., see Mittermeier et al. 2012). Therefore, the contemporary fieldwork environment presents an increasingly complex landscape in which to address human and nonhuman primate needs and interests. While ethical concerns have been discussed amongst field primatologists for decades, the scope of these conversations has widened in the last five to ten years, particularly with regard to anthropogenic processes (e.g., climate change, altered landscapes, conservation/management issues for dwindling populations) and the training of primatologists in host countries. Our motivation to explicitly address the ethics of field primatology derives from a dissatisfaction with the irrelevancy for field primatology of most of the parameters that constitute the key governing protocol regarding the ethical treatment of animals (i.e., Institutional Animal Care and Use Committee, or IACUC) and a growing concern about current and future practitioners of our field 'seeing only the primates' and not the broader community that includes human livelihoods. Here we aim to provide an overview of where we stand today in some of these conversations, and thoughts on how to move the issues forward in an applied way. To that end, this chapter summarizes recent discussions on ethical issues and outlines our expectations for future directions.

Review of Recent Discussions

In the last few years, informal and more formal ethical discussions have taken place at various professional meetings and conferences. In 2004 Trudy Turner published the edited volume, *Biological Anthropology and Ethics. From Repatriation to Genetic Identity* (see MacKinnon 2006 for review), which was the result of a 2001 American Association of Physical Anthropology symposium on 'Biological Anthropology and Ethics'. It explored many of the complex ethical issues facing the subfields of biological anthropology (including primatology) today. Authors used a case-study approach and presented information on an ethical situation they have had to face in their professional lives. This was a highly effective way to present 'hot topic' themes, and the use of case studies to illuminate ethical quandaries is something we would like to use as we move forward (especially in online formats such as blogs, and on the websites of professional organizations).

At the 2009 annual meeting of the American Society of Primatologists (held in San Diego, California) we organized a symposium titled 'Field Primatology of Today: Navigating the Ethical Landscape' (see MacKinnon and Riley 2010; and Baden et al. 2009 and Rutherford 2009 for review). This symposium addressed the concerns with ethical issues that field primatologists encounter, and was the first organized discussion on this topic at a professional meeting in several years. The themes that emerged from that session, via the papers presented and the resulting moderated discussion with the audience, included a) a need to educate our undergraduate and graduate students on contemporary ethical issues, b) a focus on multi-faceted and multi-layered ethical considerations (e.g., how to balance the wellbeing of nonhuman primates and the local human communities that surround them), and c) the necessity of self-reflection on the positive and negative effects of our presence (particularly at long-term field sites). There was also discussion about creating a formalized code of ethics for field primatology, including a review of ethical guidelines from the American Anthropological Association, the American Association of Physical Anthropology, and the Animal Behavior Society. The resulting publication by Riley and MacKinnon (2010, guest editors), which appeared as a Special Section on Ethical Issues in Field Primatology in the *American Journal of Primatology* is, we hope, representative of that symposium and a good starting point for what lays ahead.

More recently published, *Centralizing Fieldwork: Critical Perspectives from Primatology, Biological Anthropology and Social Anthropology* (edited by MacClancy and Fuentes 2011) seeks to provide a comparative exploration across primatology, biological anthropology and social anthropology, by using the practice of fieldwork as the anchoring methodology. The volume emerged from a 2007 conference held at the Anthropology Centre for Conservation, the Environment and Development (ACCEND) at Oxford Brookes University, and includes broad perspectives from an international group of researchers. Several chapters in particular help to inform and enlighten topics of ethics in field primatology: e.g., see chapters by Asquith on primate fieldwork and the anthropological method, Fuentes on context and methods, Jolly on the narrator's stance and science 'story-telling', Kutsukake on Japanese primatology and interdisciplinary approaches, Lee on local community perspectives and conservation, MacKinnon on the role of field schools in training young primatologists, Sussman on the human context of fieldwork in Southern Madagascar, and Yamagiwa on ecological anthropology and Japanese primatology, among others.

Key Lessons Learned

In this section we provide an overview of what we see as 'key concerns' that emerged from the aforementioned symposia/scholarship (MacKinnon and Riley 2010; see also Hill 2002; Carlsson et al. 2004; Nash 2005; Wolfe 2005). We hope these might serve as an effective framework for our future actions in fostering a well-rounded ethics discussion. First, how can we achieve our research goals while paying careful attention to the variable ways in which our research affects (positively and negatively) the nonhuman primates under study? This concern includes the principles of 'do no harm' (Wolfe 2005) and 'be only beneficient' (Nash 2005), as well as paying attention to issues of disease transmission (Jones-Engel et al. 2008; Wallis and Lee 1999) and the extended effects of habituation (Goldsmith 2005; Strier 2010). Strier (2010) reminds us that a long-term research presence can mean that some primates will never experience life without human observers, and that we should be cognizant of this ecological footprint. At the same time, a long-term research presence may also result in increased protection of primates from poaching, thereby outweighing the potential costs of this footprint. For example, recent work in Tai National Park, Cote d'Ivoire has demonstrated that encounter rates of primates and other wildlife were greater in research areas compared to non-research areas surveyed (Campbell et al. 2011).

Second, while our primary responsibility as field primatologists is to the nonhuman primate individuals and populations we study, we also work within a larger ethical realm that includes human primates. Increasing recognition of this reality has largely emerged as a result of recent work in ethnoprimatology (e.g., Wheatley 1999; Fuentes and Wolfe 2002; Loudon et al. 2006; Riley 2005, 2007; Lee 2010; Riley et al. 2011). Ethnoprimatology's explicit focus on the ways in which human and nonhuman primates interact has meant that primatologists are more attuned to how our data and research results can affect the local human communities in which we work (see Eudey 2002; Fuentes 2002, 2006; Garber et al. 2010; Lee 2011; Loudon et al. 2006; Riley 2005, 2006, 2007; Sommer 2011; Sussman 2011), For example, we typically live in a local community, we may hire local people in the area to assist in the research, and we might use our research results to inform conservation/management plans that will likely affect those occupied areas. How then can we mitigate potential conflicts between conservation/management plans and the local human population?

Third, how are the relationships between primate researchers living in host countries and the local people best negotiated? The ability to work within the local cultural context is often the key variable determining success in field primatology; important to always consider is that our very presence as 'outsiders' affects the communities in which we work and live (see Fuentes 2002, 2011a,b; Lee 2011; Sommer 2011). Also, as fieldwork primatologists we have an obligation to conduct ourselves in a way that will not compromise future work (Wolfe 2005). Often, the practice of field primatology does not occur in isolation from where the training of students takes place (see Garber et al. 2010; MacKinnon 2011), and the various countries and cultures in which it is practiced. There is a strong interaction among the primatologists themselves, their scientific research, and the societies in which they work.

Beyond these key concerns, we also have feedback from the broader scholarly community, and in particular, from comments raised during the aforementioned ethics symposium at the 2009 ASP meetings. There was considerable discussion about the drastically different ethical landscapes of captive and field primatology. For example, while in captive work there is on-site regulation of research, in the field, the question becomes: who monitors the research taking place? If we are doing invasive procedures (e.g. capturing primates, drawing blood), should we be required to include veterinarians in the study? This question is intricately linked to another point raised at the discussion: the countries in which we work may also have codes of ethics that we must adhere to and integrate with our own. Collectively these issues speak to the broader problem of how animal use protocol derives from laboratory-based research, and hence, many of the questions asked are of marginal relevance to the realities faced by field primatologists. Interestingly, Fedigan (2010: 766), in her survey of 105 field primatologists, found that some view it as 'better to continue going through the exercise of answering irrelevant questions (i.e., leave bad enough alone) rather than risk the possibility that a committee made up of non-field workers should learn what the relevant questions really are and then have them try to evaluate our responses on field issues about which they have little experience.' Nonetheless, there appears to be overwhelming agreement in support of change by providing the appropriate questions and context for field-based ethical issues to institutional bodies. Such questions include, but are not limited to (see Fedigan 2010, Appendix B, for a sample animal care form for field studies): (1) What are the likely benefits and possible negative effects of your presence and field methods on your study subjects, their environment, and the local human community?; (2) Do the benefits of habituating a new primate group outweigh the costs?; (3) What permits do you need to conduct research at your field site? Have you secured them? (4) Do you intend to conduct interviews with human communities? If so, have you secured IRB approval? It is promising that institutions have amended or are currently amending animal care protocol to include field-based parameters (e.g., University of Wisconsin Madison's form for wildlife observational studies in natural habitat; http://www.rarc.wisc.edu/forms/index.html; Strier, personal communication).

Discussion at the 2009 ASP symposium also centred around the responsibility of funding sources in requiring applicants to address whether they have permission to do the research, and to discuss the primary ethical concerns associated with their work, including how the issues will be addressed/mitigated. The American Society of Primatologists and other organizations already mandate attention to these issues. For example, beginning in 2011 the ASP Conservation Grant Proposal Application form requires applicants to briefly discuss ethical concerns associated with their projects. The next step is for these applications to also require applicants to acknowledge whether permits have been received and approval from IACUC and IRB (if applicable) has been secured. We recommend that other funding sources for primate research implement a similar protocol.

Finally, we discussed our obligations as teachers/mentors, and in particular the need to encourage and support co-authorship with our collaborators and assistants in the habitat countries in which we work. Wright and Andriamihaja emphasized the following: (1) Foreign scientists should participate in capacity building and fund a source-country student to train alongside them. (2) Researchers should hire local residents and provide these people with skills in language, technology and science, skills which will help them to be research assistants, tourist guides or park rangers. (3) International scientists should collaborate with host-country university colleagues and co-author publications. These colleagues should also be invited to international meetings to network and broaden their academic interests. (4) The intellectual property of the local residents should be valued, and rewarded.

Next Step: What Would a Code of Ethics Look Like?

As noted, one of the larger goals of the ASP 2009 Ethics in Field Primatology symposium (and the published commentaries and articles) was to work toward the development of a formalized code of ethics that addresses the multi-faceted dilemmas that we encounter as field-based researchers. Specifically, we noted that providing real-life examples of complex issues faced in the field might be useful for current and future primatologists.

Of course, as is noted in many professional organizations such as the American Anthropological Association (AAA), a formalized code does not 'dictate choice or propose sanctions'. Rather, codes are 'designed to promote discussion and provide general guidelines for ethically responsible decisions' (AAA Code of Ethics). Here we present suggestions for what might constitute the body of a formalized code of ethics for field primatology. We draw from the lessons learned and feedback noted above, as well as from the codes and guidelines followed by the AAA, the American Association of Physical Anthropologists, the Animal Behavior Society, National Academy of Sciences, National Association for the Practice of Anthropology, Sigma Xi, and the Society for Applied Anthropology. We envision the code as taking the following shape:

1. Responsibility/Do No Harm. One of the primary goals of an ethics code parameter involving 'responsibility' and 'do no harm' is to focus attention on the animals with whom researchers work and the people on whose lives and cultures the work affects. At the most basic level, field primatologists have fundamental ethical obligations to the species that they study and to the people with whom they work. These obligations can supersede the goal of seeking new knowledge, and can lead to decisions not to undertake or to discontinue a research project when the primary obligations conflict with other responsibilities (e.g., those

owed to sponsors or clients). Such ethical obligations might include:(a) avoiding harm or wrongdoing, understanding that the development of knowledge can lead to change which may be positive or negative for the animals studied or people with whom we work; (b) respecting the wellbeing of humans and non-human primates; (c) working for the long-term conservation and management of nonhuman primate populations; and (d) consulting actively with the affected people in a study area, with the goal of establishing a working relationship that can be beneficial to all parties involved.

2. Field primatologists must determine in advance whether their hosts/providers of information wish to remain anonymous or receive recognition, and make every effort to comply with those wishes. Researchers must present their research participants with the possible impacts of the choices, and make clear that despite their best efforts, anonymity may be compromised or recognition might fail to materialize.

3. Field primatologists should obtain in advance the informed consent of persons providing information, owning or controlling access to species being studied, or otherwise identified as having interests that might be affected by the research. It is understood that the degree and breadth of informed consent required will depend on the nature of the project and may be affected by requirements of other codes, laws, and ethics of the country or community in which the research is pursued. Further, it is understood that the informed consent process is dynamic and continuous; the process should be initiated in the project design and continue through implementation by way of dialogue and negotiation with those involved. Researchers are responsible for identifying and complying with the various informed consent codes, laws and regulations affecting their projects. Informed consent, for the purposes of this code, does not necessarily imply or require a particular written or signed form. It is the quality of the consent, not the format, that is relevant.

4. Field primatologists who have developed close and enduring relationships (i.e., covenantal relationships) either with individual persons providing information/assistance or with hosts must adhere to the obligations of openness and informed consent, while carefully and respectfully negotiating the limits of the relationship.

5. While field primatologists may gain personally from their work, they must not exploit individuals, groups, animals, or cultural or biological materials. They should recognize their debt to the societies in which they work and their obligation to reciprocate with host people in appropriate ways.

6. Field primatologists must actively encourage their students to think critically about these issues and present them with 'what if' scenarios to discuss and refer back to once they are in the field. Such initial exploration of these topics might also include: information on a particular country's history, the ethnic groups and cultural identities currently present, the socio-economic status of people in cities versus more rural areas, and cultural taboos. Field schools, coursework, and/or a required seminar before students engage in any type of

independent field research should be essential. When possible, there should be a commitment toward the training of students from habitat countries by foreign primatologists.

7. Dissemination of information is critical and work should be published in a timely manner in scholarly peer-reviewed journals and conservation reports. Field primatologists should make every effort to publish with their host country collaborators and assistants, and publications should result in formats that are accessible to habitat country nationals.

As we work on these and other statements, several relevant codes and policy guidelines will be consulted, such as:

Animal Behavior Society. 1991. 'Guidelines for the Use of Animals in Research', *Animal Behavior* 41: 183–86.

National Academy of Sciences. 1995. *On Being a Scientist: Responsible Conduct in Research*, 2nd ed. Washington, DC: National Academy Press (2121 Constitution Avenue, NW, Washington, DC 20418).

National Association for the Practice of Anthropology. 1988. 'Ethical Guidelines for Practitioners'. *Sigma Xi.* 1992. 'Sigma Xi Statement on the Use of Animals in Research', *American Scientist* 80: 73–76.

Society for Applied Anthropology. 1983 (revised). 'Professional and Ethical Responsibilities'.

Summary

Ignoring ethical issues can often lead to an abuse of science, as history readily demonstrates. While it may be far easier to not incorporate such considerations into our academic and professional goals, we need to constantly guard against carrying out our work in a vacuum, devoid of ethical contemplations. To this end, we hope that these recent discussions about ethical issues in field primatology will eventually lead to a practical set of guidelines for academic and educational use, and will continue to foster subsequent conversations on these myriad topics. We are currently developing a formalized code of ethics for field primatology, and will be exploring the facets of this endeavour by way of professional workshops, subsequent publications, and an ongoing dialogue about what a code should encompass.

Acknowledgements

We appreciate and thank our many primatological colleagues who have participated in valuable discussions of ethical issues, and in particular acknowledge the following authors and participants in the 'Field Primatology of Today: Navigating the Ethical Landscape' symposium at the 2009 American Society of Primatologists meeting in San Diego, California: B.A. Andriamihaja, Linda Fedigan, Agustín Fuentes, Paul Garber, Thomas Gillespie, Randall Kyes, Nicholas Malone, Alvaro Molina, Renee Molina, Karen Strier, Frances White, and Patricia Wright. We look forward to future collaborations at upcoming meetings via planned symposia and workshops as we build a working code of ethics for field primatology. Finally we thank the editors of this volume, Jeremy MacClancy and Agustín Fuentes, for their support and encouragement, and for inviting us to summarize our considerations thus far.

References

AAA. 1998. AAA code of ethics. Available at http://www.aaanet.org/committees/ethics/ethcode.htm.

ASP. 2000. ASP (American Society of Primatologists) policy statement on the protection of primate health in the wild. Available at https://www.asp.org/society/resolutions/primate_health.cfm.

————. 2001. ASP (American Society of Primatologists) policy statement on the ethical treatment of nonhuman primates. Available at https://www.asp.org/society/resolutions/EthicalTreatmentOfNonHumanPrimates.cfm.

Baden, A.L., A. Lu, S.R. Tecot. 2009. '2009 Annual Meeting of the American Society of Primatologists', *Evol. Anthropol* 18(5): 164–65.

Campbell, G., H. Kuehl, A. Diarrassoubal, P.K. N'Goran and C. Boesch. 2011. 'Long-term Research Sites as Refugia for Threatened and Over-harvested Species', *Biology Letters* 7 (5): 723–726.

Carlsson, H-E., S.J. Schapiro, I. Farah and J. Hau. 2004. 'Use of Primates in Research: A Global Overview', *American Journal of Primatology* 63: 225–37.

Eudey A. 2002. 'The Primatologist as a Minority Advocate', in A. Fuentes and L.D. Wolfe (eds), *Primates Face to Face: Conservation Implications of Human-Nonhuman Primate Interconnections*. New York: Cambridge University Press, pp. 277–87.

Fedigan, L.M. 2010. 'Ethical Issues Faced by Field Primatologists: Asking the Relevant Questions', *American Journal of Primatology* 72(9): 754–71.

Fuentes, A. 2002. 'Monkeys, Humans and Politics in the Mentawai Islands: No Simple Solutions in a Complex World', in A. Fuentes and L.D. Wolfe (eds), *Primates Face to Face: Conservation Implications of Human-Nonhuman Primate Interconnections*. New York: Cambridge University Press, pp. 187–207.

————. 2006. 'Human-Nonhuman Primate Interconnections and Their Relevance to Anthropology', *Ecological and Environmental Anthropology* 2(2): 1–11.

————. 2011a. 'Measuring Meaning and Understanding in Primatological and Biological Anthropology Fieldwork: Context and Practice', in J. MacClancy and A. Fuentes (eds), *Centralizing Fieldwork: Critical Perspectives from Primatology, Biological Anthropology and Social Anthropology*. Oxford: Berghahn Books, pp. 121–36.

————. 2011b. 'Being Human and Doing Primatology: National, Socioeconomic, and Ethnic Influences on Primatological Practice', *Amer. J. Primatol* 73: 233–37.

Fuentes, A. and L.D. Wolfe (eds). 2002. *Primates Face to Face: The Conservation Implications of Human and Nonhuman Primate Interconnections*. New York: Cambridge University Press.

Garber, P.A., A. Molina and R.L. Molina. 2010. 'Putting the Community Back in Community Ecology and Education: The Role of Field Schools and Private Reserves in the Ethical Training of Primatologists', *Am. J. Primatol* 72: 785–93.

Goldsmith, M.L. 2005. 'Habituating primates for field study: ethical considerations for African great apes', in T.R. Turner, editor. *Biological Anthropology and Ethics*. Albany, NY: State University of New York Press, pp. 49–64.

Hill, C.M. 2002. 'Primate Conservation and Local Communities: Ethical Issues and Debates', *American Anthropologist* 104(4): 1184–94.

Jones-Engel, L., N. Aggimarangsee, J.S. Allan, R. Chaiwarith, M.K. Chalise, G.A. Engel, M.M. Feeroz, A. Fuentes, R. Grant, L. Kuller, R.C. Kyes, M.L. Linial, C.C. May, A. Putra, A. Rompis, M.A. Schillaci, K.A. Steinkraus, S. Thongsawat, I.N. Wandia and R. Watanabe. 2008. 'Diverse Contexts of Zoonotic Transmission of Simian Foamy Viruses in Asia', *Emerging Infectious Diseases* 14(8): 1200–08.

Lee, P.C. 2010. 'Sharing Space: Can Ethnoprimatology contribute to the Survival of Non-human Primates in Human-dominated Globalized Landscapes?' *American Journal of Primatology* 72: 925–31.

———. 2011. 'Problem Animals or Problem People?Ethics, Politics and Practice or Conflict between Community Perspectives and Fieldwork on Conservation', in J. MacClancy and A. Fuentes (eds), *Centralizing Fieldwork: Critical Perspectives from Primatology, Biological, and Social Anthropology*. Oxford: Berghahn Books, pp. 69–83.

Loudon, J.E., M.E. Howells and A. Fuentes. 2006. 'The Importance of Integrative Anthropology: A Preliminary Investigation Employing Primatological and Cultural Anthropological Data Collection Methods in Assessing Human-Monkey Co-Existence in Bali, Indonesia', *Ecological and Environmental Anthropology* 2(1): 2–13.

MacClancy, J. and A. Fuentes (eds). 2011. *Centralizing Fieldwork: Critical Perspectives from Primatology, Biological Anthropology and Social Anthropology*. Oxford: Berghahn Books.

MacKinnon, K.C. 2006. '*Biological Anthropology and Ethics. From Repatriation to Genetic Identity*, edited by Trudy R. Turner, x + 327 pp., 2004, Albany, NY: State University of New York Press', *International Journal of Primatology* 27(2): 63941.

———. 2011. 'Primatology Field Schools in Central America: Playing a Pivotal Role in the Formation of Modern Field Primatologists', in J. MacClancy and A. Fuentes (eds), *Centralizing Fieldwork: Critical Perspectives from Primatology, Biological Anthropology and Social Anthropology*. Oxford: Berghahn Books, pp. 200–24.

MacKinnon, K.C. and E.P. Riley. 2010. 'Field Primatology of Today: Current Ethical Issues', *American Journal of Primatology* 72(9): 749–53.

Mittermeier, R.A., C. Schwitzer, A.B. Rylands, L.A. Taylor, F. Chiozza, E.A. Williamson, and J. Wallis. 2012. *Primates in Peril: The World's 25 Most Endangered Primates 2012-2014*. Compiled by the Primate Specialist Group of IUCN's Species Survival Commission (SSC) and the International Primatological Society (IPS), in collaboration with Conservation International (CI). Available at http://www.conservation.org/Documents/CI_Primates-in-Peril_25-Most-Endangered-Primates_2012-2014.pdf

Nash, L. 2005. 'Studies of Primates in the Field and in Captivity: Similarities and Differences in Ethical Concerns', in T.R. Turner (ed.), *Biological Anthropology and Ethics*. Albany, NY: State University of New York, pp. 27–48.

National Academy of Sciences. 1995. *On Being a Scientist: Responsible Conduct in Research*. 2nd edition. Washington, D.C.: National Academy Press.

National Association for the Practice of Anthropology. 1988. 'Ethical Guidelines for Practitioners'. Available at http://practicinganthropology.org/ethical-guidelines/.

Riley, E.P. 2005. *Ethnoprimatology of Macaca tonkeana: The Interface of Primate Ecology, Human Ecology, and Conservation in Lore Lindu National Park, Sulawesi, Indonesia*. Ph.D. Dissertation, University of Georgia.

_____. 2006. 'Ethnoprimatology: Towards Reconciliation of Biological and Cultural Anthropology', *Ecological and Environmental Anthropology* 2(2): 75–86.

_____. 2007. 'The Human-Macaque Interface: Conservation Implications of Current and Future Overlap and Conflict in Lore Lindu National Park, Sulawesi, Indonesia', *Amer. Anthropol* 109(3): 473–84.

Riley, E.P. and K.C. MacKinnon (guest editors). 'Special Section on Ethical Issues in Field Primatology (September 2010)', *American Journal of Primatology* 72(9): 749–93.

Riley, E.P., L.D. Wolfe and A. Fuentes. 2011. 'Ethnoprimatology: Contextualizing Human and Nonhuman Primate Interactions', in C.J. Campbell, A. Fuentes, K.C. MacKinnon, R. Stumpf and S. K. Bearder (eds), *Primates in Perspective* (2nd edition). New York: Oxford University Press, pp. 676–86.

Rutherford, J. 'Descent with Modification: Bioanthropological Identities in 2009', *American Anthropologist* 112(2): 191–99.

Sigma Xi. 1992. '1992 Sigma Xi Statement on the Use of Animals in Research', *American Scientist* 80: 73–76.

Society for Applied Anthropology. 1983. 'Professional and Ethical Responsibilities'. Available at http://www.sfaa.net/sfaaethic.html.

Sommer, V. 2011. 'The Anthropologist as a Primatologist: Mental Journeys of a Fieldworker', in J. MacClancy and A. Fuentes (eds), *Centralizing Fieldwork: Critical Perspectives from Primatology, Biological, and Social Anthropology*. Oxford: Berghahn Books, pp. 32–48.

Strier, K.B. 2010. 'Long-term Field Studies: Positive Impacts and Unintended Consequences', *American Journal of Primatology* 72: 772–78.

Sussman, R.W. 2011. 'Primate Fieldwork and its Human Contexts in Southern Madagascar', in J. MacClancy and A. Fuentes (eds), *Centralizing Fieldwork: Critical Perspectives from Primatology, Biological, and Social Anthropology*. Oxford: Berghahn Books, pp. 49–68.

Turner, T.R. (ed.). 2004. *Biological Anthropology and Ethics. From Repatriation to Genetic Identity*. Albany, NY: State University of New York Press.

Wallis, J. and W.R. Lee. 1999. 'Primate Conservation: The Prevention of Disease Transmission', *International Journal of Primatology* 20(6): 803–26.

Wheatley, B.P. 1999. *The Sacred Monkeys of Bali*. Prospect Heights, IL: Waveland Press.

Wolfe, L. 2005. 'Field Primatologists: Duties, Rights, and Obligations', in T.R. Truner (ed.), *Biological Anthropology and Ethics*. Albany, NY: State University of New York Press, pp. 15–26.

7

The Ethics of Conducting Field Research

Do Long-Term Great Ape Field Studies Help to Conserve Primates?

K. Anne-Isola Nekaris and Vincent Nijman

Introduction

In a recent paper entitled 'Research in Biodiversity Hotspots Should Be Free', Pitman (2010) made a convincing case that by allowing visiting researchers to conduct research at a tropical field station without obliging them to pay a fee (with all operating cost being covered by an endowment), the research output of research sites would see a dramatic increase. Using data from the Los Amigos Biological Station in Amazonian Peru, Pitman (2010: 381) concluded:

> For every 150 researcher-days logged at Los Amigos [...] an average of one peer-reviewed article or thesis was published four years later. Were the 50-bed station to maintain this rate of capacity, it would produce >120 articles and theses per year, more than twice the region's current scientific output. Twenty years after the initial investment, the cost of each article produced by the station would be approximately US$1700. In addition to giving an extra boost to the mounting productivity of tropical scientists, free field stations could also make a significant contribution to training young scientists, providing educational and other opportunities for local communities and protected areas, and collecting intensive inventory and monitoring data on the world's richest communities.

We argue here that it is not only the amount of research produced at research sites that is of importance, but also, amongst others, what species are being studied, and whether or not it is ethical to restrict studies to a limited number of species only. A large part of our research has been on non-human primates (hereafter 'primates') and hence the focus here will be on primates. Within primatology there is an imbalance with regard to the extent to which different species have been, and are being, studied, with a strong emphasis on Great Apes (chimpanzees, gorillas and orang-utans) and an under-representation of strepsirhines (lemurs, lorises, pottos, galagos) and tarsiers (K.A.I. Nekaris, unpublished data). Nekaris is trained as a biological anthropologist and Nijman as an ecologist, and we have worked on a large range of primate species. We have been professionally involved in primate conservation for the last fifteen years and currently teach on one of the few MSc courses fully dedicated to primate conservation. In addition, we are involved in teaching undergraduate anthropology students and supervising anthropology PhD students. Based on applications and interest expressed in the initial weeks, we reckon at least fifty per cent of our students are interested in working with Great Apes. Many of the research sites we will introduce below are 'household names', at least among our students and colleagues.

First we provide a short introduction outlining the need for habitat and species conservation in the tropics and then focus on the ethical obligation to maximize knowledge increase about globally threatened and otherwise little-known species. A disproportionate amount of knowledge about primates derives from a limited number of field sites, especially ones that have been operational for extended periods of time. Focusing on ten long-term field sites, we show that knowledge increase is strongly skewed, and we address the ethical issues that this raises.

The impact of humans on the natural world in the form of deforestation, natural resource exploitation, and subsequent climate change has given rise to a biodiversity crisis that some have dubbed the Sixth Extinction (Leakey and Lewin 1995). Nowhere is this destruction more apparent than in the forests of tropical South America, Africa and Asia. These forests are generally perceived to be amongst the most biodiversity-rich areas in the world, and their loss will inevitably lead to the extinction of numerous taxa. While other species-rich biomes – tropical coral reefs, geologically ancient lakes, coastal wetlands, polar regions – are in danger, and each deserves special attention on its own, the rain forest serve as an ideal paradigm of the larger global biodiversity crisis (c.f. Wilson 1988). Largely confined to the tropics and often dependent on the forest, primates also serve as important flagships for the conservation of all wildlife. With their characteristic long life histories, dietary specializations, and susceptibility to hunting, primates have proven to be especially prone to population decline (Cowlishaw and Dunbar 2000). Indeed, the IUCN Primate Specialist Group (2008) reported that nearly half (forty-eight per cent) of the world's 634 currently recognized primate taxa are threatened with extinction. As human population increases, the protected area network (national parks, nature reserves, etc.) may be the last stronghold for many primate species (Newmark et al. 1994; Harcourt et al. 2002), but competition for resources between humans and primates, lack of infrastructure, lack of local support, and insufficient funding means that even protected areas may not be secure (Newman 2007).

With such an impending crisis, twenty-first-century primatologists find themselves with an ethical obligation to record as much information as possible about species that are fast disappearing, and to use these data to inform national and international conservation policy (Wolfe 2005). This in itself poses ethical issues, especially when attempting to research species in remote areas, where, for instance, human introduced zoonoses could pose a hazard to naïve primate populations and vice versa (Woodford et al. 2002; Travis et al. 2006). Perhaps unique to primatology, however, are a large number of long-term study sites originally developed for the study of the Great Apes (common chimpanzee *Pan troglodytes*, bonobos *P. paniscus*, western gorilla *Gorilla gorilla*, eastern gorilla *G. beringei*, Sumatran orang-utan *Pongo abelii* and Bornean orang-utan *P. pygmaeus*) (e.g. Nishida and Nakamura 2008; Williamson and Fawcett 2008). Because apes are so closely related to humans, an interest in their behaviour began more than fifty years ago at some sites, primarily to understand human evolution, meaning that such studies often focus on traits that unite them to us (Wrangham et al. 1996; van Schaik et al. 2003), and to a lesser extent on ecological factors that may help to preserve wild populations (Pusey et al. 2007). Furthermore, competition between researchers to establish their 'own sites' has led to the establishment of multiple sites for the intensive study of the same species (Wolfe 2005).

The charismatic nature of these 'flagship' species has also led to an inordinate amount of funding being directed towards this mere two per cent of the living primate taxa (McGrew 2002). Since the establishment of these sites, conservation has become more critical and McGraw (2007) argued that one would now expect researchers to begin to set aside their differences, and to become bastions and models for understanding the community ecology of the many primate species within their boundaries. Indeed, the work undertaken at many long-term sites is finally being analysed from a conservation perspective (Wrangham and Ross 2008). For the Great Apes in particular, the research is said to contribute to conservation in a number of ways, including attracting funds, working towards a better understanding of Great Ape behaviour, and drawing public attention to conservation (Pusey et al. 2007). In this chapter, we examine the role of ten long-term Great Ape study sites in promoting primate conservation, and whether or not Great Apes have proven to be good umbrella taxa for other primates. We address several questions: How many primate taxa occur at each site, and what is their threat status? How many of the papers published out of each site directly address conservation questions? Is there a relationship between the threat to all primates at a site and the amount of conservation work done there? Is there evidence that the manpower and infrastructure attracted by the presence of a Great Ape has moved onto other primates who are more distantly related to humans?

Methods

1. Study Sites

For our analysis, we chose ten long-term primate study sites, many of which are well known. Criteria for inclusion were: that the site has been running for at least twenty-five years; that at least one Great Ape species is present at the site; and that other primate species occur at the site, including both diurnal and nocturnal species (Table 7.1, Figure 7.1).

At present all sites have a developed trail system, permanent staff, well-equipped camp sites, weather stations, and well-established botanical plots or trails. Many of the research areas have, as well as one or two main research stations, smaller satellite field stations; the ones listed here are the main research stations only. The information here is derived largely from McGrew et al. (1996) and Wich et al. (2009).

Table 7.1. Primate genera, with number of species in parentheses if more than one is present, at ten long-term Great Ape research sites in Africa and Asia. A question mark means that the site is in the geographical range of the species, but no data are available.

Site	Apes	Monkeys	Nocturnal Primates
Taï	*Pan*	*Cercocebus* (1), *Cercopithecus* (4), *Procolobus* (2)	*Perodicticus*, *Galagoides* (2), *Euoticus* (?), *Sciurocheirus* (?), *Arctocebus* (?)
Lopé	*Pan, Gorilla*	*Colobus, Lophocebus, Cercopithecus* (4), *Papio*	*Perodicticus*, *Galagoides* (2), *Euoticus* (?), *Sciurocheirus* (?), *Arctocebus* (?)
Salonga	*Pan*	*Allenopithecu,s Cercocebus, Cercopithecus* (4), *Colobus, Lophocebus, Piliocolobus*	*Perodicticus*, *Galagoides* (2), *Euoticus* (?), *Sciurocheirus* (?), *Arctocebus* (?)
Bwindi	*Pan, Gorilla*	*Colobus, Papio, Cercopithecus* (3), *Chlorocebus*	*Perodicticus* (?), *Galago* (?), *Otolemur* (?), *Galagoides* (?)
Kibale	*Pan*	*Colobus, Papio, Lophocebus, Procolobus* (2), *Cercopithecus* (3), *Chlorocebus*	*Perodicticus, Galagoides, Galago*
Budongo	*Pan*	*Colobus, Papio, Cercopithecus* (2), *Chlorocebus*	*Perodicticus, Galagoides, Galago* (?)
Gombe	*Pan*	*Procolobus, Papio, Cercopithecus* (2), *Chlorocebus*	*Galago* (?), *Otolemur* (?)
Mahale	*Pan*	*Cercopithecus* (2), *Chlorocebus, Colobus, Papio*	*Galago, Otolemur, Galagoides* (?)
Leuser	*Pongo, Symphalangus, Hylobates*	*Presbytis, Macaca* (2)	*Nycticebus*
Tanjung Puting	*Pongo, Hylobates*	*Presbytis, Nasalis, Trachypithecus, Macaca* (2)	*Nycticebus, Tarsius*

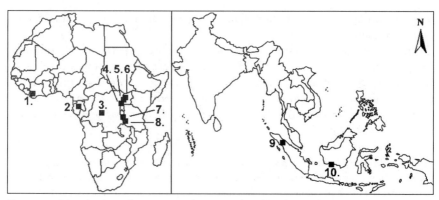

Figure 7.1. Map showing the ten research sites analysed in this study: 1. Taï, 2. Lopé, 3. Salonga, 4. Bwindi, 5. Kibale, 6. Budongo, 7. Gombe, 8. Mahale, 9. Leuser, 10. Tanjung Puting.

1. Taï forest, Ivory Coast [National Park, ~4260 km², 160-245 m a.s.l.]: this site was established in 1976 by C. Boesch and H. Boesch, and focused on the chimpanzee community and their use of tools (the use of tools by chimpanzees had been established earlier by Struhsaker and Hunkeler 1971). The primates of the Taï forest are threatened by the destruction of their habitat but especially by West Africa's relentless bush-meat trade.

2. Lopé, Gabon [Faunal Reserve, ~5000 km², 250-600 m a.s.l.]: the Station d'Etude des Gorilles et Chimpanzés was established in 1984 and has been manned continuously. The research site is situated around 12 km from the nearest village and while part of the forest was selectively logged from 1960 to 1974 there has been little human disturbance.

3. Salonga, Democratic Republic of Congo [National Park, ~3500 km², ~400 m a.s.l.]: this site was established in 1974, to study the community of bonobos. Over the years the project has expanded, with several groups now being the focus of research attention. The main threat to wildlife in the area is hunting (bow-and-arrow, snares).

4. Bwindi Impenetrable, Uganda [National Park, ~331 km², 1200-2500 m a.s.l.]: biodiversity research began in earnest in 1986 and quickly focused on the population of mountain gorillas. Later efforts focused on the sympatric chimpanzees as well, and there are now permanent teams studying these two Great Apes. The area is relatively pristine; however, there is some poaching in different parts of the forest.

5. Kibale, Uganda [National Park, ~766 km², 1390-1625 m a.s.l.]: the chimpanzees and other primates have been studied intermittently from 1978 to 1985, with a permanent chimpanzee research programme running from 1987. There is considerable anthropogenic disturbance in Kibale, with parts being affected by (selective) logging, agriculture and human expansion; hunting poses an additional threat.

6. Budongo, Uganda [Forest Reserve, ~428 km², ~1100 m a.s.l.]: studies on chimpanzees and other primates have been carried out intermittently from the 1960s onwards, more permanently from 1990. The forest has been extensively logged and large parts are now in various stages of regeneration.

7. Gombe Stream, Tanzania [National Park, ~32 km², 775-1500 m a.s.l.]: this site was established in 1960 by J. Goodall to study chimpanzees, and research has continued at the Gombe Stream research centre uninterruptedly since then. The expansion of human settlements, agriculture and infrastructure development, as well as the deliberate killing of chimpanzees by humans, have impeded the conservation of the Great Apes and their habitat.

8. Mahale Mountains, Tanzania [National Park, ~1613 km², 773-2515 m a.s.l.]: research on chimpanzees started in 1965 by a project coordinated by T. Nishida and J. Itani. Research at the Mahale Mountains wildlife research centre has been continuous apart from a brief hiatus in 1988-1994. The primates at the site have been negatively affected by habitat loss and forest fragmentation, as well as by some uncontrolled fires.

9. Gunung Leuser, on the island of Sumatra, Indonesia [National Park, ~7927 km², 0-3381 m a.s.l.]: H. Rijksen started his research on Sumatran orang-utans in 1971 and this research has been continued ever since, with a brief interruption due to political instability in the late 1990s. The main threats to the primates of Gunung Leuser are deforestation, fragmentation due to road construction (and associated deforestation) and, for selected species, capturing for the pet trade.

10. Tanjung Putting, on the island of Borneo, Indonesia [National Park, ~4150 km², 0-30 m a.s.l.]: in 1971 B. Galdikas established Camp Leaky as the main site for the study of Bornean orang-utans. The main threats to the primates of Tanjung Puting are deforestation, forest fires and, for selected species, capturing for the pet trade.

2. Data Aquisition

For each of the ten sites listed above we entered all primate species that had been recorded at the site and their conservation status as of December 2009 into a database. For a number of sites it was either unclear which species were indeed present, or there were contradicting reports (see discussion at the end of this chapter). Here we cited a conservative number based on all species actually recorded, and a more liberal number based on the number of species actually present and those that, based on their geographic and ecological distribution, were likely to occur at the site. Hence, for each site we tallied the total number of species, the number of globally threatened species (including species that are Critically Endangered, Endangered and Vulnerable), and the proportion of species that were globally threatened. We followed the standard procedure of treating threat categories as intervals of extinction risk by assuming equivalence among criteria (Isaac et al. 2007). Each site then received a threat score by summation of the number of species that were Critically Endangered multiplied by 3, the number of species that were Endangered multiplied by 2, and the number of species that were Vulnerable.

We collected data from published studies until December 2009 from each of the ten sites in the form of abstracts, book chapters, articles and reports indexed on the comprehensive primate database Primate Lit (http://primatelit.library.wisc.edu/). Through this search, we tallied the number of studies published from each site, on each primate species, and according to whether the main focus of the study was conservation. We acknowledge that not all studies from all sites will be included here, but by restricting ourselves to this single database, any bias introduced should be similar to that of any long-term study sites.

A study was considered to have a conservation component if the data had a direct impact on conservation policy, such as density estimates, fragmentation impacts, human-wildlife conflict issues, or anthropogenic effects on primate behaviour. Although we acknowledge the importance of studies which deal with topics such as the socio-biology of species, tool use, cognition, and positional behaviour, these were only considered to come under the category of 'conservation' if the authors made implicit points throughout the paper. If only one or two sentences in a final paragraph mentioned conservation, they were not considered. For each site we calculated the proportion of papers that were devoted to 'conservation' ('conservation papers / total number of papers') and the focus on Great Apes ('Great Ape papers / papers dealing with other species'). As data were not normally distributed, descriptive and non-parametric statistical tests were used accepting significance when $P \leq 0.05$ (Zar 1999). We used Yates' correction for continuity in χ^2 tests in 2×1 and 2×2 contingency tables as to prevent overestimation of statistical significance for small datasets.

Results

A total of fifty-six species (Table 7.1), including all the Great Ape species, are to be found in the ten research sites we chose, with a median of ten to eleven species at each site. One to six species at each site are considered threatened (Table 7.2). Our search yielded 1181 publications, with a median of 122 papers for each site (Range 29-212). We found no link between the age of a research site and the annual publication rate (Kendall's τ=0.19, N=10, P=0.51).

The proportion of papers that focus on conservation is not equally distributed over the different sites (χ^2=33.65, df=9, P<0.001). The two sites where orang-utans have been studied have a significantly stronger focus on conservation than the other sites combined (χ^2=5.50, df=1, P<0.02 and χ^2=3.91, df=1, P<0.05 for Tanjung Puting and Leuser, respectively). Conversely, the two sites where common chimpanzees have been studied the longest had the least focus on conservation studies (χ^2=9.09, df=1, P<0.01 and χ^2=8.02, df=1, P<0.01 for Gombe and Mahale, respectively). The proportion of papers dealing with conservation is positively correlated with the overall 'threat score' (Kendall's τ=0.62, N=10, P=0.03) but not to the number of species that are globally threatened at a site (Kendall's τ=0.51, N=10, P=0.07) or to the percentage of species that are threatened (Kendall's τ=0.25, N=10, P=0.40).

Table 7. 2. Summary of each study site, including the Great Ape species present, total number of species, number of species in each threat category, number of papers analysed, the ratio of papers published on Great Apes versus other primate species (including multi-taxa papers), and per cent of papers related directly to conservation.

Site	Great Ape	Species	CR/ EN/VU	Scientific output		
		(N)		N	Great Apes : other primates	Conservation-related (%)
Taï	*Pan troglodytes*	10-13	0/2/2	137	0.8	7
Lopé	*Pan troglodytes; Gorilla gorilla*	12-15	0/1/2	49	1.6	18
Salonga	*Pan paniscus*	13-17	1/2/0	185	3.0	4
Bwindi	*Pan troglodytes; Gorilla berengei*	12-13	0/2/1	29	6.5	21
Kibale	*Pan troglodytes*	13	0/2/1	115	2.9	13
Budongo	*Pan troglodytes*	8	0/1/0	129	2.9	13
Gombe	*Pan troglodytes*	7-10	0/2/0	212	1.3	13
Mahale	*Pan troglodytes*	8-9	0/1/0	188	8.0	5
Leuser	*Pongo abelii*	7	1/2/3	82	1.2	18
Tanjung Puting	*Pongo pygmaeus*	9	0/3/3	55	2.0	22

There was a strong focus on papers dealing exclusively with Great Apes (excluding other species of primate) for each site with a median of 2/3 of the papers dealing with Great Apes only. Taï was the only site where less than half of the papers dealt exclusively with Great Apes. The proportion of papers that focus on Great Apes is not equally distributed over the different sites (χ^2=43.26, df=9, P<0.001). Taï and Kibale had the least focus on Great Apes compared to the other sites combined (χ^2=11.06, df=1, P<0.001 and χ^2=9.40, df=1, P<0.01 for Taï and Kibale, respectively). Conversely, compared to the other sites combined, Mahale had the most focus on Great Apes (χ^2=19.96, df=1, P<0.001).

While all Great Apes are either Endangered or Critically Endangered, there was no significant correlation between the proportion of conservation-related papers coming out of a site and a focus on Great Apes (Kendall's τ=-0.21, N=10, P=0.47). The focus on Great Apes was negatively related to the number of species that are threatened (Kendall's τ=-0.50, N=10, P=0.07), that is, the less species are threatened at a site, the more the publication output deals with Great Apes only. Likewise, focus of Great Apes is negatively related to the proportion of species that are threatened (Kendall's T=-0.55, N=10, P=0.04), again showing that if fewer primates are threatened the more the focus is on Great Apes only. We found no correlation between the focus on Great Apes and the total 'threat score' for a site (Kendall's τ=-0.37, N=10, P=0.17).

While at several sites – e.g. Taï, Leuser, Gombe – diurnal monkeys are as frequently studied as Great Apes, focused research on the nocturnal primates lags behind. The sites hold twelve species of nocturnal primates representing a fifth of the total primate species of the ten long-term sites, yet we were unable to find more than a handful of published studies focusing on these taxa. With the exception of Kibale, where there have some studies of nocturnal primates, it seems that nocturnal primates are mentioned in the literature only when they are preyed upon by Great Apes. Examples of these are Sumatran orang-utans eating greater slow loris *Nycticebus coucang* in Leuser, and chimpanzees eating western potto *Perodicticus potto* in Taï, or thick-tailed greater bushbaby *Otolemur crassicaudatus* or Senegal lesser bushbaby *Galago senegalensis* in Mahale.

Discussion

1. Overview

The ten sites reviewed in this chapter provide a wealth of opportunity for the understanding of primate behaviour, ecology and conservation, being home to nearly fifteen per cent of all currently recognized primate species. Taken together, the sites have been manned for almost 350 years providing a wealth of knowledge, with numerous widely-publicized discoveries having been made. Indeed, many of the sites are household names, and the researchers that established the sites are amongst the most recognisable primatologists around. The presence of one or more Great Ape species at each site, therefore, can be argued to play a key role in the conservation of these, and indeed other non-primate species. This works through long-term research presence, the protection afforded by that presence (Struhsaker 2008; Marsh et al. 1999; but see Nijman 2005a), and subsequent conservation initiatives arising from research (Pusey et al. 2007).

In terms of the scientific study of these primates, while conservation is perhaps an outcome, it is clearly not the goal of the bulk of research being published from the ten sites. With the exception of the two Indonesian sites, researchers tend to focus on broader socio-biological and ecological questions. Considering the chronic deforestation in the vicinity of these sites (sometimes even at the sites themselves), the threat of bush-meat and the pet trade, and socio-political unrest at some sites, a change in attitude towards research will be vital for the long-term survival of these sites (Plumptre et al. 2001; Matthews and Matthews 2004; Refisch and Koné 2005; Nijman 2005b). Some researchers have reported an increasing trend towards conservation education, ecotourism and rural livelihood initiatives as a consequence of research (Pusey et al. 2007; Mugisha 2008). We urge systematic structuring and publication of these programmes so that they may serve as examples of good practice. Some sites have developed active programmes for other primate species; for example, both Taï and Kibale support long-term monkey projects (McGraw et al. 2007; Chapman et al. 2005).

2. The Balance between Research-Presence and Animal Wellbeing

A variety of negative factors arise from long-term studies that have previously been scrutinized in terms of their ethics. The first factor is the influence on the animals themselves. Habituated animals may experience high levels of stress under observation (Macfie and Williamson 2010) and extreme habituation may result in less viable research data (Carpaneto and Fusari 2000; Jack et al. 2008; see also Chapter 4 and 5 of this book). In extreme cases, habituated animals may become a danger to humans (McGrew et al. 1996; Yeager 1997), even attacking and killing villagers (Owoyesigire 2008). One must also consider the ethical implications of keeping animals under the close scrutiny of humans every hour of their waking day each day of their life. This is particularly true of animals that are as self-aware as the Great Apes (Butynski and Kalina 1998).

Habituation which results from the research process and from the often applauded means of ecotourism also has its downfalls (for a detailed overview of the pros and cons of Great Ape ecotourism, we direct the reader to Macfie and Williamson 2010). Although these practices may aid in conservation and the preservation of natural wildlife, the income derived from them may not trickle down to local people (Hill 2002). Furthermore, animals that regularly encounter humans may be more vulnerable to poachers (Carpaneto and Fusari 2000). When the same animal groups are observed by tourists day in day out, zoonoses can be a serious problem. Although at most sites protocols are in place to stop the spread of diseases, such rules are often poorly enforced (Woodford et al. 2002). When such diseases are transmitted, the results can be catastrophic (Goodall 1971; Le Gouar et al. 2009). Habituated primates may also develop stress-related illnesses or, in the case where the animals are provisioned, become obese due to being over-fed (McGrew et al. 1996). For these reasons field site controllers may pose restrictions on the number of researchers studying primates at their site. These same problems, however, are also why we believe that the positive impacts of a long-term study site (finances, infrastructure, trained assistants, supportive communities, etc.) should be shared with researchers studying as wide a range of species as possible. Inflicting the negative aspects of primatological reseach (increasing access to forest, disease transmission, over-habituation, etc.) on naïve populations should be minimized, and this can be partially achieved by maximizing the use of existing field sites. On the one hand we encourage those primatologists that study species other than Great Apes to bear in mind the option of studying their species of interest at an established site, and on the other hand we encourage those researchers that do study Great Apes to welcome colleagues that study other primates. A more equal division of funding is required in order to bridge the gap between the amount of knowledge accrued in Great Ape studies and the information known about other primate species in the same areas. As a first step we would like to see a greater emphasis on initiating long-term multi-year studies on primate species other than Great Apes at these long-term study sites.

This would allow insight in the synecology of the primate community (including interactions with Great Apes) and would be greatly beneficial in understanding the ecology of some of the lesser-known primates elsewhere. Long-term study sites may be more successful in terms of conservation if focus is placed on the environment and eco-system as a whole, as opposed to individual species (Harcourt 2000).

3. The Need for an Increased Focus on Nocturnal Primates

Throughout tropical Africa and Asia, there are a large number of nocturnal primates. Generally less is known about nocturnal primates than their diurnal counterparts, but at least with respect to their conservation some proper assessments have been made. Several nocturnal primates are suffering such pressures that they are considered amongst the most threatened primates globally (Nekaris 2006; Nekaris et al. 2009; Honess et al. 2009). Some nocturnal primates are severely range-restricted but other range over vast areas (Bearder and Nekaris 2011), and indeed around twelve species appear be living sympatrically with the Great Apes at the ten sites we have focused this assessment on. We write 'appear to be' as we were not able to come up with a definite list of nocturnal primates (Table 7.1). We were surprised to find that for most sites we could not locate a list of nocturnal primates inhabiting the forests, either in the published literature or on study site-specific web sites. The exceptions were both Indonesian sites where nocturnal primate diversity is low (with one species, the greater slow loris, present in Leuser, and the Bornean slow loris *N. menagensis* and western tarsier *Tarsius bancanus* present in Tanjung Puting) and Kibale, where a number of studies have been conducted on nocturnal primates.

Intriguingly, the first focused study of nocturnal primates at Kibale (Weisenseel et al. 1993) reported the presence of Demidoff's dwarf galago *Galago demidovii* and spectacled galago *G. inustus*, whereas in fact spectacled galago *Galago matschiei* and Thomas' dwarf galago *Galagoides thomasi* are present (S.K. Bearder, personal communication; cf. Off and Gebo 2005), illustrating the scope of further research on nocturnal primates at these sites. Even at the most famous of the study sites, Gombe, the nocturnal primate species remain completely unstudied and largely unknown. Goodall (1986: 49), Stanford (1998: 238) and Russak and McGrew (2008: 407) list southern needle-clawed bushbaby *Euoticus elegantulus* as being present at Gombe but this seems implausible as this species does not range that far east (Bearder and Nekaris 2011). In addition to southern needle-clawed galago, Stanford (1998) lists thick-tailed greater galago *Galago [=Otolemur] crassicaudatus*, noting 'seen once in 1991 in [Gombe's] Mitumbo Valley'. *Otolemur* is not included as a species present at Gombe by Russak and McGrew (2008) but they list a *Galago* sp. (i.e. an unidentified galago species of the genus *Galago*) as being present. Hence, for Gombe, a site where primatolotgists have been working for fifty years there is no consensus as to whether there are one, two, three or possibly more nocturnal primates present. In the case of nocturnal primates, little is known about species diversity, and it is likely that these long-term study sites harbour new species (Butynski et al. 2006; Bearder 1999; S.K. Bearder, personal communication) or may provide insights that could not have been gained from other sites. As stated above, we found several reports of predation on nocturnal primates by Great Apes but these were invariably reported by researchers studying the Great Apes and not the nocturnal primates.

The situation of nocturnal primates, as described above, may also be true for other small mammals, and indeed other animals as well. Smaller bodied species are generally perceived as being less charismatic (Clucas et al. 2007; Muñoz 2007; Leader-Williams and Dublin 2000), and funds associated with them, most notably those derived from tourism, are likely to be comparatively limited (Walpole and Leader-Williams 2002). It has now been repeatedly shown, however, that the habitat needs of large vertebrates often do not encompass those of smaller, yet equally or more threatened species (Bowen-Jones and Entwistle 2002).

Working at night introduces its own set of challenges, some of which can be easily addressed by working at established research sites. A well-marked established trail system allows researchers to follow animals at night without being too restricted by the terrain. Research stations with electricity (obtained with the aid of solar panels, generators, or by being connected to the grid) make it possible to recharge batteries needed for surveying, and to conduct work at night that requires adequate illumination. Finally, an established research station provides the logistics enabling researchers to work safely at night. We therefore strongly urge site managers and research coordinators of long-term sites to actively initiate or otherwise strongly encourage studies of the nocturnal species.

4. A Plea for a New Model

If the world's unique and diverse primate species are to survive into the future, local and international, governmental and non-governmental organizations and individuals, including researchers and research bodies, must take nationwide and global initiatives to aid in the conservation of the remaining biodiversity, rather than just a handful of species. The opportunities offered by the long-term presence of Great Ape research stations are, in our view, too good to be used only for Great Ape studies. We hope that the data presented in this chapter may aid in encouraging this wider use.

While we advocate the parallel study of Great Apes and other primates, and indeed other wildlife, it is important to note that Great Apes only occur in tropical Africa and on the islands of Sumatra and Borneo. Primates occur additionally throughout Central and South America, in northern and southern Africa, in Madagascar, throughout South and East Asia into the Indo-malayan and Philippine archipelagos. The arguments put forward here focusing on Great Ape research sites could be extended to other regions, and by means of this contribution we urge all primatologists to take a fresh look at long-term field sites and the opportunities offered by these sites. Following the argument put forward by Pitman (2010) in the opening paragraph, we may see a dramatic increase in the scientific output, as well as increasing opportunities for training young scientists, the provision of educational and other opportunities for local communities and protected areas, and the collecting of inventory and monitoring data on the world's richest communities. In the end it seems that making better use of existing Great Ape field sites, sharing them with as many interested parties as possible, seems to be the ethical thing to do.

Acknowledgements

We thank Jeremy MacClancy and Agustín Fuentes for inviting us to contribute to this volume, and for their patience in waiting for this contribution. We thank the participants of the Ten Year Anniversary Conference of the MSc in Primate Conservation held in Oxford in April 2010 for their stimulating discussions and insightful information. Simon K. Bearder provided valuable information about the nocturnal primates at the African sites. Our students Laura C.R. James, Andrew Arnell and Alice Akers helped with the literature search, data collection, production of Figure 1 and editing. This project was in part supported by a School of Social Sciences and Law Research Strategy Fund Grant and a Royal Society Travel Grant to Nekaris. We thank Jeremy MacClancy for constructive comments and suggestions on an earlier version of this chapter.

References

Bearder, S.K. 1999. 'Physical and Social Diversity among Nocturnal Primates: A New View Based on Long Term Research', *Primates* 40(1): 267–82.

Bearder, S.K. and K.A.I. Nekaris. 2011. 'The Lorisiform Primates of Asia and Mainland Africa: Diversity Shrouded in Darkness', in C.J. Campbell, A. Fuentes, K.C. MacKinnon, S.K. Bearder, R.M. Stumpf (eds), *Primates in Perspective.* 2nd Edition. Oxford: Oxford University Press, pp. 34–54.

Bowen-Jones, E. and A. Entwistle. 2002. 'Identifying Appropriate Flagship Species: the Importance of Culture and Local Contexts', *Oryx* 36(2): 189–95.

Butynski, T.M., Y.A. de Jong, A.W. Perkin, S.K. Bearder and P.E. Honess. 2006. 'Taxonomy, Distribution, and Conservation Status of Three Species of Dwarf Galagos (*Galagoides*) in Eastern Africa', *Primate Conservation* 21: 63 –79.

Butynski, T.M. and J. Kalina. 1998. 'Gorilla Tourism: A Critical Look', in E.J. Milner-Gulland, R Mace (eds), *Conservation of Biological Resources.* Oxford: Blackwell Science, pp. 294–313.

Carpaneto, G.M. and A. Fusari. 2000. 'Subsistence Hunting and Bushmeat Exploitation in Central-western Tanzania', *Biodiversity and Conservation* 9(11): 1571–85.

Chapman, C.A., T.T. Struhsaker and J.E. Lambert. 2005. 'Thirty Years of Research in Kibale National Park, Uganda, Reveals a Complex Picture for Conservation', *International Journal of Primatology* 26(3): 539–55.

Clucas, B., K. McHugh and T. Caro. 2007. 'Flagship Species on Covers of US Conservation and Nature Magazines', *Biodiversity and Conservation* 17(6): 1517–28.

Cowlishaw, G. and R. Dunbar. 2000. *Primate Conservation Biology.* Chicago: University Chicago Press.

Goodall, J. 1971. *In the Shadow of Man.* Boston: Houghton Mifflin.

——————. 1986. *The Chimpanzees of Gombe: Patterns of Behavior.* Cambridge: Harvard University Press.

Harcourt, A.H. 2000. 'Coincidence and Mismatch of Biodiversity Hotspots: A Global Survey for the Order, Primates', *Biological Conservation* 93(2): 163–75.

Harcourt, A.H., S. Coppeto and S.A. Parks. 2002. 'Rarity, Specialization and Extinction in Primates', *Journal of Biogeography* 29: 445–56.

Hill, C. 2002. 'Primate Conservation and Local Communities – Ethical Issues and Debates', *American Anthropologist* 104(4): 1184–94.

Honess, P.E., A. Perkin and S.K. Bearder. 2009. 'Rondo Dwarf Galago *Galagoides rondoensis* (Honess in Kingdon, 1997)', in R.A. Mittermeier, J. Wallis, A.B. Rylands, J.U. Ganzhorn, J.F. Oates, E.A. Williamson, E. Palacios, E.W. Heymann, M.C.M. Kierulff, Long Yongcheng, J. Supriatna, C. Roos, S. Walker, L. Cortés-Ortiz and C. Schwitzer (eds.), *Primates in Peril: The World's 25 Most Endangered Primates 2008–2010*. Arlington, VA: IUCN/SSC Primate Specialist Group, International Primatological Society, and Conservation International, pp. 44–46.

Isaac, N.J.B., S.T. Turvey, B. Collen, C. Waterman and J.E.M. Baillie. 2007. 'Mammals on the EDGE: Conservation Priorities Based on Threat and Phylogeny', *PLoS One* 2(3) e296.

IUCN/SSC Primate Specialist Group. 2008. 'Eaten to Extinction: 48% of All Primates Now Threatened'. Accessed on 15 March 2010 from http://www.primate-sg.org/RL08.news.htm.

Jack, K.M, B.B. Lenz, E. Healan, S. Rudman, V.A.M. Schoof and L. Fedigan. 2008. 'The Effects of Observer Presence on the Behavior of *Cebus capucinus* in Costa Rica', *American Journal of Primatology* 70(5): 490–94.

Leader-Williams, N. and H.T. Dublin. 2000. 'Charismatic Megafauna as "Flagship Species"', in A. Entwistle and N. Dunston (eds). *Priorities for the Conservation of Mammalian Diversity: Has the Panda Had its Day?* New York: Cambridge University Press, pp. 53–81.

Leakey, R.E. and R. Lewin. 1995. *The Sixth Extinction: Patterns of Life and the Future of Humankind*. New York: Doubleday Publishers.

Le Gouar, P.J., D. Vallet, L. David, M. Bermejo, S. Gatti, F. Levrero, E.J. Petit and N. Menard. 2009. 'How Ebola Impacts Genetics of Western Lowland Gorilla Populations', *PLoS One* 4(12): e8375.

Macfie, E.J. and E.A. Williamson. 2010. *Best Practise Guide for Great Ape Tourism*. Gland: IUCN/SSC Primate Specialist Group.

Marsh, C.W., M. Mohamed, W. Sinun and S. Sutton. 1999. 'The Role of Field Centers in the Conservation and Management of Tropical Forests: A Case Study of the Danum Valley', in P. Eaton (ed.), *Environment and Conservation in Borneo*. Kota Kinabalu: Borneo Research Council, pp. 211–35.

Matthews, A. and A. Matthews. 2004. 'Survey of Gorillas (*Gorilla gorilla gorilla*) and chimpanzees (*Pan troglodytes troglodytes*) in Southwestern Cameroon', *Primates* 45(1): 15–24.

McGraw, W.S. 2007. 'Vulnerability and Conservation of the Taï Monkey Fauna', in W.S. McGraw, K. Zuberbuehler and R. Noe (eds), *Monkeys of the Taï Forest: An African Primate Community*. New York: Cambridge University Press, pp. 290–316.

McGraw, W.S., K. Zuberbuehler and R. Noe. 2007. *Monkeys of the Taï Forest: An African Primate Community*. New York: Cambridge University Press.

McGrew, W.C. 2002. *Chimpanzee Material Culture: Implications for Human Evolution*. Cambridge: Cambridge University Press.

McGrew, W.C., L. Marchant and T. Nishida. 1996. *Great Ape Societies*. Cambridge: Cambridge University Press.

Mugisha, A. 2008. 'Potential Interactions of Research with the Development and Management of Ecotourism', in R. Wrangham and E. Ross (eds), *Science and Conservation in African Forests: The Benefits of Long-Term Research*. New York: Cambridge University Press, pp. 115–128.

Muñoz, J. 2007. 'Biodiversity Conservation Including Uncharismatic Species', *Biodiversity and Conservation* 16(7): 2233–35.

Nekaris, K.A.I. 2006. 'Horton Plains slender loris, Ceylon mountain slender loris *Loris tardigradus nycticeboides* (Hill, 1942)', *Primate Conservation* 20: 10–11.

Nekaris, K.A.I., K. Llano Sanchez, J.S. Thorn, I. Winarti and V. Nijman. 2009. 'Javan slow loris *Nycticebus javanicus* É. Geoffroy, 1812', in R.A. Mittermeier, J. Wallis, A.B. Rylands, J.U. Ganzhorn, J.F. Oates, E.A. Williamson, E. Palacios, E.W. Heymann, M.C.M. Kierulff, Long Yongcheng, J. Supriatna, C. Roos, S. Walker, L. Cortés-Ortiz and C. Schwitzer (eds), *Primates in Peril: The World's 25 Most Endangered Primates 2008–2010*. Arlington, VA: IUCN/SSC Primate Specialist Group, International Primatological Society, and Conservation International, pp. 44–46.

Newman, K. 2007. 'Reducing Human-Wildlife Conflict in Mozambique', *WWF*. Accessed on 15 April 2010 from http://www.worldwildlife.org/what/wherewework/coastaleastafrica/reducin ghuman-wildlife.html.

Newmark, W.D., D.N. Manyanza, D.G. Gamassa and H.I. Sariko. 1994. 'The Conflict between Wildlife and Local People Living Adjacent to Protected Areas in Tanzania: Human Density as a Predictor', *Conservation Biology* 8(1): 249–55.

Nijman, V. 2005a. 'Rapid Decline of Hose's Langur in Kayan Mentarang National Park', *Oryx* 39(2): 223–26.

———. 2005b. *Hanging in the Balance: An Assessment of Trade in Orang-utans and Gibbons in Kalimantan, Indonesia*. Petaling Jaya: TRAFFIC Southeast Asia.

Nishida T. and M. Nakamura. 2008. 'Long-Term Research and Conservation in the Mahale Mountains, Tanzania', in R. Wrangham and E. Ross (eds), *Science and Conservation in African Forests: The Benefits of Long-Term Research*. New York: Cambridge University Press, pp. 173–183.

Off, E.C. and D.L. Gebo. 1995. 'Galago Locomotion in Kibale National Park, Uganda', *American Journal of Primatology* 66: 189–95.

Owoyesigire, G. 2008. *The Interaction between Local People and Habituated Chimpanzees around Kibale National Park, Uganda*. MSc Dissertation. Oxford: Oxford Brookes University.

Pitman, N.C.E. 2010. 'Research in Biodiversity Hotspots Should Be Free', *Trends in Ecology and Evolution* 25: 381.

Plumptre, A.J., M. Masozera and A. Vedder. 2001. *The Impact of Civil War on the Conservation of Protected Areas in Rwanda*. Washington D.C.: Biodiversity Support Program.

Pusey, A.E., L. Pintea, M.L. Wilson, S. Kamenya and J. Goodall. 2007. 'The Contribution of Long-Term Research at Gombe National Park to Chimpanzee Conservation', *Conservation Biology* 21(3): 623–34.

Refisch, J. and I. Koné. 2005. 'Impact of Commercial Hunting on Monkey Populations in the Taï region, Cote d'Ivoire', *Biotropica* 37(1): 136–44.

Russak, S. M., W.C. McGrew. 2008. 'Chimpanzees as Fauna: Comparisons of Sympatric Large Mammals across Long Term Study Sites', *American Journal of Primatology* 70: 402–409.

van Schaik, C.P., M. Ancrenaz, G. Borgen, B. Galdikas, C.D. Knott, I. Singleton, A. Suzuki, S.S. Utami and M. Merrill. 2003. 'Orangutan Cultures and the Evolution of Material Culture', *Science* 299: 102–105.

Stanford, C.B. 1998. *Chimpanzee and Red Colobus. The Ecology of Predator and Prey*. Cambridge, MA: Harvard University Press.

Struhsaker, T.T. 2008. 'Long-Term Research and Conservation in Kibale National Park', in R. Wrangham and E. Ross (eds), *Science and Conservation in African Forests: The Benefits of Long-Term Research*. New York: Cambridge University Press, pp. 27–37.

Struhsaker, T.T. and P. Hunkeler. 1971. 'Evidence of Tool-using by Chimpanzees in the Ivory Coast', *Folia Primatologica* 15: 212–19.

Travis, D.A., L. Hungerford, G.A. Engel and L. Jones-Engel. 2006. 'Disease Risk Analysis: A Tool for Primate Conservation Planning and Decision Making', *American Journal of Primatology* 68(9): 855–67.

Walpole, M.J. and N. Leader-Williams. 2002. 'Tourism and Flagship Species in Conservation', *Biodiversity and Conservation* 11(3): 543–47.

Weisenseel, K., C.A. Chapman and L.J. Chapman. 1993. 'Nocturnal Primates of Kibale Forest: Effects of Selective Logging on Prosimian Densities', *Primates* 34(4): 445–50.

Wich, S.A., S.S.U. Atmoko, T.M. Setia and C.P. van Schaik. 2009. *Orangutans Geographic Variation in Behavioral Ecology and Conservation*. Oxford: Oxford University Press.

Williamson, E.A. and K.A. Fawcett. 2008. 'Long-Term Research and Conservation of the Virunga Mountain Gorillas', in R. Wrangham and E. Ross (eds), *Science and Conservation in African Forests: The Benefits of Long-Term Research*. New York: Cambridge University Press, pp. 213–229.

Wilson, E.O. 1988. 'The Current Status of Biological Diversity', in E.O. Wilson and F.M. Peter (eds), *Biodiversity*. Washington: National Academic Press, pp. 3–18.

Wolfe, L. 2005. 'Field Primatologists: Duties, Rights, and Obligations', in T.R. Turner (ed.), *Biological Anthropology and Ethics: From Repatriation to Genetic Identity*. Albany: State University of New York Press, pp. 15–26.

Woodford, M.H., T.M. Butynski and W.B. Karesh. 2002. 'Habituating the Great Apes: The Disease Risks', *Oryx* 36(2): 153–60.

Wrangham, R.W., C.A. Chapman, A.P. Clark-Arcadi and G. Isabirye-Basuta. 1996. 'Social Ecology of Kanyawara Chimpanzees: Implications for Understanding the Costs of Great Ape Groups', in W.C. McGrew, L.F. Marchant and T. Nishida (eds), *Great Ape Societies*. Cambridge: Cambridge University Press, pp. 45–57.

Wrangham, R. and E. Ross. 2008. 'Long-Term Research and Conservation: The Way Forward', in R. Wrangham and E. Ross (eds), *Science and Conservation in African Forests: The Benefits of Long-Term Research*. New York: Cambridge University Press, pp. 242–45.

Yeager, C.P. 1997. 'Orangutan Rehabilitation at Tanjung Putting National Park, Indonesia', *Conservation Biology* 11: 802–803.

Zar, J.H. 1999. *Biostatistical Analysis*. New Jersey: Prentice Hall.

8

Scrutinizing Suffering
The Ethics of Studying Contested Illness

Susie Kilshaw

Introduction

This chapter considers the ethical dilemmas and issues I faced throughout my research into Gulf War Syndrome (GWS). Despite there being ethical guidelines, ethics remains a grey area. Indeed, ethics can never be law, but instead must be enacted in particular situations and each particular circumstance may lend itself to different practice. We anthropologists are constantly faced with ethical conundrums about how we conduct our work and how others may use our publications or findings. We face challenges about how we present ourselves to and manage our ongoing relationship with informants, but also how we balance this with our relationship with funders. Pels (2000) calls this the trickster's dilemma: owing public allegiance to both research sponsors and research subjects, anthropologists can no longer hope to show either of them a 'true' face (p. 137). My work on GWS often felt rife with ethical conundrums and many of these issues can help us think broadly about ethics in the field.

From September 2001 to November 2002 I conducted fieldwork amongst the GWS community in the UK and Canada. This PhD research produced a series of publications culminating in the publication of a book: *Impotent Warriors: Gulf War Syndrome, Masculinity and Vulnerablity* (Kilshaw 2009a). Often anthropologists are drawn to conducting research within controversial, emotive and heated arenas. At the time of my fieldwork GWS was the focus of much media attention with various groups having an investment in the recognition or dismissal of the illness. Furthermore, the community itself was divided, with hostile relationships between some individuals and groups. I found participation in this arena often stressful and it resulted in constant self-examination of and anxiety about my conduct.

From a theoretical and methodological standpoint my research meant I was faced with particular ethical dilemmas from the outset. The project was situated squarely within medical anthropology and focused on sickness and suffering; this meant I grappled throughout with the role of a medical anthropologist and how it is positioned differently from other branches of the discipline. Medical anthropology 'has always had an applied edge; this is especially true of medical anthropology practiced at home. The ethics of fieldwork must include a constant assessment of the limited benefits and possible harm researchers can do' (Rapp 1999: 22). When dealing with issues of illness and suffering are we there to comment, objectively report, or are we to wade in and help sufferers and / or shine a light on inequalities and the source of such suffering?

I felt acutely what Pels has referred to as the anthropologist's 'duplex' position (Pels 1999). For Pels, the anthropologist is situated 'like a trickster, in between different moralities and epistemes' and by inhabiting such a position, 'discovers some of the impossibilities of maintaining the liberal desire for individual autonomy of choice and opinion at a distance from political struggle over existing inequalities in the world' (Pels 2000: 135–36).

Given the location of my field site, I was aware that my informants would likely examine my work. It also meant that it was difficult to disengage and disentangle myself from fieldwork in order to analyse and write (see Kilshaw 2009b). The very practice of anthropology at home means that what we do as anthropological researchers is more under scrutiny. Hartman (2007) suggests that:

> The practice of anthropology 'at home' means that anthropologists are assumed to be held to a certain standard of accountability – an ethnography in the context of a hospital will most likely be read, critiqued and reacted to by the doctors, nurses and administrators whom it considers. In this sense, conducting anthropology at home has a double heroic function: on the one hand, the ethnographer, seen to be held to standards of accountability, is assumed to be acting at the very highest level of honesty with regards to the representation of his or her informants. Secondly, an ethnography conducted at home is often absolved of any connotations of epistemological imperialism – one cannot simply represent informants in any fashion one wants with total impunity, but rather is seen to be engaging in a two-way process where the construction of knowledge is a collaborative one.

As Hartman suggests, I was aware that my work would be scrutinized by those my research considered. This meant that for much of the fieldwork and the writing up process I was a bundle of anxiety. My work involved a great many sleepless nights thinking and worrying about ethical issues and concerns. Was I acting ethically? Was I being truthful to my informants? As I moved from fieldwork to analysis and as my argument developed, these concerns became more acute. We are living in an increasingly litigious society. Some members of my study community were angry and were in the throes of legal battles already; this adds another dimension to acting ethically. In addition to the ethical concerns raised in this chapter, there is also the concern of the legal consequences of one's work.

Despite the increasing emphasis on ethics boards and the need to report on potential ethical issues, at the time of my research there was no formal ethics procedure. Although ethics were a concern, it was handled in an informal way through discussions with supervisors and colleagues. However, in my experience there was a distinct silence about the ethical issues we faced on an ongoing basis and it would seem that many of us endured these alone, feeling isolated and worried about our work or possible wrongdoings. We worried about verbalizing or drawing attention to the decisions made and actions taken in often tricky scenarios.

An early version of this chapter was presented at the 'Ethics in the Field' conference at Oxford Brookes University. I very much valued the opportunity to discuss ethical issues and receive comments upon my own experiences. Not only did I find the conference enjoyable but it also came as a relief to realize that many others had experienced ethical conundrums and remained concerned about the choices they had made. What became clear was that we are constantly faced with subtle choices and there certainly is no right or wrong action.

The first section of this chapter discusses my relationship with my informants, both in the field and beyond. I then turn to my relationship with the Ministry of Defence (MoD) and Canadian Department of National Defense (CDND) before concluding. My relationship with my veteran informants produced the most anxiety, but in the current climate I am aware there is a real interest in ethics and working with, for or on the military, so I have chosen to include a section about my work with the MoD and to highlight my ongoing relationship with military establishments. However, dividing the chapter in this way is itself problematic as the military / MoD and its inhabitants also acted as informants, as did scientists and politicians associated with the MoD.

Relationship with the GWS Community

We must bear in mind that informants are not a homogenous group. My informants included GWS sufferers, naturally, but also scientists, government officials, Gulf veterans who did not support the GWS movement; there was therefore always going to be a balance of interests. Indeed, when writing about areas of conflict and contestation one is likely to be in a position where one's work upsets or angers some (if not all) of the stakeholders. This chapter mainly considers one particular group – the GWS sufferers and members of the GWS associations – for these were the informants about whom I worried the most. Their theories and experiences comprised the central focus of my work.

One of the first ethical debates I had occurred prior to the launch of my fieldwork, and it had to do with the issue of representation. How would I present myself to my potential informants? How much information should I give? As my work continued these questions became more and more fraught as informants would ask me what my position on GWS was at that time. How do we effectively communicate what we are interested in and what we do as anthropologists and how sure can we ever be that informants are truly informed when giving their consent? People often hear what they want to hear and remain convinced that you will 'be on their side', whatever that may mean.

Furthermore, how do you keep participants informed of potential findings and their impact? At times it was difficult to feel confident that informants were entirely clear about what the potential outcome might be and how it might impact them, mainly because I did not know myself what the outcome might be. Due to the organic nature of anthropological research and the way in which we often follow threads of inquiry when they arise, it is often difficult to keep informants and participants fully informed – this is something I felt acutely. Perhaps the best way to deal with these dilemmas is to be as honest and transparent as possible and to be humane and compassionate first and foremost. Although I feel I was always com-passionate, I am not sure I was always fully transparent. My lack of transparency was due, in part, to my not knowing what my findings would be. For example, the controversial issue of GWS as an expression of unmanning, which is central to the work, only came about months after I finished the fieldwork and began the analysis.

This is not the only reason for a potential lack of transparency, however. I simply was unsure how candid I could be.[1] I remember feeling anxious at times when vet-eran informants would ask me about my particular interpretation about theories of causation or the suspected Ministry of Defence conspiracy. These were the times when I felt dishonest – consequently I was often vague. The anthropological self that has to be tutored is a potentially duplicitous self, one that may keep hidden what ought to be in public view (Pels 2000: 130).

Protection

Anthropologists say they do not harm – they do not cause problems or difficulties to those they are studying. The 1998 Anthropological Association statement on ethics asserts that 'anthropological researchers must do everything in their power to ensure that their research does not harm the safety, dignity, or privacy of the people with whom they work, conduct research, or perform other professional activities'. And yet things are rarely that easy. My greatest worry, both in the field and beyond, centred around the issue of harm and loss of dignity. I was initially concerned with potentially harming informants through the act of fieldwork, i.e. getting people to talk about things that were upsetting for them; however, I found that this anxiety soon diminished because of my confidence in my ability to handle informants with care and respect. It was the post-fieldwork period that became the primary source of anxiety. As I wrote I became more and more worried about what I was writing and the impact it might have on the GWS movement and, more specifically, my informants. I was concerned that my findings and the way I presented them would be seen as a betrayal or would upset my informants.

The first half of *Impotent Warriors* focuses on GWS explanatory models con-tained in veterans' narratives and is unlikely to cause distress, being an account of the illness in their own words. It is the latter half of the book that is potentially problematic in terms of angering members of my informant community. It is in this section that I look at GWS as a means to re-orient identity in a post-combat, post-forces environment. The central role played by the Gulf veterans' associations in this identity work is discussed. In the final chapters I develop the interpretation that GWS is, in part, an expression of lost masculinity or masculinity under threat in a changing military context. The conclusion focuses on contextualizing GWS and showing how the illness has been shaped by wider cultural forces. Throughout the book I focus on the social and cultural aspect of the condition. Importantly, I simply do not know what impact my work has had on the majority of my informants or the GWS community more generally, because attempts at contact have been largely unsuccessful (see Kilshaw 2009b).

The question of who would be afforded anonymity was a complicated issue. In publications based on this research I chose to use pseudonyms for the veterans and GWS sufferers, but not for the scientists and politicians. By only disguising the veterans I potentially reproduced a distinction between them and the medics and organizations, which may be seen as implying they are more vulnerable, or more in need of anonymity. It may have enforced a distinction between those who are seen as robust enough to be included under their real name (and hence could be seen as supported by the text) and those who are not. Despite these concerns I decided to confer on veterans and their family members pseudonyms, unlike the scientists and clinicians for whom I used their real names. There were two main reasons for this decision: firstly, the scientists had become public figures and their work was well known in the community; it was therefore difficult to disguise their identity. Secondly, and more importantly, it is the veterans who had more to lose both personally and financially. In light of ongoing pension claims and a possible mass action suit, individual anonymity was important. Despite many veterans making it clear that they were happy for me to use their names I chose not to.

Representations of Suffering

Writing about suffering is complicated. How does one even write about suffering and is it ethical to do so? What does one do if those we are studying are already suffering, as were many of my informants? Do you help lessen the pain, the problems? And, if so, what exactly does 'help' entail? Does it involve supporting informants regardless of whether or not we endorse their model or theory of causation? Does it mean helping in their fight for compensation and recognition? Or does it potentially involve presenting a different reading which may be seen as a betrayal but may be potentially helpful in rethinking the way that we perceive illness specifically and more generally?

The very focus of my work is problematic, for how are we to give a true account of suffering and what is the motivation for doing so? Spelman[2] (1997) suggests that it is our lot as humans to give form to suffering. Representing another's suffering opens it up to critique and judgement: 'whether someone is suffering, how much someone hurts, how much attention her suffering should get, how much attention one can give without suffering too much oneself, whose suffering should get attention first, whose suffering might be good for them, whose suffering isn't as bad as they think, who deserves to suffer, who doesn't' (p.2). As we conceptually make sense of suffering we compare and contrast different instances of suffering, and assign relative weights to them, whether we mean to or not (Spelman 1997).

The debate about GWS often included contestations over suffering itself. There is much discussion of the cause of the Gulf veterans' suffering, but in debating why they are afflicted do we then lose sight of the very fact that they are suffering? Indeed, I found that the investigations into understanding the illness often descended into attempts to dismiss their suffering. Judgements about what kind of suffering they were experiencing (i.e. physical or psychological) were interpreted as attempts to deny their pain. When suffering is rendered intelligible through its articulation in language it becomes primed for possible abuse by others. The 'expression of our pain or suffering that makes it available to others will mangle our account, especially if they stretch, tuck, or hem our experience in an attempt to tailor it to make sense of their own' (Spelman 1997: 4).

A huge amount of scientific research has focused on dismissing certain causes of GWS, but the effect is often that the suffering itself is denied. If, for example, it is found that depleted uranium (DU) did not cause their illness, as the veterans themselves suggest, there is a certain amount of conceptual slippage so that it appears that the veterans are not suffering at all. Although presenting an academic anthropological interpretation of GWS, I hope I was able to maintain the role of suffering as central.

Spelman discusses Harriet Jacob's *Incidents in the life of a slave girl, written by herself* to illustrate issues about suffering. Jacobs is aware of the debates going on about her suffering: she knows that something is at stake in the determination of the nature of her pain, its causes, its consequences, its relative weight, its moral, religious, and social significance. The meaning of her pain is not a given. Competing interpretations are possible, and something important hangs on which interpretation or interpretations prevail (1997: 61). Similarly, there is a great deal at stake in the meaning behind veterans' suffering.

Debates rage about the nature and cause of veterans' suffering. In the GWS discourse each cluster of symptoms and/or potential cause are divided into specializations so that the wholeness of the suffering is lost. Bauman and Giddens have both drawn attention to the way in which problems in science are broken down into particles, each of which becomes the focus of specialized research. This process of specialization is paradoxical, for 'the more minute the processes, the fuller the knowledge' and yet knowledge won in this way is 'available not as illumination, but as issue-bound instruction. Partial knowledge belongs to partial specialists' (Bauman 1992: 21–22). The 'more a given problem is placed precisely in focus', through the process breaking it down into particles, 'the more surrounding areas of knowledge become blurred for the individuals concerned' (Giddens 1991: 31). When one focuses on one small aspect of the condition the larger picture recedes. This has the effect of diminishing the overall suffering. If, for example, a researcher focuses on the role of depleted uranium in GWS and concludes that the illness is unlikely to be caused by DU, as veterans suggest, then not only is their account seen as faulty, but the suffering itself is seemingly dismissed. Furthermore, this sort of departmentalizing and specializing takes the voice of suffering away from the victims as they are no longer considered to be experts in the articulation of their own suffering.

Spelman muses that perhaps we try to make suffering intelligible so that we can make it bearable. Indeed, I must ask myself why I became interested in GWS, and what I wanted to comment upon or understand about this form of suffering. Interested in new and contested illnesses, I was searching to makes sense of what I saw around me, but also of personal experience. As a child I became very ill with something my parents, both medical doctors, could not understand. After many doctor and hospital appointments and various tests, it was suggested that my problems were probably psychological. I remember vividly the embarrassment and anger I felt when this suggestion was made. Even as a child I was aware of the stigma and the way I felt they had misunderstood my suffering. This experience stayed with me and I was often reminded of it as I pursued training in medical anthropology.

Therefore, the risk of victimizing the victim was always going to be a concern for me (i.e. see Virillo 2005)? It could also be argued that I am seeking to claim that sufferers are the victims of different forces: not necessarily of the chemicals of war or of the injections administered to them, but of cultural forces, of the medical system. Spelman argues, for Plato

> focusing on sufferers as subjects of tragedy amounts to a betrayal of them and a failure to live in accordance with our best selves. Such a focus, he insists, blinds us to the causes of human suffering, keeps us from doing anything useful about preventing further occasions of it, and indulges rather than checks or reduces our appetite-like capacity for grief. If nothing else, his claims are shockingly at odds with what appears to be a well-ingrained habit, at least in many Western cultures, of honouring the suffering of others by referring to it as tragic. (Spelman 1997: 33)

Advocacy and Accountability

The question of advocacy is at the forefront of this work. For whom is an anthropologist supposed to act as advocate, if anyone? There is a long tradition of advocacy in anthropology, but it seems to be optional rather than a requirement. Presenting the veterans' experiences and accounts of their illness could be seen as a form of advocacy in that despite the attention paid to their personal narratives of the illness in popular discourse, little credence was given to their perspective by the academic and scientific discourse. Yet I imagine some veterans will reject the claim that the book promotes their understanding of the illness. From the outset I did not intend to be an advocate for any of the various parties involved in the debate. Instead, I wanted to provide an ethnography of the illness to the best of my ability. I was not an advocate for the veteran community – this itself may be problematic – and certainly the assumption amongst colleagues was that I would be.

Cantwell, Friedlander and Tramm (2000) argue that 'the paramount ethical issue facing anthropologists in all subdisciplines today, as in the past, lies in questions of accountability' (ix). Yet accountability operates on multiple levels and its referent is subject to ambiguity (Gold 2001). Accountable to whom? Accountable to the funding source – whether governmental or private? Accountable to the scientific pursuit of truth? Accountable to every person who cooperates with the research? To who should the anthropologist be accountable first and foremost if there are various parties with contradictory aims? In my case my informants were varied, with different experiences and different accounts of the illness. My funding bodies were also varied: the ESRC, the MoD and the Canadian Department of National Defense. In the end I chose to be accountable to the pursuit of truth or at the very least to present the most accurate, informed anthropological interpretation possible.

The danger is that my work could potentially cause harm (loss of dignity, negative effect on the fight for recognition and compensation) to my informants, but there is a wider issue: rarely are the medical and political problems faced by communities directly caused by anthropologists working in them. Instead, the problems faced by research communities usually arise from the political and economic contexts they exist within. The situation in which the veterans found themselves was not caused by my work, but by larger forces and it was against these forces that I felt I had to speak out. I found myself in a situation where on a direct and personal level the veterans would potentially disagree with what I was saying, and yet I still maintained that there was a bigger picture that had to be addressed.

I felt strongly that the veterans' suffering was caused, in part, by the way in which they chose to or were encouraged (or forced) to perceive their problems and experiences. The way they experience and frame their illness is influenced by the political and medical culture in which they live. Furthermore, the way they saw the illness meant that they could never recover from it. Focusing on the physical cause and physical nature of their disorder contributes to their frustration – and this focus results from the way in which the GWS debate has been constructed along the lines of the physical versus psychological dichotomy in biomedicine. My work contends that we all, veterans included, must think beyond such mind–body dualism in order for any real progress to be made. I debate the analysis of GWS as somatization and suggest that when it is reduced simply to symptoms of a disorder, the meaningful and social dimension of distress is lost (Kirmayer 1999). I present a different approach to GWS by bringing the social dimensions back into the equation.

I am reminded that the role of the anthropologist is not to stand on the sidelines, but to witness, to speak out about what is going on (Scheper-Hughes 1995: 418–19). However, the content of such protest is not straightforward. There is the potential of causing harm to individuals, and also to the GWS movement; but what if the movement itself is harmful? During my research I began to see that the GWS associations and movement were a central and helpful means of re-working identity and providing support, but I also became concerned about how sufferers seemed locked in a negative fix. Ascribing to a GWS diagnosis / narrative seemed to mean never getting better and accepting a role as a victim. Thus, I was faced with an ethical dilemma of potentially betraying my informants or potentially betraying what I felt was my academic integrity.

Consultation

One way to potentially minimize the negative impact of my work on the community would have been to give informants the opportunity to look at and alter the work prior to publication. But is this an ethical requirement? I always felt it was and was troubled by my lack of success in doing so. Although early publications were sent to the veterans' organizations, I did not give them the opportunity to edit or alter my work. Indeed, these papers were sent with trepidation, and not without reason, as one resulted in a letter from a prominent member of the veterans' association, which furiously accused me of suggesting that the illness was fictitious. Further attempts at dialogue have been futile on the whole, although I must admit that I have not been as persistent as I could have been.

I am reminded of the Hartman quotation above which suggests that ethnography conducted at home is 'seen to be engaging in a two-way process where the construction of knowledge is a collaborative one'. In my experience the practice of anthropology at home meant a greater expectation of collaborative work, but such cooperation was not always possible.

In our role as academics, we are faced with the dilemma of needing to get work out quickly – for assessment exercises, for jobs, for funders – and any kind of co-writing or consultation will significantly slow down and impede that process.[3] Any kind of debate and discussion would have hindered the very process of feeling free to analyse and write: for what if the disagreements are too great? What if informants ask you not to publish? Or what if they asked you to radically alter the interpretation? How free do we need to be to write what we feel we need to write, and should we let this be changed by informants? How much do we allow them the opportunity to alter our interpretation? These questions were central to my experience of PhD research. I was constantly aware of and often concerned about my informants' reaction to and the impact my work might have upon them and, yet, I felt compelled to produce my interpretation unconstrained by their post-fieldwork input.

Relationship with Military Organization

One of the first decisions I was faced with concerned funding. I was awarded an ESRC studentship, and was then offered additional support from the MoD and the Canadian Department of National Defense. I was fully aware of the difficulties such funding might bring both with regard to my relationship with potential informants but also in terms of how my work might be perceived. I managed the former by contacting the two main veterans' organizations with whom I had made initial contact and asking their opinion on the matter. I was pleased to find that they felt this would not alter their cooperation with me as long as I was 'free from interference' and acted as an independent researcher. I decided to accept the funding. In the end the funding had benefits beyond the obvious – the extra funds meant that I was able to travel to my informants throughout the UK and Canada. It also gave me access to meetings and arenas that would have been difficult to gain admission to had I not been seen as somewhat 'vetted' by the MoD. This included gaining access to the Royal British Legion GWS meetings and the Gulf Veterans' Medical Assessment Programme at St. Thomas' Hospital. I was invited to sit in on patient assessments at the latter and was given office space which was extremely helpful as the clinic was the hub of medical discourse surrounding GWS.

The issue of how my work was perceived is more complicated. Interestingly, despite my veteran informants saying they were happy with my MoD funding, the funding did prove problematic to many of my colleagues. The perception was that I would be biased because of the funding and that my relationship with the MoD was problematic. This, of course, resonates with the ongoing and often dramatic debate about anthropologists' role in working with or for military establishments.

Then there is the issue of what happens beyond fieldwork. The topic of my research and my contact with and funding from the MoD led to me becoming associated with the military. I became known as a 'military anthropologist' or at least an anthropologist who had worked on the military. This has produced opportunities, but it has also affected the way in which I continue to be perceived by the academy. It was a particularly interesting and difficult time to be an anthropologist associated working on military subjects, for as I completed my PhD a debate erupted about efforts to recruit anthropologists to U.S military and intelligence projects. This particular issue meant that many of us collaborating with military organizations were seen as the enemy. In 2005 the Executive Board (EB) set up the Commission on the Engagement of Anthropology with the US Security and Intelligence Communities (CEAUSSIC) to consider these issues. As I write AAA members are voting on the resulting revisions to the association's Code of Ethics. Whether we do or do not collaborate with government or military institutions is a huge and complex issue, which requires far more attention than is possible within the limits of this chapter.

MoD as a Participant

It remained a paradox that I was funded by the MoD and yet the MoD and individuals within it were part of the investigation. However, I felt free to criticize the MoD and the military and never felt obliged to minimize these criticisms. For example, one of my main findings was that sufferers had been let down by the MoD and the military, particularly in their unsupported move from military to civilian life. On a broader level I suggest that GWS arose, in part, from to the culture of the UK military at the time. I found that the MoD representatives I met felt that GWS had resulted in such huge costs, both financially and in terms of their reputation, that they were keen to find answers even if those answers were critical of the organization. If they did not support my findings I knew they would simply neither advertise nor endorse the work.

Negotiating the relationships within these various organizations was far from easy. The GWS sufferers, the scientists, lawyers, the MoD officials and my other informants were all known to one another and the relationships between them were fraught with a great deal of mistrust. At times informants tried to get information about one another; this meant that I had to remain guarded about the information I held.

Potential Danger of Captured Work

Another concern I had was that my work could be used by stakeholders – particularly those already in powerful position – against those who are more vulnerable. What if my work was used by MoD to wash their hands of GWS or worse, to deny pensions or compensation to those who were suffering? Was I not just supporting the status quo?

I found the ASA ethics guidelines helpful as I thought about this issue:

> That information can be misconstrued or misused is not in itself a convincing argument against its collection and dissemination. All information is subject to misuse; and no information is devoid of possible harm to one interest or another... Researchers are usually not in a position to prevent action based on their findings; but they should, however, attempt to pre-empt likely misinterpretations and to counteract them when they occur.
>
> When it is likely that research findings will bear upon public policy and opinion anthropologists should be careful to state the significant limitations on their findings and interpretations. (ASA V2b (b))

There would seem to be an ethical responsibility to remain active in the debate and act to correct misconceptions or misuses. One of the ways we can do so is by continuing to stress the importance of context. Often difficulties arise when stakeholders tease out elements of our work to support their position and dispense with the important context. Strathern's 2005 paper is helpful when thinking through these issues:

> And here we come to what often makes anthropological knowledge appear useless: anthropologists hate letting go of relational coordinates. They do not like shedding the apparently extraneous bits, the shedding that others imagine essential to the speed with which ideas or objects of knowledge 'travel'. In sticking to a sense of wholeness, to the idea of something not reduced, they act as purveyors of 'contexts'.
>
> ... reduction is only apparent to those who might have entertained a more detailed version but truncate it for the sake of communication. Anthropologists, for their part, invariably and doggedly insist that the details always matter, and they give themselves the uphill task of trying to communicate *as* objects of knowledge the very effects of coordinates or contexts themselves.

In the end the concern about the impact on compensation claims diminished because the mass action suit for PTSD was concluded and the mass action claim for GWS collapsed prior to publication. This, of course, does not change the need for a careful plan of how one would proceed if called upon to act as an expert on the issue or to provide evidence. Furthermore, most of my veteran informants had military pensions based on their illness and many were involved in ongoing claims. The very fact that the issues were potentially to be played out in the legal arena adds another dimension to the ethics of such a project.

The Ethics of Knowledge Construction: Competing Forms of Knowledge

Ethical issues regarding the struggle over truth and knowledge were raised. The research process, and the subsequent writing stage, evokes important questions about authority and knowledge and the rights to speak and to be heard. The story of GWS is foremost a struggle about truth and knowledge: who can claim expertise; whose theories are taken as legitimate; whose account can be seen as a true representation of reality is constantly debated. What I witnessed was a struggle between various parties to gain legitimacy and authority for their particular perspective and theory about the illness. Of course, claims to truth and knowledge were intimately tied to political, economic and social positioning and gains. By writing about GWS I was inevitably going to be seen to support some claims to truth over others.

I often felt that as an anthropologist my very approach was at odds with the GWS community's perception of the illness. On one occasion I met with an informant and he asked me to provide him with background about my interests in GWS. I did so, outlining my usual brief that I was interested in veterans' accounts of their illness experience, their theories of causation and their beliefs about the condition. He became angered by my focus on 'belief' and suggested that I was likely to conclude that the illness was false or 'in the mind'. He said that I would be doing what the MoD would want; my focus on beliefs would support the MoD position when they said GWS was 'all in their heads'.

This interaction with an informant was representative of an underlying theme of my research and, indeed, as Good (1993) has pointed out, of anthropology more generally: the juxtaposition between knowledge and belief. As Good argues, historically 'to believe' came to connote doubt and at present implies error, whereas knowledge requires certitude and correctness. There was a sense that I was studying the 'beliefs' of veterans in relation to the knowledge of the medical and political establishment. But, in fact, I was investigating the belief of scientists, doctors, the MoD etc., and I was also investigating the veterans' knowledge about their illness. Yet, because I focused on veterans' accounts and theories about their illness, it seemed as if I had set up an opposition between their belief and the knowledge of the system.

My initial aim was to investigate GWS as it moved through different arenas; however, in the end the book focuses on the veterans' accounts. I must make clear that I could have focused on the biomedical position and / or the MoD position and the beliefs contained in these accounts (including inconsistencies). My focus on the veterans' accounts may make it appear as if they have beliefs whereas the scientific mainstream has knowledge; however, I would disagree with such a distinction. The message of the book is that the veterans feel let down by the erroneous mainstream scientific theories that suggest that the illness is probably psychological.

I was interested in the social construction of the illness and the way in which it had been influenced by cultural forces, and was not going to 'prove' the medical legitimacy of the condition and the role of the MoD in the illness. Contextualizing GWS meant I was aware of how it mirrored other Euro-American health anxieties and of its place in a wider set of new and contested illnesses. This meant I was not seeing it purely as a unique illness, but as a product of cultural forces. Social science research is likely to prove problematic to sufferers of contested illness, as has been argued in the case of Repetitive Strain Injury (RSI). Research which pointed out the social causal factors of RSI was used to imply that it was not a true, organic medical condition. Social constructionist perspectives helped to dismantle the case for RSI being a 'real' biomedical disorder by undermining the significance of the efforts of RSI proponents to use scientific methods to prove its existence (Bammer and Martin 1992).

The veteran community's aims of knowledge production or those of the MoD may not be the same as those of the anthropologist. The knowledge sought may be of a completely different nature. What if the products of knowledge or the very act of the production is at odds with our informants? I was certainly aware that various informants might not like my developing interpretation, so at times I felt duplicitous. I was not fully transparent as I did not openly discuss with them my concerns about the denial of social factors and the focus on the physical aspect of the condition. In part this was due to not wanting to alienate or anger my informants, but also because during my interaction my role was as a fieldworker. I busily observed and gathered information; I had not yet developed a theoretical focus or interpretation. As I have discussed elsewhere (Kilshaw 2006, 2009), the GWS community sees things in black and white terms – you are either for or you are against – and, thus, I was aware from the outset that my more nuanced anthropological approach might not be accepted by some of my informants. Bosk has said that ethnography is innately an unethical pursuit, arguing that we ethnographers 'betray our subjects twice: first, when we manipulate our relationship with subjects to generate data and then again when we retire to our desks to transform experience to text' (Bosk 2001: 206). Ethnography invariably involves deception. Informants 'misread the ethnographer's interest in their world, and ethnographers take no pains to correct these misreadings', says Bosk. I do not think it is as clear cut as this and I do not share his negative view of ethnography, but there is certainly an aspect of deception in our work.

As mentioned above, there are also important issues about the construction of knowledge and how much we allow informants or funders to influence or alter our representation. The propriety or ethical 'suitability' of anthropological representation cannot be detached from questions about who owns such representation, and who has the right to decide how – or indeed whether or not – it will be constructed

(Strang 2003: 181). In the end I chose to represent my findings without any input or alteration from the various and competing voices in my study community.

Conclusions

Ethics in anthropological practice is ever-changing. The ethical climate and guidelines change and this has an effect on our work. When we write and present our work it is often in a different ethical climate than when we did the fieldwork. I found this to be the case: when I started my PhD work on GWS there was no formal ethics procedures. This sometimes produces gaps and problems as our actions and work will be judged by the present climate.

In 1971, the AAA put forth the Principles of Professional Responsibility (PPR); the primary assertion was that 'in research the anthropologist's paramount responsibility is to those he studies. When there is a conflict of interest, these individuals must come first' (cited in Fluehr-Lobban 1998: 176). But whose interests? This statement is not particularly helpful when the informants themselves represent a variety of interests.

Pels suggests that we should consider the possibility of 'an emergent ethics, one that is no longer tied to a stable community but arises from contingent negotiations' (Pels 2000: 136). He suggests that such ethical discussions should be located in the negotiation of individual or communal interests that is characteristic of the practice of fieldwork. Thus, ethics should not be predetermined, but would emerge for each project through conversations and negotiations with those involved. In agreement with Pels, Strathern argues that any codification of ethics results in a reduction of anthropology's valued creativity in the moment of fieldwork encounter. She writes, 'However much talk there is of collaboration or of conserving the autonomy of subjects or recognizing their input into the research or taking power into account, this aspect of ethics in advance of anticipated negotiations, belittles the creative power of social relations' (2000: 295). Anthropologists continue to value the emergent and conversational nature of their practice and findings.

Concerned with the politics of knowledge, Barnes (1979) has argued that 'social research entails the possibility of destroying the privacy and autonomy of the individual, of producing more ammunition to those already in power, of laying the groundwork for an invincibly oppressive state' (1979: 22). But in the case of GWS, who is the hegemonic oppressor? Is the automatic logical leap that the MoD is the oppressor that must be stopped and that an anthropologist's role is to give the veterans, the sufferers, a voice against this institution? Or is it more complicated – is the oppressor actually the medical system that prevents a full understanding of this condition? Is the problem the fact that social factors have been ignored?

What does one do if the people one is studying disagree with the interpretation one is presenting? And, more worryingly, what happens when one's informants feel as though they have been betrayed by one's findings? The very nature of the way in which we are trained to think as anthropologists means we are likely to conclude in ways with which our informants do not agree. But in the end we are not there to write for our informants. We need to be free to interpret and write, even if our informants dispute our findings, indeed, even if they (or others) perceive our findings as causing harm either through questioning their firmly held beliefs or affecting their claims to compensation. In the end we have to find a balance between our relationship with informants and academic rigour, being true to our findings, being able to be free to interpret, and draw conclusions. As Amit suggests, we must find the courage to make bold statements:

> If all that we produce are carefully nuanced ethnographies which avoid clear statements of our political stance, then we will do little to advance a struggle for academic freedom however much information we gather. Our challenge will be to combine ethnographic insight with political courage … the courage to insist that the true measure of the intellectual project must be the curiosity of a critical and independent mind. (2000: 213)

I stand by what I wrote, but I maintain that it is, rightly or wrongly, my interpretation. It is not the final and definitive – the 'true' – account, but my own interpretation. I think it is necessary to emphasize the interpretive nature of what we do as anthropologists.

We anthropologists must be acutely aware of ethics and how we negotiate these sometimes murky waters. There are no black and whites and no clear answers, but I think the most important thing is that we agonize over these issues, engage in discussions about them and always remember how important they are.

Notes

1. My anxiety about my publications and their interpretation has seem.ed to cloud my memories as at the time I was simply interested in the veterans' narratives and there seemed little to be concerned about.
2. I am grateful to Vieda Skultans for recommending Spelman's work.
3. At what point are we to engage in such consultation? This research was part of a PhD and, thus, there was little possibility of consultation during this phase. As PhD students we are under pressure to complete quickly, limiting any opportunities for ongoing engagement with informants. Subsequent publications were based on the findings and interpretations contained in the PhD thesis, meaning that consultation would have come at a later stage of the process.

References

Amit., V. 2000. 'The University as Panopticon: Moral Claims and Attacks on Academic Freedom', in M. Strathern (ed.), *Audit Cultures: Anthropological Studies in Accountability, Ethics and the Academy*. London: Routledge, pp. 215–235.

Bammer, G. and B. Martin. 1992. 'Repetitive Strain Injury in Australia: Medical Knowledge, Social Movement, and de facto Partisanship', *Social Problems* 39(3): 219–37.

Barnes J. A. (1979), *Who Should Know What? Social Science, Privacy and Ethics*. Cambridge: Cambridge University Press.

Bauman, Z. 1992. 'Death as a Social Construct', *Theory, Culture and Society* 9: 21–22.

Bosk, C. 2001. 'Irony, Ethnography, and Informed Consent', in B. Hoffmaster (ed.), *Bioethics in Social Context*. Philadelphia: Temple University Press, pp. 199–220.

Cantwell, A., E. Friedlander and M. Tramm. 2000. 'Introduction', in Anne-Marie Cantwell, Eva Friedlander and Madeleine L. Tramm (eds), *Ethics and Anthropology: Facing Future Issues in Human Biology, Globalism, and Cultural Property*. New York: The New York Academy of Sciences, pp. vii–xv.

Fluehr-Lobban, C. (1998) 'Ethics', in H. R. Bernard (ed.), *Handbook of Methods in Cultural Anthropology*. Walnut Creek, London, New Delhi: Altamira Press.

Giddens, A. 1991. *Modernity and Self Identity*. Cambridge: Polity Press.

Gold, A. 2001. *www.researchethics.org/uploads/word/anthropologist.doc.*

Good, B. 1993. *Medicine, Rationality and Experience: an Anthropological Perspective*. Cambridge: Cambridge University Press.

Hartman, T. 2007. 'Beyond Sontag as a Reader of Lévi-Strauss: "Anthropologist as Hero"', *Anthropology Matters Journal* 9(1).

Kilshaw, S. 2006. 'On Being a Gulf Veteran: An Anthropological Perspective', *Philosophical Transactions of the Royal Society* B. 361 (1468) (2006): 697–706.

———. 2009a. *Impotent Warriors: Gulf War Syndrome, Vulnerability and Masculinity*. Oxford: Berghahn.

———. 2009b. 'Obligations to Veteran Informants: Contentious Research and Stakeholder Engagement', *Anthropology News* 50(5): 28–29.

Kirmayer, L. 1999. 'Rhetorics of the Body: Medically Unexplained Symptoms in Sociocultural Perspective', in Y.Ono, A. Janca, M. Asai and N. Sartorius (eds), *Somatoform Disorders: A Worldwide Perspective*. Keio University Symposia for Life Science and Medicine, Vol. 3. Tokyo: Springer, pp. 271–286.

Pels, P. 1999. 'Professions of Duplexity. A Prehistory of Ethical Codes in Anthropology', *Current Anthropology* 40(2): 101–136.

———. 2000. 'The Trickster's Dilemma: Ethics and the Technologies of the Anthropological Self', in M. Strathern (ed.), *Audit Cultures: Anthropological Studies in Accountability, Ethics and the Academy*. London: Routledge, pp. 135–172.

Rapp, R. 1999. *Testing Women, Testing the Fetus: the Social Impact of Amniocentesis in America*. London: Routledge.

Scheper-Hughes, N. 1995. 'The Primacy of the Ethical: Propositions for a Militant Anthropology', *Current Anthropology* 36(3) (June), 409–420.

Spelman, E. 1997. *Fruits of Sorrow: Framing our Attention to Suffering*. Boston: Beacon Press.

Strang, V. 2003. 'An Appropriate Question? The Propriety of Anthropological Analysis in the Australian Political Arena', in P. Caplan (ed.), *The Ethics of Anthropology: Debates and Dilemmas*. London: Routledge, pp. 172–194.

Strathern, M. 2000. 'Afterword', in M. Strathern (ed.), *Audit Cultures: Anthropological Studies in Accountability, Ethics and the Academy*. London: Routledge, pp. 279–304.

———. 2005. 'Useful Knowledge'. British Academy: Isaiah Berlin lecture Proceedings of the British Academy 139, 2005 Lectures.

Virilio, P. 2005. *The Original Accident*. Cambridge: Polity Press.

9

Messy Ethics

Negotiating the Terrain between Ethics Approval and Ethical Practice

Tina Miller

All types of research raise and encounter ethical considerations. But what is ethical research, how is it practised and how far can/should it be regulated? In all social science disciplines there is evidence of growing ethical regulation set against a societal backdrop of increased concerns with risk, safety, accountability, surveillance and litigation. Across the UK, universities are now required to appoint ethics committees in order to ensure that ethical procedures are followed in research. These shifts have evoked different responses from research communities, ranging from viewing increased ethics regulation as helpful in providing guidance and frameworks, to concerns about how codes of ethical practise are interpreted, and alarm at the potential dangers inherent in claims of 'ethical expertise' (Hammersley 2009: 212; Morrow 2009). Certainly the social worlds and contexts in which individual lives are lived and relationships experienced have become increasingly complex and the methods of research we may employ, correspondingly more various (Marsden 2004). At the same time ideas of ethical regulation imply – and draw upon – standardized codes of practice in which 'ethical rules are context free' (Mattingly 2005: 453; Truman 2003). A misfit then emerges between complex social and cultural worlds, a regulatory discourse which invokes ideas of universal research ethics, and practices and experiences which unfold 'in the field' (Reissman 2005). This chapter will follow certain aspects of the unfolding research process once ethics approval has been successfully negotiated. It will focus in particular on qualitative longitudinal research in sociology and so shares some practices associated with ethnographic research more generally.

An overarching concern for members of ethics committees is the protection of those who are to be subjects/participants in research and, more recently, the protection of the researcher too. This emanates from the philosophical and ethical principles of justice and respect for research subjects and their protection through the avoidance of 'coercion', 'harm', and 'risk'. These principles have become enshrined in ethical codes and guidelines of professional practice. It was the legacy of the horrors of Nazi experiments on human subjects during the Second World War and the resulting Nuremberg Code (1947) followed by the Universal Declaration of Human Rights (1948) and the declaration of Helsinki in 1964, which have subsequently shaped medical and, latterly social science, research ethics (Miller and Boulton 2007). In addition and more recently there has also been public outrage following various medical research scandals involving unethical research practises which have resulted in claims of a subsequent loss of public trust in those carrying out such research[1] (O'Neill 2004). The ethical regulation of social science research emanates from biomedical research codes of ethical practise, which do not translate straightforwardly across to the social sciences, and whose generality can obscure the 'subtleties' encountered in practice (VanderStaay 2005: 373; Hammersley and Atkinson 2007). Indeed, some would argue that they hardly translate at all to research practices in disciplines such as anthropology and sociology which often employ ethnographic and qualitative longitudinal approaches when exploring individuals, groups, events, settings and practices over time and in the field (Mattingly 2005: Miller and Boulton 2007; Truman 2003).

Notwithstanding this lack of fit, most researchers in these disciplines are now required by University research ethics committees (URECs) to gain 'informed' consent from participants, and the way in which these participants are accessed may well also be regulated by the ethics committee in order to ensure that subjects participate voluntarily in the research. A particular concern has been to protect those participants who could be 'vulnerable' in some way: yet definitions of vulnerability are open to interpretation, and competing conceptions of vulnerability between researchers and ethics board has recently been noted (Buckle, Dwyer and Jackson 2010). Methods of planned data collection are also considered by the ethics committee but interestingly, the process of departing the field and ending the research attracts much less attention than gaining access to it (Iversen 2009). Each of these areas – access and consent, data collection and leaving the field – is considered below alongside the ethical issues which can arise in exploratory, qualitative longitudinal research projects. Two qualitative longitudinal studies will be drawn upon in order to illuminate each of these stages in the research process in which it will be argued that unforeseen and ongoing ethical issues can and do arise. These two pieces of sociological research focus on unfolding personal experiences in the transition to first-time motherhood (Miller 2005, 2007) and first-time fatherhood (Miller 2011).

A defining characteristic of qualitative research is the rich data which the method can produce through, for example, 'discovery-oriented' interviews (Buckle, Dwyer and Jackson 2010: 112). In qualitative longitudinal research the richness and intensity of the data elicited can be heightened through the collection of data over time, but in a landscape of uncertain trajectories, which can give rise to a range of ongoing ethical considerations for the researcher. This is because personal transitions often sit at the core, and provide a distinctive feature of, qualitative longitudinal research in sociology. These transitions have outcomes which can be individually imagined and anticipated, but which at the commencement of a research study and relationship cannot be known by either/any party. Qualitative longitudinal research therefore shares characteristics of ethnographic research and provides a temporally sensitive means of capturing individual transitional life events as part of everyday experiences as they are lived and unfold (Thomson and Holland 2003). But it is their unfolding nature which can prompt unforeseen – and unforeseeable – ethical considerations. Similarly, relationships with participants in this type of research are established in ways that are not so possible, or likely, in research using one-off, 'snapshot' interviews. These relationships will develop and change across the course of a project and may even continue long after the research has ceased (McLean and Leibing 2007; Hammersley and Atkinson 2007). The ways in which research boundaries are metaphorically drawn are therefore more permeable in longitudinal research, prompting questions that require continual ethical reflection in the field (McLean and Leibing 2007; VanderStaay 2005). These questions are of course much more familiar to anthropologists whose research more commonly involves prolonged periods of being in the field, but are much less familiar or relevant to those engaged in one-off interviews (Atkinson, Coffey and Delamont 2007; Hammersley and Atkinson 2007; Mattingly 2005; VanderStaay 2005). So whilst responding to the question of what constitutes ethical research is, at one level, relatively straightforward, achieved by meeting the conditions set by, and approved by (any number of) ethics committees, doing the research is in practice usually a much messier business. Through a focus on issues of access, 'informed' consent, data collection and leaving the field, as experienced in the two research projects noted above, I will highlight the ethical concerns which can arise in this type of longer view and exploratory research.

The Research Studies

The studies on transition to first-time motherhood and first-time fatherhood which will be used to explore ethical issues in longitudinal research were conducted consecutively in the UK. The first of these, the motherhood study, commenced in the mid-1990s when formalized university ethics approval was not required, although disciplinary guidelines on ethical practice were consulted. The fatherhood study began in 2005 by which time formalized ethics committee procedures were in place across universities in the UK and ethics approval had to be, and was, gained before this piece of research could commence. In both pieces of research unforeseen ethical issues arose at different times and in different ways as the research unfolded and were addressed in ways that were sensitive to the specific circumstances and contexts. The motherhood study explored how changes in women's lives around the birth of their first child impacted on their experiences and identities as mothers (Miller 2005). Potential participants (women in late pregnancy with their first child) were identified using snowballing techniques[2] through my own social networks and were invited to then contact me by letter or telephone. Eventually seventeen women were accessed in this way and were invited by telephone to take part in the longitudinal study, to which they agreed. 'Consent' (in any sense) was taken to be given as interview arrangements were made. This study then involved the women being interviewed (usually in their home) on three separate occasions over a period of approximately one year from late pregnancy onwards about their experiences of transition to motherhood. Following the final interview a short postal questionnaire was sent to the women in order to collect demographic data and to ask about their experiences of being a participant in the study.

The fatherhood study, which was also UK-based, was undertaken as a companion and comparative study to the earlier motherhood study. It focused on how men experience the changes associated with the birth of their first child and how they construct their roles and identities as fathers. University ethics approval was required before the research could commence. A total of seventeen participants eventually responded to posters and/or leaflets in shops and work premises and opted in to the study. For this study obtaining written 'informed' consent was a requirement set by the ethics committee and this was initially negotiated through email once potential participants had provided details of their preferred means of contact. This also involved information sheets being sent by email to the participants – another condition set by the UREC – and then interview arrangements were agreed in subsequent email exchanges. At the first interview the longitudinal study was again explained and the men were then asked to sign a consent form at that time, consenting to all three planned interviews. The conditions set by the ethics committee prolonged the access period in this second study and made the initial contacts with the participants feel much more formal than in the earlier motherhood study: the metaphorical reach of the University research ethics committee shaped this first interview encounter.

Access and 'Informed' Consent

A common requirement set by ethics committees is that potential participants must opt in to research projects in order to ensure that coercion has not been exerted and that participation is voluntary. This requirement will have shaped the type of sample eventually accessed in the fatherhood study. Even though the research was advertised in a wide range of places in order to try to attract a diverse sample, the eventual sample in many ways reflected those individuals conjured up in normative western discourses of the 'good', involved father. The men were all employed,[3] partnered, resident in couple households and intending to 'be there' for their as yet unborn child. Their impending fatherhood was occurring at a stage in their adult life where it appeared that (particularly economic) responsibilities for a child could be met. The requirement that men must opt into research on fatherhood – especially when they are not yet fathers – is hardly likely to produce a sample of men who may feel ambivalent, uncertain or (even) in denial and/or fear of this impending life event. Rather, such a requirement will appeal to those who feel confident about having a 'story' to tell and who are engaged and anticipating being a 'good' involved father (Dermott 2008; Miller 2011). The further requirement that the men must sign a consent form, having first been provided with an information sheet, will also have influenced the type of sample accessed: clearly reading information sheets and providing written consent assumes, at the very least, literacy (Mattingly 2005; Miller and Bell 2012; Reissman 2005). It is of course possible to think more creatively about how to inform (as much as is ever possible) potential research participants about what their involvement in research might mean (Morrow 2009), but there remains a sense that in a period of increasing litigation, gaining consent is also about 'institutional self-protection' (Mattingly 2005: 461; Truman 2003). Paradoxically, there is also a danger that a 'tick box' mentality can be encouraged through the meeting of ethics committee requirements, and so once a consent form has been signed the inexperienced researcher may feel that 'ethics' have been 'done' and can be mentally ticked off (Miller and Boulton 2007).

The problematic nature of 'informed' consent has received increasing attention, especially amongst anthropologists in regard to ethnographic research and being 'in the field' and more recently, qualitative research which has a longitudinal dimension (Atkinson, Coffey and Delamont 2007; Boulton and Parker 2007; Hammersley and Atkinson 2007; Thomson and Holland 2003). Amongst other things, critiques have included discussion about what it is that is being consented to and by whom, and at what point consent can be regarded as being 'informed' or indeed freely given (Miller and Bell 2012). Similarly, whilst many 'ethnographers would accept the principles of informed consent, there is considerable disagreement about what this requires in particular cases' (Hammersley and Atkinson 2007: 212). As ethnographic and qualitative longitudinal approaches are necessarily exploratory, how can the researcher know what will emerge through the process and how can participants be expected to provide informed consent in such circumstances? In both the motherhood and fatherhood studies the research was described to the participants (in person at the first interview in the motherhood study and in an information sheet ahead of the first interview and again in person at the first interview in the fatherhood study). In both studies I was struck by how willingly the participants gave their verbal – and written in the fatherhood study – consent that they would participate in three in-depth interviews over a period of approximately a year before and following the birth of their first child. At this entry point they could not know how their journeys into first-time parenthood would unfold or what might occur in unpredictable research encounters.[4] Interestingly, their willingness to participate during this period of personal transition underscores many things, including how unproblematic becoming a mother/ father is perceived to be in western societies. Their eventual narratives of transition told a different story (Miller 2005; 2011).

Research has also shown that people can, for a host of reasons, disclose more than they had intended once a research interview is underway irrespective of consent being given (Birch and Miller 2000; Sinding and Aronson 2003). For example, at the end of a first interview[5] with a participant in the fatherhood study I asked if there was anything else he would like to add, to which he replied 'No, very thorough questions. You've got me from every angle'. The implication was that the interview had been much more probing than he had expected, or had consented to. Unintended disclosures may also be more likely in longitudinal research where research relationships can move beyond perfunctory attempts at establishing rapport and/or 'faking friendship' (Duncombe and Jessop 2012). Following a first interview another of the fatherhood study participants (off tape) said that the interview had been 'good' for him because 'to be honest I don't really talk about these things other than to my wife'. Unintentionally, and in ways which could not be captured in any formulaic notion of ethics, the participants in the fatherhood study came to experience the interviews as opportunities for personal reflection. The interviews with the men were usually longer than those with women in the earlier motherhood study. Over the course of the research it became clear that this group of men had limited opportunities – and so culturally and socially acceptable spaces – in which to talk about the significant personal transition they were experiencing. The research, again unintentionally, had provided the participants with a space and opportunities to talk in ways that several described as being 'like counselling' and 'as a time for reflection and as such very useful'. Interviews were also described as 'cathartic' and 'thought provoking' and were often looked forward to, as the following extract from an end-of-study questionnaire[6] illustrates:

> I didn't really know what to expect from the interview process. However Tina explained the process fully before the first interview started and during the interview made me feel very comfortable. I looked forward to the second and third interviews. (Stephen,[7] end-of-study questionnaire)

The successive interviews prompted the participants to reflect on their experiences in ways that they probably otherwise would not have done, as the following extract shows:

> I enjoyed being part of the study. It provided a space to reflect and think about the whole process – not just during the interviews themselves, but before and after, anticipating and reflecting on them, what came up, what didn't. I would quite happily have been interviewed more often and for longer! (Richard, end-of-study questionnaire)

For these participants the research permeated areas of their lives outside of the recorded interviews in ways that could not be precisely known or anticipated or indeed consented to in any 'informed' sense.

Most exploratory longitudinal research has an unknowable trajectory that underscores the impossibility of truly 'informed' consent. As Mattingly has suggested, it is only after participants have experienced being part of our research study – had us 'on a trial basis' – that they can really 'make a truly informed decision' (Mattingly 2005: 455). There is a risk then that requiring increasingly formal (written) consent will reduce the pool of willing participants to those who will also feel confident enough to 'opt in' to our research. There is a paradox too that the consent form once signed can only act as a fig leaf to cover the complex individual experiences and disclosures which can unfold – and must be sensitively and ethically managed – in research on personal transitions. The increasingly regulatory approach to ethics in research will no doubt make some groups of potential participants much harder to access whilst others, by default, will become the 'professionally researched' (Miller and Boulton 2007: 2208). For example, in the fatherhood study three of the participants volunteered that they had also signed up for 'a hospital study'. But even when consent is willingly given/signed over, who actually ends up 'peopling' the data we collect in longitudinal research and who informs our data analysis? In the following section the ways in which data is constituted, and how its collection is shaped, is considered further.

Collecting Data

At one level, having negotiated the difficult terrain of accessing a sample and gaining consent, the process of data collection can be viewed as much less problematic – by the ethics committees and researcher alike. This is especially the case where more traditional methods in sociology such as face-to-face interviews, which are audio-taped, are to be employed. In both the motherhood and fatherhood studies face-to-face interviews, as well as the end-of-study questionnaire, were the 'formal' methods of data collection which were approved (in the case of the fatherhood study) by the University ethics committee. But in both studies the question of when data was actually being collected, from whom, and more importantly what constituted the data, became concerns. What appeared quite straightforward – that data is being collected from participants once the interview has begun and the recording device is switched on, and ends as the recording device is switched off – was in fact much more complicated. Data of course usually include descriptions of others who are not the participants in the research (and have not given consent),[8] but in the fatherhood study the wives and partners of the participants quite often contributed in subtle and less subtle ways to the data that was being collected. For example, as the interviews were usually carried out at the men's homes in the evenings or weekends (around their paid work commitments), their wives/partners were also usually around, although not sitting in the same room. They would on occasion walk through the room during the interview, pass the baby to the new father, raise their eyebrows at what they heard said, smile, shake their heads and sometimes add their own thoughts. The men too would call out to their wives/partners to check or confirm aspects of their accounts. These interactions did not form part of the data collection described on the ethics application form but they would later be recalled, and would therefore inform the data analysis. Indeed, during the analysis it was these, apparently inconsequential, interruptions that, at times, helped to illuminate intricate dimensions of gendered caring practises (for examples see Miller 2011, chapter 5).

The mismatch and messiness of what happens in the field around the formal, ethics-committee-approved data collection activities are illuminated further through the data collection process. Once I had accessed a sample for the fatherhood study, email became the usual mode of contact and, as noted earlier, was used to set up initial and subsequent interviews. At the outset of the project this was envisaged as a means of access only and not as part of the data collection phase of the research (Ison 2008; Meho 2006). But it turned out to serve both as an organizing tool as well as a way of providing other 'informal' data, a source that had not been anticipated by me in this first piece of research in which email was used. So were these 'email conversations' data? They were not part of the formal data collection activities described in my research application (in-depth interviews and end-of-study questionnaire) and which had been approved by the university research ethics committee, and they fell outside the interviews which the participants had 'consented' to. But I could not 'unknow' what had been communicated to me via these emails, or prevent them from being a factor in my interpretations during data analysis, for example in relation to emotional displays and masculinities. In longitudinal research email can provide an apparently straightforward way of setting up interviews and staying in touch with participants in between these interviews, but it can also redraw, in subtle and less subtle ways, research boundaries. For example, in the fatherhood study my personal email details were regularly added by the participants to block email birth announcements. Developments in IT such as email and mobile phones can clearly facilitate channels of access, project management (especially in longitudinal research) and innovative communication[9] (Meho 2006; Ison 2008). But these developments also require the researcher to think carefully about how their own privacy and researcher relationships may be affected. On the one hand, being added to block email birth announcements signalled to me a sense of rapport having been established, and I was always very pleased to receive any news via email, but it also reminded me of the practical need, in future research, to have both a dedicated project email address and mobile phone number.

The use of unstructured or semi-structured interviews and questionnaires, which are widely used in sociology, have not attracted the same ethical scrutiny as observation, field notes and participatory methods routinely used in anthropology. But approaches to data collection are becoming increasingly varied across disciplines in order to understand more complex social and cultural worlds (Keats 2009). The increasing use and current interest in qualitative longitudinal research in sociology to chart personal and social change (see, for example, http://www.timescapes.leeds.ac.uk/), together with the developments in IT noted earlier, make it almost impossible to know in advance 'what will constitute relevant data' in a research project (Mattingly 2005: 460). Yet university research ethics committees appear to work with ideas of data itself as unproblematic, provided that informed consent has been obtained from those participating and that collection methods appear to be ethical and will not cause harm or involve coercion. But in the longitudinal fatherhood study the concern became not just what will constitute 'relevant data' but, more fundamentally, what the data was and when it was being collected.

The activity of data collection has been historically shaped and constructed in significant ways in social sciences and particularly sociology as a consequence of developments in recording technologies (Lee 2004). In the same way the developments in IT noted above have also introduced new possibilities concerning when and where and what 'data' is collected. But notwithstanding the important and complimentary developments in the types of data that can now be captured in social science research, for example through film and photography, the transcribed words and language – 'voice' – of the research participant can remain privileged as constituting the accurate, authentic and objective data in interview-based research. Indeed, the ability to record an interview, which had become common research practice by the mid-1950s, was seen to eliminate 'the conscious or unconscious bias associated with note-taking' (Lee 2004: 878). This assertion clearly invokes a particular epistemological position which many would contest and find problematic: that 'objective' technically recorded, and therefore 'unbiased', data results from the research interview. As noted above data collection is in practice a much messier and less controllable endeavour than is suggested by this. But nevertheless the recorded interview in western sociology has continued to be largely regarded as an unproblematic – ethical – method of data collection and one with which ethics committees are both familiar and comfortable (Taylor 2002). Yet, the apparently unproblematic face-to-face interview is always a co-construction (Rapley 2001), often experienced as highly problematic and as a result can be ethically fraught (Birch and Miller 2000). Given these different data collection methods (and there are of course many others), ideas of 'ethical universalism' across (and within) disciplines is both implausible and probably impossible (Reissman 2005: 487). Returning then to the question of what constitutes relevant data, clearly this cannot be known in advance and may, in the field, be collected in the spaces and places around the specified data collection process just as much as through it.

Leaving the Field/Letting Go

As noted earlier, a defining characteristic of ethnographic and qualitative longitudinal research is that it involves establishing longer term relationships – which can involve emotional involvement and/or friendship – with those whose lives are studied. It is surprising then how little attention is paid to how these research relationships are to be ended. Gaining ethics approval involves detailing the sample, access, consent procedures, data collection, methods of analysis and (sometimes) dissemination, but not usually how the researcher will 'let go' or eventually leave the field. It has been recognized that in research which takes an ethnographic approach there is a greater tendency for it 'to lack a sense of an obvious endpoint', an observation which can be levelled at qualitative longitudinal research too (Bryman

2008: 309). In a similar vein Iversen has also recently noted that 'despite the global increase in ethnographic publications and methodological sophistication … little attention has been paid to "getting out"' (2009: 10). Endings to research can of course be prescribed by funding bodies and other resource considerations including researchers' own time availability. But ending research relationships may not be nearly so clearly drawn and will 'often take a considerable amount of negotiation' (Letherby 2003: 116). Even where a 'fixed termination or end point' for a study is pre-specified, practices of 'disengagement' can be conceptualized, negotiated and experienced, even amongst researchers working together, in widely varying ways (Iversen 2009: 11). It is surprising then that this ethically sensitive terrain has not attracted the attention of ethics committees to the same extent as access and 'getting in'. This is not to suggest that the ethics committee gaze should be extended, but rather to reiterate a concern that research should involve thinking and acting in ethically responsible ways throughout and sometimes beyond a piece of research. As it is currently constructed, ethics committee approval can over-emphasize apparently 'critical points' in the research process, so that research becomes framed in distorted and potentially unethical ways. It is clear then that there is a difference between meeting the requirements set by an ethics committee and 'the kind of continual reflexive exploration of methodological and ethical issues in which researchers ought to be engaged' across the life of a project (Hammersley 2009: 218).

In the motherhood and fatherhood studies outlined earlier in this chapter the research was designed to capture women and then men's transitions to first-time motherhood and fatherhood across a period of one year. Whilst managing the end of the motherhood study felt quite straightforward – by the time of the last interview the women were busy trying to deal with (in most cases) a return to work and the demands of their growing baby – the experience has been different in the fatherhood study which remains 'live' even though the proposed (and consented to) interviews have all been carried out. Channels of communication were left open in the earlier motherhood study through, initially, the end-of–study questionnaire and my commitment to let the women know about any publications that came from the study.[10] In practice there was little continued communication.[11] In the fatherhood study the research design was changed as the research unfolded to include a later interview at around the time of their child's second birthday (and additional university ethics approval was sought, and granted, for this change). At this two-year interview the possibility of future interviews was discussed and the participants verbally agreed to participate in further interviews as their children reach school age (this will depend on funding). Reflecting on why 'getting out' in this second project has felt less clear-cut than in the earlier study I have a mixed sense of achievement and gratitude at managing to recruit a group of men into a longitudinal project and having gradually built up a rapport. Others too have observed that leaving the field in research related to families can be less clear-cut as 'parents often come to perceive the researcher as a friend or trusted resource' (Iversen 2009: 17; Mattingly 2005). In the fatherhood study the researcher relationship has come to feel comfortable as the participants know what the interviews involve (reflecting on events since we last met), will often have thought about this in advance ('I thought I must remember to tell Tina that') and I have listened to their stories around the significant life event of new fatherhood as these have unfolded. I have also become aware, through the interview encounters, of the lack of acceptable spaces in which emotional and 'caring masculinities' can be narrated: a consequence of the ways in which normative, hegemonic displays of acceptable masculinities are narrowly prescribed in some western societies (Plantin, Mansson and Kearney 2003; Johansson and Klinth 2007; Kimmel, Hearn and Connell 2004; Miller 2011). It seems all the more important then to continue to explore these men's experiences (which are not routinely voiced) beyond transition into different phases of unfolding fatherhood. Without the ethics committee requiring me to – and how could they when this has been an unforeseen dimension of the research process? – I have a sense of responsibility to this group which involves a commitment to keeping them informed of any publications arising from the research and looking for funding opportunities to enable further interviews. Even though it was originally anticipated that the fatherhood study would mirror the motherhood study, my responsibilities have been differently construed, and 'letting go' has not yet happened.

Of course the end of being in the field does not have to always mean severing research relationships completely; equally, some researchers may feel considerable relief at the end of research and 'getting out' – and some participants will feel similarly (Hammersley and Atkinson 2007). A year after the last end-of-study questionnaire had been returned in the motherhood study I contacted all the women by letter to confirm that their address details had not changed in order to honour a 'research bargain' I had made – that I would send them the tapes on which their interviews had been recorded (Hammersley and Atkinson 2007; Miller 2005). I received a reply back from one of the participants who confirmed that she would like me to send her tapes. She finished her note: 'It seems so long ago that to be honest I'd forgotten about it' (Abigail). Abigail's remark shows the different perspectives that researcher and participant can have in relation to research, in this case once the field has been left. But whilst Abigail had 'forgotten about it', in other circumstances the relationship may be experienced in different, more emotionally dependent and problematic ways in which participant expectations (and those of gatekeepers) can be heightened as a consequence of the research. Expectations can be raised, intentionally or otherwise, through 'research bargains' as entry to research sites or groups or individuals are negotiated and managed. Striking and honouring 'research bargains' is yet another activity which may be necessary in the field but cannot be known in advance, or regulated in any meaningful way by an ethics committee before the commencement of the research: however, significant ethical and moral dilemmas may ensue which need to be managed in situ (VanderStaay 2005). Again, this highlights the need for researchers to be ethically equipped, to know 'how to act in any given circumstance', to be able to think and practise ethically as they undertake research in ways that are context specific both in the field and as they analyse, write up and disseminate their findings (Mattingly 2005: 469). But developing a capacity to research people's lives in ways that are ethically and morally acceptable clearly requires much more than successfully negotiating the university research ethics committee.

Concluding Discussion

This chapter has argued that regulatory styles of ethics and research practice and notions of 'ethical universalism' do not map neatly onto everyday research experiences in the field (Riessman 2005; Mattingly 2005). Indeed, this approach may emphasize particular aspects of the research process, for example acceptable modes of access and informed consent, and as a consequence distract attention away from other aspects in ways that could even be considered unethical. As a result of this, and because obtaining ethics approval is increasingly a pre-requisite for a piece of research and a condition of funding councils, researchers may convey particular versions of their research plans to ethics committees in which, paradoxically, ethical concerns are downplayed or minimized. There have been numerous challenges to the dominant 'static audit and accountability model of ethics' and calls for an appreciation of ethics as context specific, fluid, pragmatic and unfolding across research encounters (Corrigan 2003; Mattingly 2005; Miller et al. 2012; Miller and Boulton 2007). As Mattingly notes, 'the notion that tricky ethical matters can be handled by a single set of universal standards (embodied in a legal sounding document) is itself problematic' (2005: 455). At the same time, increased litigation, audit and accountability have become more familiar features of western societies, resulting in regulatory discourses around ethics and institutional concern. What is clear is that ethical issues and dilemmas can be encountered in even the most apparently innocuous piece of research and that it is vital that researchers are adequately equipped to make, and balance, ethical and moral judgements and decisions. But how can this be achieved?

The impossibility of knowing in advance what issues might arise in the field has proved to be a dominant thread across this chapter. But this does not preclude the importance of planning and being as prepared as possible. Ethnographic and qualitative longitudinal research is often concerned with the 'small details' which intricately and subtly pattern everyday lives and which means that 'no exact recipe for ethical fieldwork can be written' (VanderStaay 2005: 406). Similarly, it is impossible for university research ethics committees to be able to capture all the (unknowable) ethical and moral issues that might arise in researching such aspects of everyday lives. Yet groups of individuals with expertise in research practises in the field could provide a useful 'support forum' rather than a regulatory role across the life of a research project. Indeed, researchers with less experience would probably welcome the opportunity to discuss ethical and/or other issues or dilemmas as they arise and new information technologies now make this more possible, even when in the field. It is also essential that research training equips and prepares researchers in order that they can better navigate problems as they are encountered. Consideration of ethical issues in longitudinal (and indeed single-interview) research should be woven through the research methods syllabus rather than be dealt with as a discrete topic, often aligned to jumping institutional hurdles and getting ethics approval. Making ethical decisions – 'walking the ethics tightrope' – involves judgements which can have critical importance to someone else's life or circumstances, or that of the researcher, and necessitates being able to weigh up matters and make decisions as and when they arise (Morrow 2009:18). Requiring those new to ethnographic/longitudinal research to read the accounts of others 'can provide a vicarious experience of the dilemmas and circumstances a researcher should be prepared to encounter' (VanderStaay 2005: 406; Miller et al. 2012). There is a need then to broaden out ethical thinking, planning and practice, before, during and after being in the field. To concentrate ethical jurisdiction in the hands of university research ethics committees and prioritize ethics approval clearly runs the risk of narrowing ethical thinking. Ethics committees can have a role to play – even if in this litigious age it is only at the level of institutional protection if things go wrong – but ethics and ethical dilemmas in the practice of research must be much more broadly conceived and understood. Researchers in the field require ethical support, not regulation.

Notes

1. Most recently in a case in the UK where Dr Andrew Wakefield was found to have acted 'unethically' by the General Medical Council in research which was found to be 'fatally flawed'. In his study into the link between the MMR injection and autism Dr Wakefield collected blood samples from children attending his son's birthday party by paying them £5. (http://news.bbc.co.uk/1/hi/health/8483865.stm)
2. It had been decided not to contact potential participants through more formal health provider channels, e.g. antenatal clinics as I did not want the research affiliated in any way with the delivery of health services or the participants to feel more obliged to provide accounts of transition that mirrored health service discourses of motherhood. At the same time (mid-1990s) I was also aware that using health service routes of access would require me to gain ethics approval from the local health authority and this I knew, from the experiences of others, to be a long, protracted and difficult process in which an understanding of qualitative research methods often seemed to be lacking in the expertise represented in the ethics committee.
3. The men were employed in a wide range of skilled jobs that would mostly position them as middle-class.
4. See the extract from my field diary about these concerns in Miller and Bell (2012).
5. The interviews were loosely structured and guided by (if/as necessary) a short prompt sheet of areas relating to changing identities and transitions.
6. An end-of-study questionnaire was sent to all the participants in the motherhood and fatherhood studies. The main aim in using this instrument was to confirm participant's age, educational level and to ask them which social class they would place

themselves in if asked to do so. In addition, and most interestingly, the participants were also asked to describe how they had found being a participant in the study.

7. All participant names have been changed.

8. Most researchers would accept that it is good practice to change any identifying features (of people and places) if their publication could cause harm or distress, but this may not always be possible.

9. In a small pilot study on teenage fatherhood which was undertaken alongside the main fatherhood study, mobile phones were found to be the most effective way of keeping in touch with the participants whose lives were lived in often 'chaotic' circumstances.

10. I met one of the women several years later and we exchanged email addresses and she arranged to get the book that had been written about the research from the library, and to let me know what she thought about it. She did this and emailed me to say she had enjoyed reading the book but it now all seemed such a long time ago.

11. One mother did contact me to let me know the very sad news that her sister who had been suffering from postnatal depression (a topic which had come up in the interviews) had committed suicide. She also added the equally devastating news that a friend's young child had died in a horrific accident in the participant's garden. Although I could only offer condolences and support, I was glad that I had made it possible for this participant to be able to contact me.

References

Atkinson, P., A. Coffey and S. Delamont. 2007. *Handbook of Ethnography*. London: Sage.

Birch, M. and T. Miller. 2000. 'Inviting Intimacy: the Interview as Therapeutic Opportunity', *International Journal of Social Research Methodology* 3(3): 189–202.

Boulton, M. and M. Parker. (eds). 2007. 'Informed Consent in a Changing Environment', *Social Science and Medicine* 65(11): 2187–2408.

Bryman, A. 2008. *Social Research Methods*. Oxford: Oxford University.

Buckle, J.L., S.C. Dwyer and M. Jackson. 2010. 'Qualitative Bereavement Research: Incongruity between the Perspectives of Participants and Research Ethics Boards', *International Journal of Social Research Methodology* 13(2): 111–125.

Corrigan, O. 2003. 'Empty Ethics: The Problem with Informed Consent', *Sociology of Health and Illness* 25(7): 768–792.

Dermott, E. 2008. *Intimate Fatherhood*. London: Routledge.

Duncombe, J. and J. Jessop. 2012. 'Doing Rapport' and the Ethics of 'Faking Friendship', in T. Miller, M. Birch, M. Mauthner and J. Jessop (eds), *Ethics in Qualitative Research*, 2nd ed. London: Sage.

Hammersley, M. 2009. 'Against the Ethicists: On the Evils of Ethical Regulation', *International Journal of Social Research Methodology* 12(3): 211–225.

Hammersley, M. and P. Atkinson. 2007. *Ethnography: Principles in Practice,* 3rd ed. London: Routledge.

Ison, N.L. 2008. 'Having their Say: Email Interviews for Research Data Collection with People who have Verbal Communication Impairment', *International Journal of Social Research Methodology* 12(2): 161–172.

Iversen, R. 2009. 'Getting Out in Ethnography: A Seldom-told Story', *Qualitative Social Work* 8(1): 9–26.

Johansson, T. and R. Klinth. 2007. 'Caring Fathers. The Ideology of Gender and Equality and Masculine Positions', *Men and Masculinities*. Online First, published on 9 March 2007.

Keats, P.A. 2009. 'Multiple Text Analysis in Narrative Research: Visual, Written and Spoken Stories of Experience', *Qualitative Research* 9(2): 181–195.

Kimmel, M.S., J. Hearn and R.W. Connell. 2004. *Handbook of Studies on Men and Masculinities*. London: Sage.

Lee, R.M. 2004. 'Recording Technologies and the Interview in Sociology, 1920-2000', *Sociology* 38(5): 869–889.

Letherby, G. 2003. *Feminist Research in Theory and Practice*. Buckingham: Open University Press.

Marsden, D. 2004. 'The Changing Experience of Researching Family and Intimate Relationships', *International Journal of Research Methodology* 7(1): 65–71.

Mattingly, C. 2005. 'Towards a Vulnerable Ethics of Research Practice', *Health* 9(4): 453–471.

McLean, A. and A. Leibing. (eds). 2007. *The Shadow Side of Fieldwork*. Oxford: Blackwell Publishing.

Meho, L. 2006. 'Email Interviewing in Qualitative Research: A Methodological Discussion', *Journal of the American Society for Information Science and Technology* 57(10): 1284–1295.

Miller, T. 2005. *Making Sense of Motherhood: A Narrative Approach*. Cambridge: Cambridge University Press.

————.2007. '"Is This What Motherhood is all About?" Weaving Experiences and Discourse through Transition to First-time Motherhood', *Gender & Society* 21: 337–358.

————.2011. *Making Sense of Fatherhood: Gender, Caring and Work*. Cambridge: Cambridge University Press.

Miller, T. and L. Bell. 2012. 'Consenting to What? Issues of Access, Gatekeeping and "Informed" Consent', in T. Miller, M. Birch, M. Mauthner and J. Jessop (eds), *Ethics in Qualitative Research*. 2nd ed. London: Sage.

Miller, T., M. Birch, M. Mauthner and J. Jessop. (eds). 2012. *Ethics in Qualitative Research*. London: Sage.

Miller, T. and M. Boulton. 2007. 'Changing Constructions of Informed Consent: Qualitative Research and Complex Social Worlds', *Social Science & Medicine* 65: 2199–2211.

Morrow, V. 2009. 'The Ethics of Social Research with Children and Families in Young Lives: Practical Experiences', Working Paper No. 53. Oxford University: Young Lives.

O'Neill, O. 2004. 'Accountability, Trust and Informed Consent in Medical Practice and Research', *Clinical Medicine* 4(3): 269–276.

Plantin, L., S. Mansson and J. Kearney. 2003. 'Talking and Doing Fatherhood: On Fatherhood and Masculinity in Sweden and Britain', *Fathering* 1(1): 3–26.

Rapley, T.J. 2001. 'The Art(fullness) of Open-ended Interviewing: Some Considerations on Analysing Interviews', *Qualitative Research* 1(3): 303–323.

Reissman, C.K. 2005. 'Exporting Ethics: A Narrative about Narrative Research in South India', *Health* 9(4): 473–490.

Sinding, C. and J. Aronson. 2003. 'Exposing Failures, Unsettling Accommodations: Tensions in Interview Practice', *Qualitative Review* 3(1): 95–117.

Taylor, S. 2002. *Ethnographic Research: A Reader*. London: Sage.

Thomson, R. and J. Holland. 2003. 'Hindsight, Foresight and Insight: the Challenge of Longitudinal Qualitative Research', *International Journal of Research Methodology* 6(3): 233–244.

Truman, C. 2003. 'Ethics and the Ruling Relations of Research Production', *Sociological Research Online* 8(1).

VanderStaay, S.L. 2005. 'One Hundred Dollars and a Dead Man: Ethical Decision Making in Ethnographic Fieldwork', *Journal of Contemporary Ethnography* 34(4): 371–409.

10

Key Ethical Considerations which Inform the Use of Anonymous Asynchronous Websurveys in 'Sensitive' Research

Em Rundall

Introduction

With internet usage and accessibility ever escalating, both in the UK and internationally, online research methodologies are an increasingly popular avenue of research both within and without the academe. Web research frequently provides a cost-effective, convenient, and in many cases highly efficient method of collecting data, particularly where a sample is widely geographically distributed, or where a high level of participation is sought and economic, temporal, and personnel constraints are in place. A diverse repertoire of online research tools is available, each with their own characteristics and associated ethical and methodological considerations. In some instances, the characteristics of an online research tool may mean it is especially suited for the sample or topic based on ethical or ethically driven methodological grounds.

Anonymous asynchronous websurveys present a modern approach to fieldwork that is particularly useful when focusing on 'sensitive' or potentially taboo topics, where respondents may, if identified, be reluctant to participate, or choose to modify their responses to be perceived more favourably by the researcher. Examples include research into electoral polling and sexual practice (Brady et al. 2004; Mustanski 2001a; Van Eeden-Moorefield et al. 2008). Furthermore, these websurveys are increasingly favoured in research with private or 'at risk' populations, such as sufferers of domestic violence, in a variety of areas of healthcare, and with Lesbian, Gay, Bisexual, Trans, and Queer-identified[1] populations (Dillon 2000; Gordon et al. 2006; Stewart and Williams 2005; Kanzaki et al. 2004; Bull et al. 2004; Koch and Emrey 2001; Riggle et al. 2005; Morris and Rothblum 1999; Whittle et al. 2007; Mustanski 2001a and b). As discussed later in the chapter, the asynchronicity of these websurveys, where the participants' and the researchers' online presence are unrelated, enables increased convenience, privacy, and safety during participation, which may be of particular concern for some participant cohorts. These websurveys provide a flexible platform from which to collect both quantitative and qualitative data, depending on the nature of the investigation. Moreover, with a multitude of user-friendly and inexpensive online research providers available, students and researchers who lack specialized technological knowledge may straightforwardly and securely construct and launch their own online research tools.

However, despite numerous methodological and ethical benefits of online research approaches, these are frequently neglected in higher education training courses. This leads to students and established offline-researchers lacking the knowledge and skills to construct and implement ethically responsible online research. Subsequently, students and researchers may discount or fail to consider an effective, ethically sound methodological approach which is admirably suited to the characteristics of their research. This is further exacerbated by a lack of international, pan-discipline consensus regarding online ethical practices and procedures (Hammersley 2006, in Madge 2007; Brownlow and O'Dell 2002; see also Madge 2007 for multiple examples), although suggestions of online ethical best-practice abound in methodological literature (Sharf 1999; ESOMAR 1999, in Brownlow and O'Dell 2002; Barchard and Williams 2008). These suggestions range from advocating the application of conventional offline ethics to internet research, to constructing updated ethical guidelines tailored specifically to the online research setting (cf. Binik et al. 1999; Brownlow and O'Dell 2002). Accompanying this lack of consensus is what Haggerty (2004: 394) persuasively describes as an 'ethical creep' on the part of research ethics boards. Whiteman (2007: 3), drawing on Haggerty's notion of ethical creep, suggests that due to a misplaced fear of litigation, these panels are unnecessarily reluctant to approve sensitive online research, applying notions of morality and legality instead of ethical soundness.

In this chapter I discuss key issues, benefits and pitfalls in relation to what I suggest are five of the most important ethical considerations when using anonymous, asynchronous websurveys, especially in sensitive research: inequalities of internet accessibility; informed participation and consent; anonymity and confidentiality; safety of participants and researchers; and security of data. I base my discussion on my research experiences, in addition to referring to empirical literature. My experience using websurveys has included research into: transsexual employees' experiences of discrimination and protection in UK workplaces (Rundall 2010; Rundall and Vecchietti 2009); the construction of 'lesbian' and lesbian identity by the British lesbian community (Rundall 2005); staff experiences of age discrimination in higher education (Manfredi 2008); and the taboos, grooming practices and beauty ideals surrounding women's face, head, and body hair in the UK (Rundall 2004). I conclude with a call for increased focus to be placed on ensuring that current and future researchers are taught the necessary skills in order to make ethically and methodologically informed choices about the felicity of online research tools in their investigations.

Inequalities of Internet Accessibility

Internet accessibility and technological knowledge vary internationally, both within and between national populations, as do technological infrastructures and server speeds (see reports compiled by Akamai [e.g. Akamai 2008] for international data). Additionally, the traits of a research sample frequently dictate how an online rather than an offline approach might affect the eventual cohort. It is the combination of the above which determines the feasibility and practicality of online approaches in a given research situation. In light of the above, this subsection focuses on two main considerations. Firstly, it is necessary to consider barriers faced by sections of the population either nationally or internationally, depending on the remit of the research, regarding internet access and the possession of skills required to engage in online research. Secondly, of the proportion of people who do have access to the internet and do possess the necessary skills, one must consider who is likely to agree to participate online, and who will be deterred by the distanced web-forum.

In the UK, for example, whilst sixty-five per cent of households possess an internet connection (ONS 2008), many people's internet usage takes place in a workplace or communal setting, such as in internet cafés or public libraries. Consequently, where access is restricted to public spaces additional ethical considerations come to the fore regarding the *mise en scène* of respondents' participation. This has a notable bearing in research on sensitive or potentially taboo topics, as participation may potentially result in negative repercussions for the participant in a social or professional capacity. For example, employers frequently retain legal access to employees' data-files and email accounts (Keller and Lee 2003: 215; see also Binik et al. 1999; Flanagan 1999; Frankel and Siang 1999), and may monitor websites that employees visit. In public-computer spaces, there is also the potential for a user's screen to be viewed by others. Therefore, a number of issues must be considered to ensure that asynchronous anonymous participation is what it purports to be. A key way to minimize these potential repercussions is to use a generic online research provider or university server rather than one linked too closely to the topic in question. Moreover, ensuring that the websurvey is accessible via URL only, and that prospective participants are furnished with enough information to make an informed decision about whether or not, and indeed where, to log onto the websurvey and participate, may also help to ensure participant privacy and safety (these topics are discussed later in this chapter).

Another accessibility consideration centres on the proportion of national populations whose knowledge or use of computers and the internet is limited or nonexistent, and who thus remain excluded from online research. Therefore, when considering whether to use an online approach, it is necessary to consider who will be excluded from the research, and how this will impact upon generalization of the findings. Whilst under-representation of proportions of society is by no means unique to internet-based research, it is exigent to consider how exclusion will impact upon those less/un-able to participate. For example, Flanagan (1999, in Keller and Lee 2003: 214) reminds researchers that those who are under-represented 'are less likely to reap the benefits of the research'. This is of particular concern in research with populations that are already marginalized by, or within, their wider society, and whose 'voices' or experiences may be less likely to be heard.

A further consideration in web-research concerns those who will choose to participate, and those who will experience a web-based approach as a disincentive, despite the benefits of convenience and anonymity. Whilst some research has suggested that web-respondents are increasingly representative of a cross-section of society (O'Connor and Madge 2001), other research has highlighted the potential for sampling errors and bias (Couper 2000; Bryman 2004; Brady et al. 2004). For example, depending on the target population, previous research has suggested that web-participants tend to be younger, better educated, enjoy greater economic security, and are ethnically unrepresentative of the general population (Couper 2000; Mann and Stewart 2000; O'Connor and Madge 2001; Varoga 2005; Mustanski 2001a; Graham and Marvin 1996).

However, some of these considerations may be offset by intersectional characteristics of a target population. When considering whether to employ a websurvey in my research with LGBTQ populations, I was mindful of their considerable online presence internationally. Furthermore, Jones (1997) advises that minority populations frequently use the internet as an avenue of support. Having employed reflexive on- and offline recruitment approaches,[2] I was able to avoid all but one of the above accessibility issues. In my research projects with transsexual employees and lesbians in the UK there was a significant under-representation of individuals from ethnic minorities, considerably less than the national average. Despite careful consideration of the ethics of accessibility, sampling discrepancy remained. Websurvey research with both similar and wider research focuses has reported comparable under-representation. One could posit that a range of issues are involved, from inequalities of social capital, to notions of propriety regarding research participation and the internet.

Whilst there are multiple barriers to online participation, one must bear in mind that under-representation also occurs in offline research. Providing researchers remain cognizant of: the potential impact an online approach may have on their sample, the traits of the target population, and the overall suitability of a websurvey for the research in question, many sampling discrepancies may be overcome through reflexive tailoring of recruitment procedures. It is an awareness of these issues which enables researchers to take the first steps towards designing and implementing responsible and ethically driven primary research.

Informed Participation and Consent

The process of ensuring informed participation comprises one of the foundations of ethically responsible research, and is no less important in an anonymous online setting than in a non-anonymous offline one. It is particularly important in research which centres on topics that may potentially cause participants to experience discomfort, or even distress. Ensuring that respondents are aware, not only of the overarching theme of the research, but also of the sub-components upon which the questions are based, enables them to weigh up the pros and cons of participation. As ever, care should be taken to pitch information in an accessible manner, and researchers should refrain from using language that privileges individuals with higher educational attainment. This may potentially lead not only to misunderstandings, but to less educated participants feeling that the research is not aimed at them. Use of academic or research jargon should be minimal and, where justifiably used, be clearly defined. When researching a minority group, informed use of jargon and preferred terms is an important and ethically necessary demonstration of respect for the participant sample (for further discussion of this, see Madge 2007; Martin and Meezan 2003). Failure to do so may cause offence, and demonstrate a lack of awareness, or even prejudice.

Achieving informed participation in an asynchronous anonymous websurvey setting is eminently achievable. For example, whereas in an offline setting participants may be provided with an information sheet and then invited to seek clarification, the characteristics of anonymous asynchronous websurveys require an approach which is tailored to the setting. I, and many other proponents, advocate the presentation of a condensed welcome/information page as soon as the website is accessed. It is useful to incorporate an organizational or university logo as well as text cues to define the research affiliations of the project and its legitimacy, and to set the researcher in context. This is necessary where an external or unrelated server or survey platform has been used to host the websurvey. Institutional affiliation and researcher context are both primary means that participants use to quickly decide whether or not to continue forward and read the project information, or whether they feel uncomfortable proceeding. The subsequent information provided should be sufficient to enable respondents to decide whether or not to participate, and should summarily answer the following standard ethical questions:

- Who is conducting the research and why?
- Who else is involved in the project?
- How is it funded?
- Who will be included in the research?
- What level of confidentiality is afforded to participants?
- What, if any, are the legal barriers to this?
- How secure is the data?
- What are the risks and benefits of taking part?
- What incentives, if any, are offered?
- Who can participants contact if they have any questions or concerns?

The page should also specify the participant's right to remit from the study without prejudice or penalty (which can be further enabled by providing an onscreen 'exit' button on each page of the survey). However, unlike non-anonymous instances of data collection, where it may be possible for participants to withdraw from a study at a later stage, in an anonymous setting this becomes unfeasible. As will be discussed in the following subsection, the provision of anonymity may lead participants to respond in a considerably less guarded manner than they otherwise might, which can potentially lead to feelings of overexposure. Therefore, it is crucial that researchers make clear from the start the impossibility of data retraction after submission. Provided participants are aware of this potential 'cost' and related limitation of anonymity, they may approach participation with necessary prudence.

In addition to a condensed welcome/information page, a hyperlink to a more detailed, printer friendly version may also be used to allow participants to retain the information for future reference. Ultimately, however, the key to facilitating informed participation is to present the information in a highly digestible manner. There is a propensity, both on- and offline, for participants to skim-read research information, to skip whole tracts of text, or to fail to comprehend fully the information provided (see Varnhagen et al. 2005 on this issue). The use of attention-directing text-formatting is an excellent way to tackle this (the benefits of which are thoroughly dealt with by literature on the psychology of visual perception; see Poder 2007; Abrams et al. 2007; Holmes et al. 2009). Indeed, text-formatting is useful throughout websurveys. For example, where I chose to date-restrict questions in the main body of my websurvey on transsexual employees' workplace experiences, I found the use of colour-formatting to be an invaluable presentation tool.

A pitfall of asynchronous anonymous websurveys is that there is considerably less room for clarification should a respondent misconstrue the information provided. As previously mentioned, in a face-to-face or interactional/synchronous setting, researchers have greater scope to address this. Dialogue between participants and the researcher is not impossible in websurvey research, but it does present limitations to anonymity. In each of my research projects I have included both on- and offline contact details for myself,[3] my supervisor, and the University Research Ethics Officer. To date, participants have chosen to contact me only via email to ask questions about a websurvey. On balance, I would argue that confidentiality, and indeed, participant anonymity, were maintained despite this email contact. Whilst these individuals' identities, or pseudonyms, and their contact details became momentarily known to me, it signified only an expression of interest in the research. Contact could only be initiated by participants, and remained totally unlinked to any information they may have previously provided, or later chosen to provide, via the websurvey. Furthermore, in order to maintain confidentiality, once I had responded to an enquiry, I deleted both the received and sent emails. Thus, whilst contact does present a limitation to complete anonymity, it is a limitation which may reflexively be recognized and addressed.[4]

Obtaining or inferring consent in an anonymous asynchronous websurvey setting is relatively straightforward. To use a form of consent which could lead to the identification of a participant would be ludicrous where a methodological approach has been used specifically for the anonymity it affords participants. Therefore, in some cases websurvey researchers may choose to assume consent by the participant's submission of their responses at the end of the survey. Other researchers, myself included, favour the use of an 'I agree and wish to proceed' button at the bottom of participant information pages (others include Birnbaum 2000; Mustanski 2001a; Keller and Lee 2003). Keller and Lee (2003) make the notable point that this approach is similar to that used when accepting software downloads, and thus the majority of web-participants will have experience of such consent procedures. I would add to this that the use of an 'I agree' button may also encourage participants to reread participant information if they find they are unclear. However, I acknowledge the questionability of this suggestion, as web-users may be used to disregarding 'terms and conditions' details when agreeing to other web-facilities and downloads, and may exhibit the same behaviour in web-research. A fail-safe in websurvey, and particularly in sensitive websurvey research, is to provide an 'exit survey' button on each page presented, as previously mentioned, so that should respondents become uncomfortable, or wish/need to discontinue participation for any reason, they may do so quickly and easily.

Anonymity and Confidentiality

The level of anonymity that asynchronous websurveys can afford participants is one of the overriding benefits that govern their propriety and increasing popularity in sensitive research. By collecting data anonymously, questions may be asked on topics that, in a non-anonymous setting, might otherwise deter participation, or at the very least result in skewed or potentially unreliable responses. Indeed, online anonymity is noted for its desirable effect upon respondents' social desirability awareness,[5] reducing the extent to which participants seek to manipulate the impression they give to the researcher compared to non-anonymous forums (Agnew and Loving 1998).

However, this reduction in respondents' self-surveillance presents the researcher(s) with certain ethical responsibilities. Firstly, participants may complete questions with a frankness they later regret. I have already mentioned the importance of ensuring participants understand the limitations of data withdrawal after submission, in order to encourage prudent participation and to guard against possible feelings of overexposure. Whilst online interactions take place in a space which is frequently perceived to be suspended from offline frameworks of socio-culturally determined notions of propriety, these notions may regain potency after participation, leading to feelings of distress. This may be pertinent in cases where participants fear identification, post-participation consequences, or where the security of the data they provide is in question. Secondly, although the levels of anonymity provided by anonymous asynchronous websurveys are usually sufficient for the purposes of sensitive research, there are a number of potential limitations and pitfalls to this, which I discuss later in the subsection on data security. Therefore, in order to minimize potential emotional and corporeal repercussions, researchers' responsibilities are twofold. Ensuring that participants are aware of the boundaries to anonymity is incumbent upon the researcher, as is the onus of avoiding the collection of 'identifiers'[6] during the course of participation. Researchers can achieve this by taking an informed and holistic approach to their websurvey construction.

In my research, I have found the sense of distance and security engendered by an anonymous asynchronous websurvey approach to be advantageous in instances where respondents fear potential negative repercussions either socially or professionally. For example, this was an essential consideration in my research with transsexual employees, primarily because of the significant and pervasive levels of discrimination and harassment faced by transsexual and other gender diverse people, notably, but not only, in work spaces (Rundall 2010; Rundall and Vecchietti 2009; Whittle et al. 2007). In addition, many respondents were not 'out' about their trans- identity, status, or history, to more than a few select people at the time of participation, and it was imperative that this confidentiality was maintained and respected. Concomitantly, not all participants who were 'out' would necessarily wish to be linked to accounts of their experiences in the workplace. Furthermore, some participants may have been concerned about the possibility of being identified by their employer, colleagues, family, or friends should the results be published. Thus, in this project, the needs of the target population and the topics under investigation specifically warranted an anonymous and distanced approach. Participants could be secure in the knowledge that I would be unable to deduce their identities from the dataset, and the data would be inaccessible to others who might be able to do so (see Fox et al. 2003).

Given the above information, fledgling researchers could be forgiven for assuming that data collected via anonymous asynchronous websurveys maintains a greater level of honesty and thus a purer sense of validity than is the case with non-anonymous methodological approaches. To do so, however, is to ignore the bipartite repercussions of web-facilitated anonymity, which are concurrently beneficial and potentially detrimental to data validity. Whilst anonymity may encourage legitimate participants to provide honest and uninhibited responses, potentially some members of a research sample may not genuinely meet the inclusion criteria, which may be difficult to discern immediately in an online setting, if at all. Furthermore, respondents may, either intentionally or unintentionally, present an online persona which is quite different to their 'real' offline persona (see Rheingold 2000), potentially bringing the validity of the data into dispute.

Illegitimate participation occurs for a number of reasons, including the desire to obtain incentives offered as part of participation, or as prank-based or malicious sabotage (see Keller and Lee 2003 and Mustanski 2001a for wider discussion of these issues). In my experience, prank-based and malicious sabotage is, to a great extent, linked to the topic or group being researched. In the web-survey I conducted on lesbian identity construction I received a number of sexually based responses from men who thought their responses were humorous or even seductive. I also received a number of threatening and violent responses from homophobic individuals. Malicious sabotage may be prevented somewhat by using direct or focused avenues for advertising one's research study. For example, due to the pervasiveness of transphobia and related violence (Rundall and Vecchietti 2009; Whittle et al. 2007; Martin and Meezan 2003; Levi 2003; Riggle et al. 2005), and in view of my experiences in the lesbian identity project, I chose to advertise my research focusing on transsexual employees only via relevant advocacy, support groups, and networking organizations. This proved successful, as no 'saboteurs' were detectable in the ensuing data (see also Mustanski 2001a, Morris and Rothblum 1999 on the issue of sabotage). It is important to be cognizant of safe practice; for instance if the URLs for online research tools are advertised in an unrestricted manner, they may be circulated by individuals beyond the inclusion criteria, which may lead to increased levels of prank-based or malicious sabotage. I discuss these issues again in the following section on participant and researcher safety.

In anonymous asynchronous websurvey interactions it is impossible to validate the authenticity of the persona or self-reported characteristics presented (see Varnhagen et al. 2005 on this issue). Indeed, there may be significant discrepancies between who the online participant presents themselves to be, and who they actually are. However, this issue of discrepancy is not exclusive to online research and can also affect face-to-face and vocal research interactions. Additionally, it may be difficult to detect duplication, errors of self-selection (Brady et al. 2004; Koch and Emrey 2001; Dillman 2000) or misunderstandings which may arise in distanced research, and it is imperative that the impact of these be considered, both when deciding to use an online approach, and when evaluating the possible impact these variables may have on the data collected. Mustanski (2001a) persuasively asserts that to some extent all research, both on- and offline, and indeed inter-personal interactions, are affected by the issues of lying, sabotage, and the individual's awareness of social desirability, regardless of the methodological approaches utilized.

Indeed, the potential fluidity of representation of persona presented an intriguing conundrum in my research in terms of the multi-faceted nature of identity construction and interactional recognition, where the divide between personas and externally accepted identity is of key relevance. These considerations informed the research design of my various websurvey-based research projects, where I employed both quantitative and qualitative questions for key topics under investigation to enable me to compare and if possible, triangulate, the information, and thus provide a degree of complementarity. However, I recognize that the epistemologically-driven methodological allegiances which frequently permeate research processes, combined with the construction of methodological fiefdoms (Tinsley 2005) and ensuing paradigm wars (Oakley 1999; Kelle 2006), may make a mixed-method approach methodologically undesirable (Rundall 2010). Nevertheless, I argue that, providing researchers remain reflexive and holistic in their research design and later analysis, the many benefits of online anonymity frequently outweigh the potential pitfalls.

Safety of Participants and Researchers

The safety of both participant and researcher comprises a significant consideration in ethically responsible research. Safety considerations are frequently determined by the methodological tools employed, the research focus, and the target sample. As well as maintaining their own safety, researchers are responsible for ensuring that appropriate steps are taken to maintain their participants' emotional and physical safety, particularly where the research focus is of a sensitive or potentially taboo nature, and where the research sample may consequently be considered at risk. It is imperative that researchers consider how participation will impact on the wellbeing of respondents during and following participation. This should include participants' emotional wellbeing, their social position, and any future interactions with gatekeepers or others involved in the research. Antagonists may expend a surprising amount of energy in communicating their negative views, or in attempting to sabotage the research. Therefore, where research is of a sensitive or taboo nature, or the characteristics of the participant sample have the potential to attract negative or unwanted attention, researchers need to maintain a reflexive and informed approach.

Anonymous asynchronous websurveys offset many of the physical risks applicable to offline or non-anonymous forums, and give the participants themselves the power and responsibility to guard their own physical safety. Distanced asynchronicity allows respondents to choose a time and place which is convenient, safe, and private for them to log on to the internet and participate (numerous websurvey proponents discuss the benefits of this, including O'Neil 2001; O'Connor and Madge 2001; Dillon 2000; Mann and Stewart 1999, in O'Connor and Madge 2001). Despite these benefits, researchers should remain cognizant of the impact that such self-determined participation may have on the validity of the data (Dillman 2000; Rheingold 2000; Joinson 1999 in Mustanski 2001a), because participation could occur when the respondent is tired, distracted, or intoxicated (Mustanski 2001a). Nevertheless, I suggest that these limitations can and do apply to other methodological approaches. Indeed, even in face-to-face interactions it may be difficult to fully discern a participant's level of focus.

As I have highlighted earlier, the anonymity provided by a websurvey may also somewhat lessen potential emotional risks, although participants may still have concerns. For example, respondents may justifiably experience apprehension about reprisals if they participate. Concerns may arise surrounding the legitimacy of the research, the motive of the researcher(s), the utilization of the data, and potential security breaches regarding access to identifiers. These concerns can be assuaged by a respectful and thorough approach to informed participation. It is also useful to provide contact details to enable participants to discuss any concerns with the research team prior to participation, although, as previously mentioned, communication which involves a degree of identification may discourage dialogue. As a compromise, in my websurveys I provide a space for participants to leave anonymous feedback. Whilst this is not a dialogue, it does provide respondents with an outlet should they feel uncomfortable about making email or postal contact, as discussed earlier in this chapter.

In order to proceed responsibly when designing and instigating fieldwork, investigators should possess a basis of empirically derived knowledge of the topics and populations under focus. In research which centres on topics that could invoke distress or discomfort, it is imperative that care is taken not to ask unnecessarily sensitive or ethically reckless questions. For example, Chen et al. (2004: 160) emphatically remind researchers that to do so may open 'old wounds to a significant extent'. The suitability of topics or questions should be reviewed through an ethical lens to determine the impact they may have on participants, both during and after data collection. Participating in research can be therapeutic and cathartic for some respondents (see Birch and Miller 2000 for an extensive discussion on this issue), and indeed may be one of the factors on which individuals base their decision to participate. However, not all participants find the research experience positive, and Stern (2003) makes the notable suggestion that a researcher and their supervisory or ethics team must contemplate their legal, ethical, and moral responsibilities. Courses of action need to be considered in case the researcher is exposed to upsetting information, or responses, such as threats of self-harm, suicide, or harm to others. I would suggest that the possibility of receiving 'upsetting' responses in a research setting, and the researcher's approach to these, is an issue which can be neglected or underemphasized in academic training. Indeed, fledgling researchers may initially fail to consider the possibility of negative reactions, and dialogue needs to take place between the researcher and their supervisor regarding appropriate and necessary action. In anonymous online research, responding to threats of self-harm, suicide, or harm to others may be distinctly problematic due to the unknown identities of participants. Therefore, in combination with an attention-directing, clear participant information page, as previously discussed, it is vital that the contact details of relevant support organizations are supplied in the 'welcome' and 'debriefing' material/web pages to enable participants to pursue this avenue should they require it. Whilst highlighting these avenues of support, it is also beneficial for researchers to specify the level of support or information they are qualified to provide participants in relation to the research issues, as well as the limitations to this. It is crucial to clarify this, in order to prevent participants from wrongly assuming that the researcher has greater power, influence, or ability to support them than is actually the case.

Researchers in the social sciences face a variety of risks when undertaking research. An asynchronous websurvey approach alleviates many of the potential hazards participants and researchers may be subject to in synchronous and offline research. In an online research setting, risks for the researcher relate primarily to inappropriate circulation of contact and project details. This frequently results in nuisance emails or spam, which, in my experience, appear to stem from an individual/participant placing the 'point of contact' email address on to a mailing list. In some instances this may proceed further. For example, Madge (2007: 664) raises the potential for researchers to be subject to 'cyberstalking', which, although rare, may have a serious impact.

As previously mentioned, my research into lesbian identity construction attracted much prank-based and malicious sabotage. To combat this in my subsequent research I developed a set of simple and effective safety procedures. Initially, careful consideration must be given to the routes chosen to advertise requests for participants. In my most recent research, which focused on transsexual employees, I approached only trans-friendly organizations to prevent prejudiced individuals trying to 'sabotage' the research. This meant that individuals outside the target population would be less likely to become aware of the research, thus minimizing potential interference from undesirable parties. Interference is a problem frequently faced in LGBTQ and other sensitive research, and is raised time and again in the methodological literature (for example, Mustanski 2001a; Morris and Rothblum 1999). To prevent my departmental email address from being circulated widely in the public domain I constructed an email account specifically for the study in question. In addition, I supplied the departmental postal address for offline correspondence, which I chose to make obtainable only by logging onto the participant information page of the web-survey: this approach successfully eliminated less focused pranksters and saboteurs.

Security of Data

Data security is a multi-faceted issue which transects all aspects of primary research, from the commencement of the websurvey construction and data collection, to analysis, and lastly, to both short- and long-term storage. Anonymous asynchronous websurveys confer numerous ethical and methodological benefits. Despite these, online data collection presents various risks with regard to data security which are not applicable to offline research. Seasoned online researchers warn of the ever developing threat to the security of electronic data (Spinello 2001), and the speed with which security measures can become obsolete (Keller and Lee 2003). This is further exacerbated by the researcher's potentially limited understanding of the complexity and nuances of web-based data security.

The issue of data security needs to be addressed from the outset: this begins in the research design phase of the primary research. It is here that researchers lay the foundations of the anonymity which comprises one of the distinguishing features of the websurvey approach. As is elaborated later in this section, maintaining anonymity and data security in an anonymous asynchronous web-setting is not solely concerned with foiling external attempts to access data, it also includes maintaining the safety and confidentiality of participants should a third party succeed in gaining unauthorized access. Therefore, it is at this stage that researchers must ensure that the questions neither require nor encourage participants to provide identifying information. This is both ethically and methodologically advantageous, because to fail to do so may result in respondent anxiety and could ultimately deter their continued participation.

The next stage is to ensure that the websurvey itself is secure, and that no one other than the researcher is able to edit the questions, survey format, security settings, or data once collected. Administrative tools, editing functions, and the data reservoir should be password protected, regardless of the platform used to create and launch the survey, for example, if it is an internal (affiliated university/organization) or external provider and server. When using an external platform provider it is of utmost importance, before the survey is constructed, launched, and any data collected, that researchers ensure they, rather than the survey-platform operator, retain ownership of the questionnaire, data, and intellectual property rights. It is also prudent to enquire about the provisions the platform provider has in place to back up and secure subscribers' data and surveys should their servers suffer technological difficulties.

The implications of data security can vary for different participant groups and varying research topics, particularly where the research is of a sensitive, personal or illegal nature (see Madge 2007; Brownlow and O'Dell 2002). Therefore, the issue of data security presents an ethical conundrum for researchers, particularly given the propensity for participants to be less self-policing or restrained in their online responses. This has implications both in terms of identification and the respondents' wellbeing. During the process of gaining informed consent, the researcher must inform participants of the potential limitations to data security in a way that does not deter participation all together (see Brownlow and O'Dell 2002 for a persuasive discussion of this issue). Researchers should be mindful of the global nature of the internet. The impact of the laws and customs of the territory or country from which participants are drawn will also impact upon data security, and potentially, participant safety. The extent to which respondents' internet usage is potentially monitored, and the topic or website restrictions in place, should all be considered when determining the propriety and feasibility of a project on an ethical level. Moreover, Kramarae (1995, in Brownlow and O'Dell 2002: 687) adds the caveat that, ultimately, whilst researchers can conscientiously promise confidentiality and security with regards to methods of data process and storage, they cannot promise that data is immune to unauthorized third-party access. It is therefore an expedient stratagem to ensure that identifiers are not collected during the course of participation. Despite all these potential security pitfalls, researchers do collect data which, for research purposes, may be considered to be both private and anonymous.

As ever, where identifying details have been collected as part of the research process, researchers themselves are subject to the possibility of being subpoenaed to reveal the identity of their participants (see Brownlow and O'Dell 2002; Binik et al. 1999; Keller and Lee 2003). Additionally, the risk of hacking or tracing by government, security, or civilian parties, regardless of encryption and other measures in place, remains ever present (see O'Dochartaigh 2002, in Madge 2007; Binik et al. 1999; Keller and Lee 2003). If data is intercepted, any identifying details contained may be linked to other sites which, in combination, may reveal the identity of the participant or provide further information to exact that result. 'WebCrawlers', programmes which 'automatically find and download web-pages' (Thelwall and Stuart 2006: 1771), and thus potentially sensitive or private information, are an integral component of this threat to data security. These programmes remain largely unnoticed by web-users, and are increasingly used for more suspect intentions such as by spam creators, in addition to commercial search engines (Thelwall and Stuart

2006 discuss this issue in detail). However, where data lacks identifying material, the risk of participants being identified in connection with their responses, or at all, is significantly diminished.

Once the data have been downloaded, and throughout the analysis period, its security must be maintained, regardless of the format. Academic or institutional procedures on electronic and physical data storage and academic integrity should set out the specific guidelines for affiliated researchers. However, standard good practice is simply achieved through password protection in electronic formats, which extends to back-up copies. Physical copies must be maintained in a secure fashion, for example, in a lockable filing cabinet. Where a participant has made contact, either via email or post, any headers or identifying information should be removed. Once complete, the main body of the correspondence may be retained in the same manner as the data itself, with any ingoing or outgoing emails deleted from the researchers' email account. However, even after the process of de-identification has been completed, correspondence should be stored separately to any websurvey data or analysis for good measure. Each institution's research data storage policy should set out the length of time that data must be retained after the study has been completed.

It is useful for researchers, including students, to contemplate how the security of research data would be maintained if they were unable, for example through long-term illness or death, to maintain it themselves (a consideration detailed in Keller and Lee 2003). Whilst such precautions are standard practice in medically-affiliated disciplines such as psychology, this is not the case in many other social science disciplines, and is thus unlikely to be foremost in many researcher's minds. However, this scenario does illustrate the importance of security with regard to data of a sensitive nature, and its enduring security requirements. Anonymous data pose significantly less risk to a participant than in an identified setting. Nevertheless, I suggest that awareness of the need to ensure enduring data security would benefit researchers, particularly those at an early stage of their research career, even where the immediate research project does not warrant such levels of security. I believe that contemplation of this issue would help to increase a reflexive consideration of the ethics of data security, and help fledgling researchers in particular to approach their investigations through an ethical lens.

Conclusions

In this chapter I have sought to illustrate the ethical and methodological appropri-ateness of anonymous asynchronous websurveys as a modern approach to sensitive fieldwork. I have suggested that web-research is an area that can be easily neglected in ethical and methodological training, and have indicated that this chapter seeks to encourage fledgling web-researchers, as well as those already in the field, to consider anonymous asynchronous web-surveys in their future investigations. I have drawn on both my own web-research experience, and relevant empirical literature, to high-light what I suggest are some of the key issues, benefits, and pitfalls in relation to five key ethical considerations, and the ways in which researchers may address these. I have asserted that anonymous asynchronous websurveys present a cost-effective and convenient methodological tool which is straightforward to design and implement, even for those researchers who possess limited technological knowledge. Furthermore, I have argued that ethically and methodologically, the anonymity and asynchronicity engendered by web-surveys make this research tool an excellent choice when collecting data from hidden or widely geographically dispersed populations. Additionally, I have demonstrated that this modern approach to fieldwork is also eminently suitable for research where, in an identified/synchronous setting, the sensitive or potentially taboo nature of the research topic may deter participation or result in skewed responses due to participant awareness of social desirability. However, future research is needed to address a number of outstanding issues. For example, the field, and indeed participants, would benefit from a means of secure and completely anonymous dialogue between participant and researcher that is not email or post-based. Additionally, where a sensitive research project incorporates a broad participant focus and requires a wide circulation, additional consideration is needed with regards to the deterrence of saboteurs and pranksters. Lastly, research is needed to determine why individuals from ethnic minorities are frequently underrepresented in web-research, and how this may be addressed.

1. Frequently referred to by the acronym LGBTQ. 'Trans' incorporates all transsexual, transgender, and other gender-diverse people.
2. I used on- and offline sampling approaches with key LGBTQ centred organizations. Additionally, I encouraged further snowball sampling in an attempt to access prospective participants who were not linked directly to formal community networks.
3. As discussed later, I construct email accounts specifically for individual research projects.
4. If a researcher possessed the web-design knowledge necessary to design the following, or found a websurvey platform that provided such a facility, completely anonymous asynchronous dialogue would be possible. For example, participants could enter their query or concern anonymously in to a secure online dialogue space linked to the websurvey, but retained separately from the data. Once the participant had submitted their response they could be provided with a temporary identification number linked to that question, and visible only via that number (and so not visible to other participants). Queries would then be viewed by the researcher. Using the identification number, participants could log back in at their leisure to view the researcher's response. This process could be repeated as necessary, with dialogue threads remaining linked by the initial identification number.
5. Where respondents mediate their responses in light of social conventions in order to be perceived favourably by others.
6. Information that may directly, or indirectly in conjunction with other 'identifiers', reveal the identity of an individual.

References

Abrams, A.B., J.M. Hillis and D.H. Brainard. 2007. 'The Relation Between Color Discrimination and Color Constancy: When Is Optimal Adaptation Task Dependent?', *Neural Computation* 19(10): 2610–37.

Agnew, C. and T. Loving. 1998. 'The Role of Social Desirability in Self-reported Condom Use Attitude and Intentions', *AIDS and Behavior* 2(3): 229–39.

Akamai. 2008. *Akamai Report: The State of the Internet.* http://www.akamai.com/stateoftheinternet/, accessed March 2009.

Barchard, K.A. and J. Williams. 2008. 'Practical Advice for Conducting Ethical Online Experiments and Questionnaires for United States Psychologists', *Behavior Research Methods* 40(4): 1111–28.

Binik, Y.M., K. Mah and S. Kiesler. 1999. 'Ethical Issues in Conducting Sex Research on the Internet', *Journal of Sex Research* 36(1): 82–90.

Birch, M. and T. Miller. 2000. 'Inviting Intimacy: the Interview as Therapeutic Opportunity', *International Journal of Social Research Methodology* 3(3):189–202.

Birnbaum, M.H. 2000. *The Online Laboratory: Experimental Research on the Internet. Psychological Experiments on the Internet B2 – Psychological Experiments on the Internet.* San Diego, CA: Academic Press.

Brady, D., M. Fiorina and S. Iyengar. 2004. 'A New Frontier in Polling', *Hoover Digest* 1, http://www.hooverdigest.org/041/brady.html.

Brownlow, C. and L. O'Dell. 2002. 'Ethical Issues for Qualitative Research in On-line Communities', *Disability and Society* 17(6): 685–94.

Bryman, A. 2004. *Social Research Methods.* Second edn. Oxford: Oxford University Press.

Bull, S.S. et al. 2004. 'Recruitment and Retention of an Online Sample for an HIV Prevention Intervention Targeting Men Who Have Sex with Men: the Smart Sex Quest Project', *AIDS Care* 16(8): 931–43.

Chen, S.S., G.J. Hall and M.D. Johns. 2004. 'Research Paparazzi in Cyberspace: the Voices of the Researched', in M.D. Johns, S.S. Chen and G.J. Hall (eds), *Online Social Research: Methods, Issues, and Ethics.* New York, NY: Peter Lang, pp. 157–75.

Couper, M. 2000. 'Web Surveys: A Review of Issues and Approaches', *Public Opinion Quarterly* 64: 464–94.

Dillman, D.A. 2000. *Mail and Internet Surveys: The Tailored Design Method.* 2nd edn. New York, NY: John Wiley and Sons.

Dillon, J. 2000. 'Battered Women to Tell Their Stories Via Email', *The Independent on Sunday*, 30 January 2000, 3.

ESOMAR. 1999. 'ESOMAR Guideline. Conducting Marketing and Opinion Research Using the Internet', *Journal of the Market Research Society* 41: 439–41.

Flanagan, P. 1999. 'Cyberspace: The Final Frontier?', *Journal of Business Ethics* 19(1): 115–22.

Fox, J., C. Murray and A. Warm. 2003. 'Conducting Research Using Web-based Questionnaires: Practical, Methodological, and Ethical Considerations', *International Journal of Social Research Methodology* 6(2): 167–80.

Frankel, M.S. and S. Siang. 1999. *Ethical and Legal Aspects of Human Subjects Research on the Internet.* Washington, DC: American Association for the Advancement of Science. http://www.aaas.org/spp/dspp/sfrl/projects/intres/main.htm, accessed March 2009.

Gordon, J.S. et al. 2006. 'Successful Participant Recruitment Strategies for an Online Smokeless Tobacco Cessation Program', *Nicotine and Tobacco Research* 8: 35–41.

Graham, S. and S. Marvin. 1996. *Telecommunications and the City: Electronic Spaces, Urban Places*. London: Routledge.

Haggerty, K.D. 2004. 'Ethics Creep: Governing Social Science Research in the Name of Ethics', *Qualitative Sociology* 27(4): 391–414.

Hammersley, M. 2006. 'Are Ethics Committees Ethical?', *Qualitative Researcher* 2: 4–8.

Holmes, A. et al. 2009. 'Neurophysiological Evidence for Categorical Perception of Color', *Brain and Cognition* 69(2): 426–34.

Joinson, A. 1999. 'Social Desirability, Anonymity, and Internet-based Questionnaires', *Behavior Research Methods, Instruments, and Computers: a Journal of the Psychonomic Society, Inc* 31(3): 433–38.

Jones, S.G. (ed.). 1997. *Virtual Culture: Identity and Communication in Cybersociety*. London: Sage.

Kanzaki, H. et al. 2004. 'Development of Web-based Qualitative and Quantitative Data Collection Systems: Study on Daily Symptoms and Coping Strategies Among Japanese Rheumatoid Arthritis Patients', *Nursing and Health Sciences* 6(3): 229–36.

Kelle, U. 2006. 'Combining Qualitative and Quantitative Methods in Research Practice: Purposes and Advantages', *Qualitative Research in Psychology* 3(4): 293–311.

Keller, H.B. and S. Lee. 2003. 'Ethical Issues Surrounding Human Participants Research Using the Internet', *Ethics and Behavior* 13(3): 211.

Koch, N.S. and J.A. Emrey. 2001. 'The Internet and Opinion Measurement: Surveying Marginalized Populations', *Social Science Quarterly (Blackwell Publishing Limited)* 82(1): 131.

Kramarae, C. 1995. 'A Backstage Critique of Virtual Reality', in S. Jones (ed.), *Cybersociety: Computer-mediated Communication and Community*. Thousand Oaks, CA: Sage, pp. 36–56.

Levi, J. 2003. 'Protections for Transgender Employees', *Human Rights: Journal of the Section of Individual Rights and Responsibilities* 30(3): 12–13.

Madge, C. 2007. 'Developing a Geographers' Agenda for Online Research Ethics', *Progress in Human Geography* 31(5): 654–74.

Manfredi, S. 2008. *Developing Good Practice in Managing Age Diversity in the Higher Education Sector: An Evidence Based Approach*. Oxford: Oxford Brookes University.

Mann, C. and F. Stewart. 1999. 'Internet Methodologies and Qualitative Research', Unpublished conference paper, BSA, Glasgow, April 1999.

———. 2000. *Internet Communication and Qualitative Research: A Handbook for Researching Online (New Technologies and Social Research Series)*. London: Sage Publications.

Martin, J.I. and W. Meezan. 2003. 'Applying Ethical Standards to Research and Evaluations Involving Lesbian, Gay, Bisexual, and Transgender Populations', *Journal of Gay and Lesbian Social Services* 15(1/2): 181–201.

Morris, J.F. and E.D. Rothblum. 1999. 'Who Fills Out a "Lesbian" Questionnaire?', *Psychology of Women Quarterly* 23(3): 537–57.

Mustanski, B.S. 2001a. '*Getting Wired*: Exploiting the Internet for the Collection of Valid Sexuality Data', *Journal of Sex Research* 38(4): 292.

———. 2001b. *Semantic Heterogeneity in the Definition of 'Having Sex' for Homosexuals*. Manuscript in review. Bloomington, IN: Department of Psychology, Indiana University.

Oakley, A. 1999. 'Paradigm Wars: Some Thoughts on a Personal and Public Trajectory', *International Journal of Social Research Methodology* 2(3): 247–54 (248).

O'Connor, H. and C. Madge. 2001. 'Cyber-Mothers: Online Synchronous Interviewing Using Conferencing Software', *Sociological Research Online* 5(4). www.socresonline.org. uk/5/4/o'connor.html, accessed June 2008.

O'Dochartaigh, N. 2002. *The Internet Research Handbook. A Practical Guide for Students and Researchers in the Social Sciences.* London: Sage.

O'Neil, D. 2001. 'Analysis of Internet Users' Level of Online Privacy Concerns', *Social Science Computer Review* 19(1): 17–31.

ONS (Office for National Statistics). 2008. *Internet Access.* [Online]. http://www.statistics. gov.uk/CCI/nugget.asp?ID=8, accessed January 2009.

Poder, E. 2007. 'Effect of Colour Pop-out on the Recognition of Letters in Crowding Conditions', *Psychological Research* 71(6): 641–45.

Rheingold, H. 2000. *The Virtual Community: Homesteading at the Electronic Frontier.* (Rev. ed.). Cambridge, Mass.; London: MIT Press

Riggle, E.D.B. et al. 2005. 'Online Surveys for BGLT Research: Issues and Techniques', *Journal of Homosexuality* 49(2): 1–21.

Rundall, E. 2004. *A Study of Women's Face, Head, and Body Hair, Focussing on its Relation to Gender Distinction and Gender Identity: Seeking to Question Related Attitudes Which Reflect Social Trends and Taboos Bsc.* (Hons) thesis, Oxford: Oxford Brookes University.

———. 2005. *What is a 'Lesbian'?: The Deconstructive Constructive of the Category 'Lesbian' by the British 'Lesbian' Community.* MA thesis, Oxford: Oxford Brookes University.

———. 2010. *Transsexual People in UK Workplaces: An Analysis of Transmens' and Transwomens' Experiences.* PhD Thesis, Oxford: Oxford Brookes University.

Rundall, E. and V. Vecchietti. 2009. '(In)Visibility in the Workplace: The Experiences of Trans-Employees in the UK', in S. Hines and T. Sanger (eds), *Transgender-Identities: Towards a Social Analysis of Gender-Diversity.* London: Routledge, pp. 127-150.

Sharf, B. 1999. 'Beyond Netiquette: the Ethics of Doing Naturalistic Discourse Research on the Internet', in S. Jones (ed.), *Doing Internet Research. Critical Issues and Methods for Examining the Net.* Thousand Oaks, CA: Sage, pp. 243–57.

Spinello, R. 2001. 'Code and Moral Values in Cyberspace', *Ethics and Information Technology* 3(2): 137–50.

Stern, S.R. 2003. 'Encountering Distressing Information in Online Research: a Consideration of Legal and Ethical Responsibilities', *New Media and Society* 5(2): 249–66.

Stewart, K. and M. Williams. 2005. 'Researching Online Populations: the Use of Online Focus Groups for Social Research', *Qualitative Research* 5(4): 395–416.

Thelwall, M. and D. Stuart. 2006. 'Web Crawling Ethics Revisited: Cost, Privacy, and Denial of Service', *Journal of the American Society for Information Science and Technology* 57(13): 1771–79.

Tinsley, C.H. 2005. 'The Heart of Darkness: Advice on Navigating Cross-Cultural Research', *International Negotiation* 10(1): 183–92.

Van Eeden-Moorefield, B., C.M. Proulx and K. Pasley. 2008. 'A Comparison of Internet and Face-to-Face (FTF) Qualitative Methods in Studying the Relationships of Gay Men', *Journal of GLBT Family Studies* 4(2): 181–204.

Varnhagen, C.K. et al. 2005. 'How Informed is Online Informed Consent?'; *Ethics and Behavior* 15(1): 37–48.

Varoga, C. 2005. 'Internet Polling Perils: Wonky Policy Papers or Concise Slogans?', *Campaigns and Elections.* http://findarticles.com/p/articles/mi_m2519/is_/ai_n11841402, accessed July 2008.

Whiteman, E. 2007. 'Just Chatting': Research Ethics and Cyberspace', *International Journal of Qualitative Methods* 6(2): 1–9.

Whittle, S., L. Turner and M. Al-Alami. 2007. *Engendered Penalties: Transgender and Transsexual People's Experiences of Inequality and Discrimination.* The Equalities Review.

11
Covering our Backs, or Covering all Bases? An Ethnography of URECs

Jeremy MacClancy

'A few days ago I received from Canada, as a curiosity, the questionnaires, forms, and other papers that must now be filled out in multiple copies before a "band" (that is the official term) of Indians in British Columbia will grant anyone permission to do fieldwork. They will not tell you a myth unless the informant receives written assurance that he retains literary ownership, with all the legal consequences it entails. You must admit that this meddlesome bureaucracy, this mania for paperwork – a caricature of our own customs – has eliminated much of the old attraction of fieldwork!'

(Claude Lévi-Strauss, in Lévi-Strauss and Eribon 1991: 44)

Until relatively recently British social scientists were left to their own ethical devices, as were their French counterparts. It was assumed that, while researching, they would do no harm, that they would uphold a broadly humanitarian ethos. These days, those attitudes are often considered out of date. In the last decade UK academics have become obliged to submit research plans to the ethical review board of their employing institution, known as a University Research Ethics Committee (UREC). Causal factors for this change include: the ever-more widespread discourse and implementation in Europe of human rights legislation; British research councils' increasing concerns about accountability; UK emulation of similar practice in the USA; British universities' rising fears about the possibility of litigation, and also of complainants not just turning to the courts, but to the press as well.

In the United States, Institutional Review Boards (IRBs) dedicated to the ethical regulation of academic research, came into being in the mid-1970s (Shweder 2006: 507). Criticism of their practice has since become legion (Schrag 2010; on Canada, Van den Hoonaard 2011). Critics have repeatedly accused IRBs of misapplying an ethical model derived from medical experimentation to social scientific research. This mismatch is particularly acute with fieldwork-based research, which is by definition open-ended, unpredictable, contingent. Unlike those involved in fixed-design research, fieldworkers do not control the activities they investigate; they do not direct, but rather follow those they study. Some also consider the IRB model of research far too narrow, and not taking account of a range of alternatives (Denzin and Giardina 2007: 20; Ellis 2007: 209–10). Further questions are raised about whether one can, and should, differentiate between research activities and personal life, and if so, where would or should the border lie (Katz 2006: 500). Others have argued the present workings of IRBs create a significant financial burden 'with virtually no counterbalancing good': they call for the exemption of minimal-risk research from IRB review (Kim, Ubel, and De Vries 2009: 535). On top of that, some more politically engaged social scientists judge the supposed neutrality of IRB criteria as but a thin mask for imperialism (e.g. Christians 2007: 55). According to some, concern about the apparent obstacles to IRB approval of research has led to an uncomfortable culture of evasion or dishonour:

> When I judge that the issue of what one might call 'institutional honor' is highly salient – that is, when public recognition that research took place without IRB approval stands a high likelihood of providing serious, negative notoriety, for example, in the study of drugs – I assume that it is prudent to seek IRB approval. When the converse is so, I am – and, I suggest, others are – likely to decide to let things slide. (Bradburd 2006: 495)

Others adopt a more cynical pose, ensuring their applications achieve a barely minimal compliance with IRB requirements (Schwandt 2007: 92). Critics also argue that present practice appears more concerned with protecting the university rather than the subject. As such, they are 'more an impediment than a boon' (Bradburd 2006: 497). The stated, primary function of an IRB is to fulfil the ethical requirements of federally funded research; however many university hierarchies have been accused of extending this regulatory concern to a broadening swathe of research, no matter how funded, or even whether funded. Critics term this worrying phenomenon 'mission creep' (Lederman 2006b; Shweder 2006). In sum, the incorporation of social scientific research within the remit of IRBs has led to widespread disquiet and in some quarters to active, creative resistance.

In the UK, some social scientists had high hopes for the newly-established URECs. In 2004 an early review of their emerging practice stated that ethical scrutiny mechanisms foster 'better dialogue' and 'would not be so independent of the researchers that they would risk becoming bureaucratic and unresponsive' (Tinker and Coomber 2004: 7). Today, these attitudes seem at best halcyon, at worst innocent of how committees function. In this chapter I compare the workings of URECs at two very different British universities. So far no anthropological work has been carried out on the practice of British URECs. Moreover, as the American anthropologist Rena Lederman underlined in her introduction to an 'American Ethnologist' Forum devoted to discussion of ethical regulation, 'a comparative perspective would help clarify the specificity of the US case'. To her, such a comparison might inform the debate between the present system of IRBs and the right of academic freedom, bolstered by the First Amendment (Lederman 2006a: 479). At the same time, a study of URECs should highlight what aspects of their practice appear to be functioning in the UK, in an at least satisfactory manner, and what is causing agitated debate.

A Tale of Two URECs

In 2009, after some negotiation, I managed to obtain permission from the UREC of my home institution to study two URECs: one in a prestigious, well-established British university with a confederate structure, which I will call University A; the other in a leading new university, which had converted from polytechnic status in the early 1990s, which I call University B. In the first half of 2009, I endeavoured to interview as many members, whether internal or external, of both URECs as possible. I was generously granted access to a meeting of the UREC at University A.

University A

The UREC at University A was established in 2002. According to its inaugural chair, it 'took quite a long time to set up a workable system'. Very few models of ethical review were at the time available for research in the social sciences, and the Committee's members were particularly keen not to reproduce the overburdensome approach of medical ethical review: special issues of the British Medical Journal had recently given voice to the great discontent of medical researchers over the increasing onus on them caused by government regulations. Since University A is research-intensive and thus the potential amount of regulation was very great, it was decided to establish a university-wide committee which would develop policy and oversee the functioning of three divisional URECs, each charged with ethical review of the disciplines within its remit: medical sciences, social sciences, overseas medical research. To prevent the overloading of these bodies, it was agreed that undergraduate research would be ethically reviewed within their respective departments. Undergraduate simulations and exercises on humans, so long as the students were told to carry them out by their teachers, were designated as part of the educational process and therefore not requiring ethical regulation.

An initial question concerned the limits of research. In other words, when is an academic off-duty? Some scholars in the humanities on the Committee pointed out that most scientists go to their lab, lock up at the end of day, and go home. In contrast, as one historian put it, 'We're never civilians'. A further question was whether or not to produce a common form for all proposed research. One member, a visiting professor in medical ethics from a country where the academic culture of ethical regulation was already much more developed, wanted the highest level of ethical review for all research. Others responded, 'That won't work. There is too much research being done in my department.' The respondents saw themselves as realists, and him as an idealist. Generally, members of the UREC recognized key differences between medical and social scientific research, i.e. that much of the latter carried no or a very low degree of risk. For instance, despite their initial wishes and efforts, Committee members were unable to produce a unified protocol for work with children; one had to be derived for medical researchers, one for those in the social sciences. The protocols which were derived have been revised several times. Members expect to have to revise them in the future, in response to comments from users.

One general principle formulated by the Committee was that of matching the level of scrutiny to the level of risk. They wished to minimize paperwork and were desirous not to put obstacles in the way of research. Most thought making ethical review onerous would only breed a culture of non-compliance. Committee members wanted their research-active colleagues to work together with them; otherwise the committee's efforts would defeat their own point. An external member of the UREC, who had previously managed a secondary educational institution, saw the problem in terms of leadership, or of proselytizing the message in the right way: 'getting people at lower levels to believe in what they are doing, in order to extend the message, rather than raise hackles as seeing it imposed'.

On the topic of informed consent, they decided that if, for a certain research proposal, written consent was difficult to obtain, or unobtainable, they would look at best practice already extant in the discipline concerned. As one stated, they were keen not to reinvent the wheel. If the proposed research followed pre-existing best practice, there would be no need for a full review of it by the UREC.

Members of the Committee acknowledged that questions could also be raised about the safety of researchers. They realized that they had to consider the possibility of writing generic principles, not just for the practice of research and its potential effects on those studied, but to safeguard the physical and mental health of researchers themselves.

Committee members recognized that training in research ethics was a difficult area and a weak point in their policy. Some founding members of the UREC had experience from work in their own disciplines; others had almost none. These original members assisted one another in their general education in ethical regulation, outside experts were occasionally brought in to give talks, and the principle of distributing the latest, relevant literature at each meeting was established. With respect to the research ethics training of staff and students, committee members recognize there is a continuing lack of clarity as to who or what level of the institution is responsible for its delivery. An external member of the UREC said that some training did cascade down the hierarchy, but was not too sure how much.

University A did not initially allocate any funding for its UREC. Its members donated their own time. The need for more administrative support soon became evident but proved very difficult to obtain. The Committee did manage to secure some funding after making a strong bid to the University, but its members felt the level of support granted was still minimal. An external member on the UREC stated that his colleagues were well aware of the tension over resources: 'Its members worry that they cannot do a comprehensive and complete set of procedures to be able to say to the outside world that they have a rock-solid approach. For example, how do you know every piece of research has gone through the process?' As another Committee member pointed out, the perceived implication of the University hierarchy's tightfistedness was that 'One doesn't matter'.

While Committee members regard their system of assessing proposed research as working relatively well, they acknowledge that monitoring the ethical practice of research once it is in progress remains a cause of concern. A commitment to monitoring was made in its original policy statement, but was later removed as the UREC came to recognize it had neither the time nor the resources to put it into effect. On the whole, self-evaluation forms, already in use in some UK universities, were seen as patronizing. As a trial, some researchers were asked to produce their own reports, but their level of compliance was not itself monitored. The Economic and Social Research Council, the main British Government funding body for the social sciences, has stated that monitoring is to be a requirement for winning its grants. University A is considering how best to monitor its ESRC-funded research.

How has the system functioned? Since the establishment of the divisional URECs, the chief UREC has not had to carry out a review of any application submitted to a divisional UREC. To that extent ethical regulation appears to be working satisfactorily, with each divisional UREC able to deal with all its applications without any applicant seeking further appeal. However, given that University A is research-intensive, the level of applications to the Social Sciences divisional UREC compared to those to its Medical Sciences counterpart remained suspiciously low. Committee members interpreted this low level as a sign of non-compliance. One member of the UREC guessed that the level of compliance within his own department, which he headed, was about seventy per cent. He thought that where the need for ethical approval was patent, for example when working with children, the level was high; where the need was less evident, the level, he estimated, was lower. While there was discussion between committee members about the possibility of disciplinary action for researchers who did not comply, this was regarded as being the very last option they would wish to pursue. An external member of the UREC had raised the question of what one can do to find out what is going on. His colleagues on the Committee agreed, but he judged the query was 'usually parked, because they have so much to do'.

Representatives from social sciences disciplines reported that the system of ethical regulation was not working successfully within their departments. Legal academics in particular strongly criticized the wording of the relevant forms, e.g. the insufficiently precise concept of 'harm'. They argued that, generally, the wording was such that, if interpreted critically, no research would be allowed. For them, a verbal assurance by the UREC of common-sense interpretations of the written code was insufficient. In the terms of one Committee member, these critics wanted 'to unpick the whole process and make it water-tight'. They also worried that the University was overly compliant with the Data Protection Act, implemented by the British Government in the 1990s, and that full advantage should be taken of opt-out clauses. Some anthropologists had learnt from other universities that the presumption there was that researchers would do bad unless boxed in by a process of ethical review. They wished the UREC to make the contrary presumption: to explicitly recognize that all researchers intended not to do harm, and that this intention was integral to why one became a social scientist.

In response, the Committee established two working groups, whose membership included the original complainants about the system: one group was to examine fieldwork, the other the interviewing of elites and oral history; both subsequently submitted reports and series of recommendations. The members of the group concerned with elites and oral history noted a repeated complaint that the initial ethics clearance form was 'intimidating and overly complicated'. They recommended greater clarity in the research ethics policy on the UREC website. The continuing tension here appears to be between producing a form written in accessible prose and ensuring that prose is sufficiently precise to satisfy legal requirements. The group also underlined the need for the University to employ 'clear and consistent definitions', e.g. to choose and use one term out of the several current phrases indicating accepted standards ('protocols, code of practice, best practice'). While recognizing that relevant professional associations, such as the Association of Social Anthropologists, had produced their own codes of best practice, these were to be viewed as guidelines only. The group recommended that 'researchers must be trusted to make informed judgements where necessary between conflicting principles'.

On a more general note, some members of University A were opposed to its UREC because they saw it as another, unwanted example of the increasingly bureaucratic, legalistic style of the institution. Some opponents raised the flag of academic freedom. According to one of its external members, the UREC was 'reasonably dismissive' of articles circulated to them which were critical of ethical review on grounds of academic freedom. In response to critics who argued the case of academic freedom, Committee members replied that they wished to facilitate research, not stop it. One member stated that within his department no one saw ethical regulation as an infringement of academic freedom: researchers 'are not free to give our subject a bad name'. Members of the UREC considered that in their University, the issue of ethical regulation had been elided with another one then current there, which was against major changes to the governance of the institution. For some Committee members, these two issues became blurred into a more general posture of opposition to the university administration. This style of argument was outside the control of the UREC and complicated its work.

University B

B Polytechnic was granted university status in 1992. As one of the new universities, University B has striven to develop a research culture. While generally successful in this aim, it still cannot yet be classified as research-intensive, and is certainly nowhere near the level of University A. Like its counterpart in University A its UREC, set up in 2000, established a two-tier system of ethical regulation, the initial form being little more than a checklist, which was reviewed by an Ethics Officer within each of the University's Schools. If the applicant was unable to answer all questions on the list negatively, he/she had to fill in a much more thorough form, reviewed by their School Ethics Officer, and then assessed by the UREC. This longer form is revised regularly, with Committee members taking into account comments made by applicants. Since there is a much lower volume of research carried out in this university compared to University A, there is no assessment of full applications by any body other than the UREC. Because of an increasing number of applications, each application is read by only two members of the Committee and its Chair.

Resourcing the Committee was an initial concern. One member of the UREC said that it was only very begrudgingly resourced by the University and Schools. It took major arguments by Committee members to get their time included in their respective Schools' workload planning for individual academics. Its membership has proved to be very stable. Though staff were often pushed into accepting the duty of serving on it, many then came to like it.

A founding member reported that its early years were an educative process for both UREC members, who received some specific research ethics training, and for research-active staff in general. In initial discussions, members of the Committee wondered whether they should be reflecting on the quality of the research design of the application. After internal debate, they decided it was ethically appropriate for them to do so, whether the application was from the medical or social sciences. In the review of applications, they realized they had to make applicants become much more explicit and informative about their proposed methods and analysis. Too much, it seemed, was assumed, or even unexamined by those submitting proposals. At the same time, Committee members engaged in much debate over what was the nature of research: they eventually decided that vicarious information gathering was quotidian scholarly practice and not the business of the UREC, while the conduct of an organized research program was. Committee members also queried cases where there were no apparent plans to publish the results of the research. They felt they sometimes needed to point out to some researchers that they were under an obligation to publish; otherwise they could be accused of wasting the time and goodwill of the researched. Some applicants were not pleased to be told this. During these early years, the Committee also received 'some quite tart responses' from supervisors: 'How can you do this to me?' Such supervisors had to be told that it was their job. Some research-active supervisors were unhappy at the way in which this Committee functioned. These critics regarded its comments as unhelpful and its requirements as unrealistic. One, when he complained about the restrictive consequences of certain questions on the initial checklist, was surprised to be told to interpret them 'creatively'. He then wondered what exactly was the status of the initial form. Some anthropologists thought the Committee's reactions to fieldwork-based research proposals showed insufficient understanding of the ethnographic realities of fieldwork. Some thought the Committee was too directive, and its practice openly tending towards the restrictive.

The UREC had noted that the number of applications from certain schools within the university was surprisingly low, suggesting that certain departments were not as compliant as others. No disciplinary action was taken but the relevant departments were notified that the UREC was aware of their low level of submissions.

Ethical Regulation at Work

In both universities, the establishment and maintenance of their URECs is a continually evolving process. Even though the wording of their forms might imply commandments written on stone, their phrasing in fact undergoes steady modification. One might say, the supposed ethical absolute is always relative to its time. A key tension here, as mentioned above, is between generating a readable, accessible form and producing one which satisfies the relevant legal requirements. Neither should be sacrificed for the other, theoretically. But a legally valid form might be unreadable to all but those trained in law, and so avoided by most of those for whom it was intended. Rates of non-compliance would continue to rise, as would the need for unwanted, disciplinary action. An unreadable form would tempt the legally untrained either to bypass ethical regulation and so feed an uneasy academic culture of subversion, or to adopt a cynical posture of minimal form-filling, which teaches them little about ethics and further distances them from the administrators with whom they are meant to be co-operating. Disciplinary action, if it did come, is an unattractive, very time-consuming option to increasingly pressured academics, and would only damage an already imperilled tradition of collegiality. At the same time, a very easy-to-read form might provide little legal defence to researchers and their university and so, in its own way, negate the very aim of the paperwork. In sum, the tension between legal rigour and accessibility is one which does not go away, and an alienating culture of academics quietly subverting their bureaucracies becomes slowly but cumulatively established. Nobody wants this outcome.

The suggestion made by a member of the UREC of University B, that one adopt a strategy of 'creative interpretation' of a readable but seemingly over-restrictive form, might be attractive to some applicants, but would stand on very weak legal grounds. Among other considerations here, the limits of acceptable creativity are not worked out in advance and are hence unknown, but would most likely be practised in an unchecked, informal manner by individual academics. Related to this, I noted above that in both URECs, members at times argued that 'common sense' had to prevail, in conflictive or difficult cases. While this is a tempting recourse of last resort, it is, of course, a very dangerous ground for argument, as common sense is uncodified, contested, dynamic, and historically contingent. What strikes me as common-sensical might appear an unjustifiable assumption to you, even if we work in the same discipline. This is especially the case in the social sciences, where internal contestation about their very nature and methods is integral to the disciplines themselves.

I could argue that investment in training staff and research students might ameliorate some of these difficulties: the better-briefed the reader, the more legalistic in tone and hence legal robustness the form can be; in the process, indulgence in creativity or the necessity for recourse to claims based on 'common sense' might well diminish. The theory is good; the reality less so. In University A, training for UREC members was somewhat uneven and appeared over-reliant on their trained intelligence, their respective professional codes of practice, and internal debate. Worse, they were unsure how much training was carried out down the hierarchy. The training for UREC members in University B appeared to be somewhat more methodical, but no formal monitoring was made of how many research-active staff across the institution, usually feeling pressed for time, attended the ethics training events which were staged.

In both universities, the relative lack of support from the higher reaches of the University hierarchy was noteworthy. The UREC of University A had to argue forcibly for financial support; that of University B was forced to campaign for recognition of their duties in personal workload planning. The statement, quoted above, 'One doesn't matter' only reinforces the feeling that in the highest levels of University A, ethical regulation is regarded as a resource-consuming burden which they are obliged to recognize but which they will not perform at anything but the most minimal of levels.

The predicament of monitoring, as we have seen, is even worse. Getting researchers to monitor themselves is seen as patronizing, but there is no funding for others to carry it out. Thus it does not occur. But if there is no monitoring, what then is the point of the initial ethical regulation? If one argues that researchers are to be trusted to carry out their work in an ethically upright manner, then that argument should apply as much to initial regulation as it does to monitoring. Once again, trust can be viewed as a perilously weak ground on which to base a system of ethical regulation. And if this argument is not accepted, i.e. that we should not trust researchers, then the process of ethical regulation is fundamentally flawed, as its key final stage is missing. At this reduced rate, the best argument for keeping a system of ethical regulation, however lopsided it be, is founded on its educational power, especially for fledgling researchers. In other words, the central value of URECs and their sub-units is making researchers more ethically aware. But this argument turns an application to an UREC into just a training exercise, and one which is therefore only relevant to first-time applicants. The rest could justifiably ignore the forms.

There are interesting differences between the two URECs. Membership is particularly stable on that of University B. Perhaps it is over-stable. Though long-term membership might lead to a knowledgeable committee which develops a coherent approach, the fear is that a low rate of turn-over can promote a culture of intellectual complacency and a static consensus. If we accept that the derivation of ethical principles is a negotiated process, forever open to the possibility of a scrutinized revision, then membership of a UREC should by definition be by fixed terms. One benefit of this might be to further disseminate knowledge of ethical regulation (if that is so desired), as the percentage of staff who have served on a UREC or any of its sub-units slowly rises.

A second difference between the two URECs is in the way they treat their applicants. Those in the UREC of University B thought it appropriate to comment on the design of the proposed research; their counterparts in University A very much did not think that appropriate. As one of its members put it:

> People here would hit the roof if the UREC questioned their research, partly because they know they're international standard. There is more a sense that they are not here to be managed. They take pride in their independence as academics. They have internalized the standards of research.

Members of the UREC in University B were also much more prepared to be assertive towards their peers. In marked contrast, members of the UREC in University A described their approach, in approving terms, as 'gentle', 'evolutionary', 'softly, softly', 'gentlemany'. An external member of this UREC stated that he was surprised 'how delicate, how sensitive Committee members had been with people. They don't wish to tread on toes. They need to be directive at times.' He went on, 'This is the most difficult group I've ever been on. I have to be careful what I say there, though I'm a reasonably confident person. I have found it quite hard.' I thought at first this difference between the two URECs a consequence of the relative prestige of the two universities, those in a famed institution having greater respect for their peers who, after all, were meant to be at the top or near the top of their respective disciplines, globally. When I stated this at the conference on which this book is based, American participants immediately responded with examples of very prestigious universities in the United States, staffed by renowned academics, recipients of the greatest prizes, which were managed in a very hierarchical manner and where the IRBs were as directive as the UREC of University B, if not indeed more so. This suggests that the 'softly, softly' approach of University A is, to a significant extent, caused by its relative lack of hierarchy and the fact that academics still control much of that hierarchy. It also suggests that any analysis of ethical regulation at a university needs to take its general management structure into account. 'Management' here includes the effect of a university's insurance policy, for evidence is already emerging how this can restrict the range of research carried out by a university's researchers. In the case of one British university, discussed at a 2009 conference on research ethics scrutiny, its system of ethical regulation was reportedly powered by insurance concerns. The senior management of the institution wished to lower its premiums.[1]

In both universities, some academics judged the work of their UREC as restrictive. This is a particular version of a more general suspicion raised by some

British academics that ethical regulation is a covert means of curtailing academic freedom. Further, one member of the UREC at University A said he had gained the impression that the NHS sometimes uses ethical regulation as a way to slow down or impede research. It is thus depressingly noteworthy that when an undergraduate research assistant of a UK professor carried out telephone interviews of British university employees concerned with ethical regulation, one administrator replied:

> What came in then was much more greatly managed research which perhaps the academics may not have particularly liked. But because there was such wholesale change in the university, I think probably it went through unaccepted, so that we actually do have a much more managed regime now, which could be seen as a curb on academic freedom. (Quote in Dingwall n.d.: 15)

Her mentor, commenting on this quotation, stated that some universities were exploiting the introduction of ethical regulation to control their academic employees; that is, the establishment of URECs was being used by managers as a welcome, cloaked opportunity for them to further curtail academic freedoms (Dingwall n.d. 15–16).

The history of ethical regulation may be recruited to bolster this critical approach. Its conventional history starts with the public exposure of Nazi doctors' abuse of fellow human beings. This led to the Nuremberg Medical Trials of 1946–1947 which set out a code of permissible medical experiments. This declaration became the template for subsequent codes of ethical regulation of biomedical research. In time, these codes became the inspiration for similar guidelines for the conduct of social scientific investigation. However, revisionist historians regard this conventional version as a creation myth, devised to legitimate those who benefit from the present, cumulative expansion of ethical regulation in academia (Dingwall 2008: 1). They point out that Germany in the 1930s already had a particularly developed regulatory code for scientific research which was subsequently not respected; that the code produced at the Nuremberg Trials was rapidly assembled in order to be able to indict the Nazi doctors; that the Allies did not seriously apply the code to themselves; and that US scientists in the 1930s sustained an informal mode of professional control. Instead, revisionists argue the massive postwar expansion of biomedical research could not be controlled by the pre-existing professional mechanisms. This loss of control led traditional elites to exploit regulation as one means to regain power and influence (Dingwall 2008: 2). These opposed versions of the past of ethical regulation are polemically stark alternatives: we should not have to follow either unquestioningly. But the existence of these versions should make us query any attempt to justify present practice in terms of the past. History is no guide when it is so disputed.

So where are we left?

An End to Ethical Regulation of the Minimally Risky?

British social scientists had raised fears and worries about ethical regulation almost as soon as its implementation was suggested. In an early discussion prompted by the ESRC, some stated concerns it would be an off-putting, time-consuming hurdle which could generate 'considerable hostility'. 'Most felt that it was not usually relevant to the kind of research they did. Most also indicated that, amongst their colleagues, there was a general resistance to and disquiet about the increasing regulation of research by RECs' (Webster et al. 2004: 8). A separate, contemporary review had already identified non-compliance: 'where there is a UREC, in a significant number of cases they do not appear to be scrutinizing all the research that is being done' (Tinker and Coomber 2004: 11).

There is further evidence, beyond Universities A and B, that these worries and concerns endure in the UK (e.g. Macdonald 2010). In a 2009 conference on ethical regulation of the social sciences, the Chair of the UREC at the Open University admitted that it was easy to be over-bureaucratic, and that they still lacked tools to adequately identify the risks and benefits of proposed research (Oates 2009). At the same meeting, when I asked the twenty-six participants in a workshop on URECs whether they felt their respective committee under-financed and over-burdened, about one-third raised their hands.[2] Moreover, fears that URECs can be more regulatory than facilitative, laying down the rules rather than entering into educative discussion, are not assuaged when, for instance, the Chair of the UREC at Oxford Brookes University speaks of their work as 'an objective review process' (Taylor 2009: 7).[3] It is perhaps revealing that two sociologists who also work at Oxford Brookes have called for a shift from a static audit and accountability model of ethics review to one which is more democratic, supportive, and sensitive to process (Miller and Boulton 2007). Other social scientists have voiced concern that URECs are even determining what kinds of research get done, and that research which they find difficult to approve is not being considered by researchers (Dingwall 2009; Dyer and Demeritt 2009: 47). Some worry that academics are being subjected to stricter scrutiny than those studying the same or similar topics extra-murally. One Cambridge psychologist worried, after seeing his team's work misrepresented in the British national press, that if academics are regulated because their work 'can do harm to the public', shouldn't journalists be monitored in a similar manner (Baron-Cohen 2009: 27)?

Of course, there are irreducible differences between research in the medical sciences and that in the social sciences. Social scientists do not insert potentially nasty substances into people's bodies and then sit back to watch the consequences. In the name of medical advance, research clinicians may take very real risks and face genuine ethical concerns. It is little wonder, in fact reassuring, that the National Health Service has such a rigorous process of ethical regulation. But for social scientists, the very great majority of their work involves very little or no identifiable risk towards those studied. Confidentiality and anonymity must be upheld, if need be, the vulnerable protected, and potential commercial exploitation of the data carefully controlled and prescribed. But, beyond those areas and specific exceptions, the possibility of doing any harm to those studied is extremely small. So why bother?

My argument so far is that, because of lack of resources, the present system of ethical regulation of the social sciences in British universities is best defended as a training exercise for fledgling researchers, and almost nothing more. For the ESRC, it appears primarily a rhetorical exercise, a way of publicly stating its commitment to safeguard all those involved in research, especially the researched, even if that commitment cannot be properly backed up. Furthermore, even if resources were endlessly available, the tension would still remain of producing an ethical review form which was both readable and legally binding. I fear that these tensions and inadequacies will be most clearly exposed and put to the test if or when a case is brought by a researched person against a researcher, for whatever reason.

In the United States, some universities have already declared that they will no longer be reviewing applications for ethical review of research, except for that of federally funded research, because the present system has proved so burdensome and time-consuming. Given all the above, it is very difficult not to agree with this strategy, or to retain ethical regulation for anyone other than first-time applicants. Time for a rethink?

Notes

1. 'URECs – how they are working' workshop, Academy of Social Sciences/Social Research Association conference on 'Ethics in Social Sciences: Regulation, Review or Scrutiny?', 11 May 2009, London.
2. 'URECs – how they are working' workshop, Academy of Social Sciences/Social Research Association conference on 'Ethics in Social Sciences: Regulation, Review or Scrutiny?', 11 May 2009, London.
3. It seems matters are little better in the much longer-established RECs of the National Health Service. An analysis of 100 decision letters written by NHS RECs 'found evidence of poor communication … Typos and grammatical mistakes were found in almost thirty per cent of letters; sometimes wording was impolite and demonstrated a lack of respect towards applicants; and there was often lack of clarity about the nature of a revision' (Angell and Dixon-Woods 2008). In a 2008 conference, Sir John Lillyman, former President of the Royal Society of Medicine and a strategic adviser to the NHS National Research Ethics Service, recognized that 'RECs can stray into arrogance' (Atkinson 2009: 41).

References

Angell, E.L. and M. Dixon-Woods. 2008. 'Style Matters: an Analysis of 100 Research Ethics Committee Decisions Letters', *Research Ethics Review* 4(3): 101–105.

Atkinson, R. 2009. 'Now is the Winter of our Discontent: Contentious Issues in Research Ethics. AREC Conference Report, London, November 2008', *Research Ethics Review* 5(1): 40–41.

Baron-Cohen, Simon. 2009. 'The Distorting Lens', *New Scientist* 28 March, 26–27.

Bradburd, D. 2006. 'Fuzzy Boundaries and Hard Rules: Unfunded Research and the IRB', *American Ethnologist* 33(4): 492–98.

Christians, C.G. 2007. 'Neutral Science and the Ethics of Resistance', in N.K. Denzin and M.D. Giardina (eds), *Ethical Futures in Qualitative Research. Decolonizing the Politics of Knowledge*. Walnut Creek, CA: Left Coast Press, pp. 47–66.

Denzin, N.K. and M.D. Giardina. 2007. 'Introduction: Ethical Futures in Qualitative Research', in N.K. Denzin and M.D. Giardina (eds), *Ethical Futures in Qualitative Research. Decolonizing the Politics of Knowledge*. Walnut Creek, CA: Left Coast Press, pp. 9–43.

Dingwall, R.T. 2008. 'The Ethical Case against Ethical Regulation in Humanities and Social Science Research', *Twenty-First Century Society* 3(1), February, 1–12.

————.2009. 'The Current System, Do we Need a Paradigm Shift?', Academy of Social Sciences/Social Research Association Conference *Ethics in Social Science: Regulation, Review or Scrutiny?*, London, 11 May. Attended by author.

————.n.d. 'Interim Report on 2008 Study of the Implementation of the ESRC Research Ethics Framework', http://www.academia.edu/2166575/Interim_Report_on_2008_Study_of_the_Implementation_of_the_ESRC_Research_Ethics_Framework, accessed on 20 October 2012.

Dyer, S. and D. Demeritt. 2009. 'Un-ethical Review? Why it is Wrong to Apply the Medical Model of Research Governance to Human Geography', *Progress in Human Geography* 33(1): 46–64.

Ellis, C. 2007. '"I Just Want to Tell *my* Story": Mentoring Students about Relational Ethics in Writing about Intimate Others', in N.K. Denzin and M.D. Giardina (eds), *Ethical Futures in Qualitative Research. Decolonizing the Politics of Knowledge*. Walnut Creek, CA: Left Coast Press, pp. 209–27.

ESRC Research Ethics Framework Project. 2004. *ESRC Developing a Framework for Social Sciences Research Ethics. Project Update*. http://www.york.ac.uk/res/ref/docs/update250604.pdf, accessed on 1 March 2010.

Katz, J. 2006. 'Ethical Escape Routes for Underground Ethnographers', *American Ethnologist* 33(4): 499–506.

Kim, S., P. Ubel and R. De Vries. 2009. 'Pruning the Regulatory Tree', *Nature* 457, 29 January, 534–35.

Lederman, R. 2006a. 'Introduction: Anxious Borders between Work and Life in a Time of Bureaucratic Ethics Regulation', *American Ethnologist* 33(4): 477–81.

————.2006b. 'The Perils of Working at Home: IRB 'Mission Creep' as Context and Content for an Ethnography of Disciplinary Knowledges', *American Ethnologist* 33(4): 482–91.

Lévi-Strauss, C. and D. Eribon. 1991. *Conversations with Lévi-Strauss*. (orig. pub in French, 1988, trans. P.Wissing). Chicago: University of Chicago Press.

Macdonald, Sharon. 2010. 'Making Ethics', in M. Melhuus, J.P. Mitchell, and H. Wulff (eds), *Ethnographic Practice in the Present*. Oxford: Berghahn, pp. 80–94.

Miller, T. and M. Boulton. 2007. 'Changing Constructions of Informed Consent: Qualitative Research and Complex Social Worlds', *Social Science and Medicine* 65(11): 2199–2211.

Oates, J. 2009. 'Towards Principled Ethics Review', Academy of Social Sciences/Social Research Association Conference *Ethics in Social Science: Regulation, Review or Scrutiny?*, London, 11 May. Attended by author.

Schrag, Z. 2010. *Ethical Imperialism. Institutional Review Boards and the Social Sciences, 1965--2009.* Baltimore, MD: Johns Hopkins University Press.

Schwandt, T.A. 2007. 'The Pressing Need for Ethical Education: a Commentary on the Growing IRB Controversy', in N.K. Denzin and M.D. Giardina (eds), *Ethical Futures in Qualitative Research. Decolonizing the Politics of Knowledge.* Walnut Creek, CA: Left Coast Press, pp. 85–98.

Shweder, R.A. 2006. 'Protecting Human Subjects and Preserving Academic Rreedom: Prospects at the University of Chicago', *American Ethnologist* 33(4): 507–18.

Taylor, S. 2009. 'Dr Elizabeth T Hurren: Interview', *Research Forum,* Oxford Brookes University 5(2), February, 6–7.

Tinker, A. and V. Coomber. 2004. *University Research Ethics Committees. Their Role, Remit and Conduct.* London: King's College London.

Van den Hoonaard, W.C. 2011. *The Seduction of Ethics. The Transformation of the Social Sciences.* Toronto: University of Toronto Press.

Webster, A., G. Lewis, N. Brown and M. Boulton. 2004. *ESRC Developing a Framework for Social Science Research Ethics. Project Update.* ESRC Research Ethics Framework. June. http://www.york.ac.uk/res/ref/docs/update250604.pdf, accessed on 3 March 2010.

Notes on Contributors

Tim Allen is Professor in Development Anthropology at the Department of International Development, the London School of Economics and Political Science. He has carried out long-term field research in Sudan and Uganda and has also researched in Ghana, Botswana, Zimbabwe, Kenya and Tanzania. His books include *Trial Justice: The International Criminal Court and the Lords' Resistance Army*; *Culture and Global Change* (edited with Tracey Skelton) and *Poverty and Development* (edited with Alan Thomas).

Dr Catherine M. Hill is a Reader in Anthropology in the Department of Social Sciences, Oxford Brookes University. Her research focuses on costs to rural populations of living alongside wildlife, including protected species, and how this affects rural livelihood security, perceptions of risk and ultimately people–wildlife relationships.

Agustín Fuentes is Professor of Anthropology at the University of Notre Dame. He completed a B.A. in Zoology and Anthropology, and an M.A. and Ph.D. in Anthropology at the University of California, Berkeley. Fuentes' recent published work includes *Evolution of Human Behaviour* (Oxford University Press, 2008), *Health, Risk, and Adversity* (co-edited, Berghahn Books, 2008), *Core Concepts in Biological Anthropology* (McGraw-Hill, 2006), and *Primates in Perspective* (co-edited, Oxford University Press, 2006).

Susie Kilshaw is a Senior Research Fellow in the Department of Anthropology, University College London. She currently has two research projects in Qatar, funded by the Qatar National Research Fund: one is a cross-cultural comparison (Qatar and UK) of the experience of miscarriage and the other investigates the social impact of genetic knowledge, particularly in relation to consanguinity. Her book *Impotent Warriors: Gulf War Syndrome, Vulnerability and Masculinity* (Berghahn, 2009), whose writing was supported by a Wenner Gren Hunt Fellowship, explored how Gulf War Syndrome has been influenced by the culture in which it developed.

Nobuyuki Kutsukake is Lecturer at the Department of Evolutionary Studies of Biosystems, The Graduate University for Advanced Studies, Japan. His research focuses on behavioural ecology and evolutionary biology in social mammals (primates, carnivores, rodents, etc.). Awards received include the first Primates Top Impact award (2007, Springer), and a Commendation for Science and Technology from the Minister of Education, Culture, Sports, Science and Technology, Japan (2010).

Jeremy MacClancy is Professor of Anthropology and Director of the Anthropological Centre for Conservation, the Environment and Development, Oxford Brookes University. He has conducted major fieldwork in Vanuatu and Basque Spain, and writes on the history of anthropology, and the anthropologies of art, food, sport, and nationalism. His books include *Expressing Identities in the Basque Arena* (James Currey, 2007), (edited with A. Fuentes), and *Centralizing Fieldwork* (Berghahn, 2011). His latest work is *Anthropology in the Public Arena. Historical and Contemporary Contexts* (Wiley, 2013), a critical history of academic and popular anthropologies in the UK.

Katherine C. MacKinnon is Associate Professor of Anthropology at Saint Louis University. She holds a B.A. and Ph.D. in Anthropology from the University of California at Berkeley, and an M.A. in Anthropology from the University of Alberta. She has published on primate behaviour and ecology, and co-edited the volume *Primates in Perspective* (2nd edition, Oxford University Press, 2011). MacKinnon has carried out fieldwork in Costa Rica, Nicaragua, Panama, Suriname and Zambia, and her research interests include infant and juvenile development, evolution of social complexity, conservation issues in Latin America, and ethics in field primatology.

Matthew R. McLennan is an Honorary Research Associate at Oxford Brookes University. His research concerns the interactions between humans and wildlife, and the challenges of conservation outside of protected areas, with a special focus on human–great ape sympatry in Africa. His doctoral research on the chimpanzees in Bulindi was the first detailed study of co-existence between humans and African great apes in the context of rapid deforestation, agricultural expansion and escalating human–wildlife conflict.

Tina Miller is a Professor of Sociology at Oxford Brookes University with research and teaching interests in the areas of gender, family and reproductive lives, transitions, caring and paid work. She has an expertise in qualitative longitudinal research methods, narrative analysis and research ethics. Her published work has undergone translation into Mandarin, Turkish and Italian and her most recent monograph is *Making Sense of Fatherhood: Gender, Caring and Work* which was published by Cambridge University Press in 2011.

K. Anne-Isola Nekaris is Professor of Anthropology, Oxford Brookes University, and Head of the Nocturnal Primate Research Group. Specializing in nocturnal primates and primate conservation, she has worked on (extinct and extant) primates in five continents, and is best known for her work on slow and slender lorises. For the latter she earned the 2012 Lawrence Jacobsen Conservation Award from the Wisconsin National Primate Research Center.

Vincent Nijman is a Reader in Anthropology, Oxford Brookes University, specializing in primate conservation and assessing the impacts of wildlife trade. Trained as an ecologist, he has published over 100 scientific papers including contributions in most major biodiversity conservation journals. Each year Nekaris and Nijman teach some thirty-five students on the MSc in Primate Conservation, which, in 2008, was the recipient of the UK's Queen's Anniversary Price for Excellence in Higher Education.

Melissa Parker is director of the Centre for Research in International Medical Anthropology and a senior lecturer at Brunel University. She has undertaken anthropological research in Sudan, Uganda, Tanzania, Ghana and the UK on a wide range of global health issues including HIV/AIDS, tropical diseases, female circumcision, and health and healing in the aftermath of war. Her publications include *Learning from HIV/AIDS* (edited with George Ellison and Cathy Campbell) and *The Anthropology of Public Health* (edited with Ian Harper).

Erin P. Riley is an Associate Professor in the Department of Anthropology at San Diego State University where she teaches undergraduate and graduate courses in biological anthropology, anthropological primatology, and research design. In 2007, she was awarded *Most Influential Faculty* by the department's outstanding graduating senior. Along with co-author Katherine MacKinnon, she was guest editor of and contributor to a special issue in the *American Journal of Primatology* on Ethics in Field Primatology. Her primary research interest lies in human–nonhuman primate interconnections (ethnoprimatology) with notable publications in *American Anthropologist*, *American Journal of Primatology,* and *Oryx*.

Em Rundall is currently a Policy Official in the Civil Service, having previously been a Postdoctoral Teaching Associate in the Department of Social Sciences, Oxford Brookes University. She recently completed her PhD on trans-employees' experiences in UK workplaces, and has published on her research. Her findings have been circulated to the Equality and Human Rights Commission, and the Government Equalities Office. She also contributed to a research project commissioned by the Equalities Review. Em has previously conducted research into constructions of lesbian identity, and taboos surrounding women's hair. Her interests include identity construction, sociological theory, employment equality, and methodological and ethical issues arising from research into 'sensitive' topics.

Karen B. Strier is Vilas Professor and Irven DeVore Professor of Anthropology at the University of Wisconsin-Madison. Her long-term field study on the critically endangered northern muriqui in Brazil's Atlantic Forest has contributed to the conservation of the species and to comparative perspectives on primates. She is a Fellow of the American Association for the Advancement of Science and a member of the US National Academy of Sciences and the American Academy of Arts and Sciences. She is the author of *Primate Behavioral Ecology*, 4th edition (Pearson, 2011) and *Faces in the Forest: The Endangered Muriqui Monkeys of Brazil* (Harvard University Press, 1999), in addition to other works.

Index